Islam and Israel
Muslim Religious Endowments and the Jewish State

Michael Dumper

Islam and Israel
Muslim Religious Endowments and the Jewish State

Michael Dumper

Institute for Palestine Studies
Washington, D.C.

The Institute for Palestine Studies, founded in Beirut in 1963, is an independent nonprofit Arab research and publication center, not affiliated with any political organization or government. The opinions expressed in its publications do not necessarily reflect those of the Institute.

Library of Congress Cataloging-in-Publication Data

Dumper, Michael.
Islam and Israel : Muslim religious endowments and the Jewish state / Michael Dumper.
p. cm.
Includes bibliographical references and index.
ISBN 0-88728-254-7 (hc)
1. Waqf--Israel. 2. Waqf--West Bank. 3. Waqf--Gaza Strip. 4. Waqf--Palestine--History. I. Title.
KMK2168.5.D86 1993
297' .65--dc20

93-31040
CIP

Printed in the United States of America

CONTENTS

For my mother and father

ACKNOWLEDGMENTS

I would like to thank Professor Walid Khalidi for first giving me the idea of this subject and then continuing to encourage me through the many years of its execution. His faith and patience in my ability were wonderful incentives and provided a great boost to my early lack of confidence. I would also like to thank Dr. Nazih Ayubi, who supervised the thesis from which this book was derived. His criticisms helped me to see the pattern hidden behind all the details I was amassing.

A great number of people helped me during the course of my fieldwork in Israel and the occupied Palestinian territories, partly with introductions, partly as interviewees, and partly as a sounding board for ideas. These include Dr. Haydar Abdul Sha'fi and Khadr Abu Sha'ban in the Gaza Strip, Ibrahim Daqqaq, Adnan Husayni, Mahmud Hawari, Mazen Qupti, Yusuf Natshe, Jihad Nummari, Raja Shehadeh, and Shaykh Hasan Tahbub in the West Bank and East Jerusalem, and Dr. Yitzhak Reiter, Professor Aharon Layish, Fathi Furani, and the late Professor Sami Mar'i in Israel. I would particularly like to thank Haydar and Hayfa' Khalidi for introducing me to the Old City of Jerusalem. Without the assistance of all these people, this research could not have been carried out.

A number of other people also helped me in providing friendly hospitality, advice on grant applications, contacts, and encouragement. My warmest thanks go to Cat Essoyan, Chris Smith and Tina Schmallenbach, Ghada Rabah, Ora and (the late) Blanca Davis, Kamel al-Asali, Tim Niblock, Alistair Duncan, Michael Adams, and George Abed. I would also like to thank the secretaries of the Politics Department at Exeter University, Faye Burgoyne, Sue Ridler, and Sandy Condron, for creating a friendly and congenial atmosphere in which to work. A special thanks also to the staff of the Institute for Palestine Studies, particularly to Philip Mattar, Linda Butler, and Mark Mechler for sticking patiently with this project and giving the final result a more accessible shape and style. Finally, I would like to thank my partner Ann for her perseverance and encouragement.

Financial assistance for this research came from the Diana Tamari-Sabbagh Foundation, the Economic and Social Research Council, and the Palestine Studies Trust. I am most grateful to these bodies for their support.

LIST OF MAPS AND TABLES

Preface

Waqfs are Islamic religious and social institutions that have played an important political role in the history of Muslim society and the development of Middle Eastern states. This book explores the role of Palestinian Muslim waqfs both inside Israel and in the areas under Israeli control (excluding the Golan Heights) that are frequently referred to as the occupied Palestinian territories.

Because Israel is a modern non-Muslim state in the Middle East, its relations with traditional Islamic institutions, such as waqfs, deserve attention. This is particularly the case since waqfs have strong associations with Palestinian nationalist sentiment. The purpose here is to establish a framework for understanding Israeli policies with regard to the Palestinian Muslim waqfs and to account for their simultaneous marginalization and persistence as politically significant institutions.

The Arabic word *waqf* (plural, *awqaf*) can be loosely translated into English as "religious endowment," although this term does not convey the sense of religious piety and grace with which waqfs are associated in Islam. G.C. Kozlowski has provided the most concise description of waqfs:

> *Awqaf* are "endowments" in the general sense that they are gifts made to individuals as well as institutions. Throughout the history of the Islamic world, such settlements provided for many of the spiritual and temporal wants of Muslims. Funds derived from endowments built and sustained places of worship, established schools and hospitals, supported scholars and preachers, provided paupers with graves and supplied weapons to warriors fighting in the cause of faith. At the same time, founders rarely ignored those dear and near to them. A clause in the deed of endowment could set aside a sum of money for the founders and their dependents.[1]

Waqfs have proliferated during the course of Islamic history. In many parts of the Middle East, the revenue derived from the waqfs—the endowed properties and lands—provided a veritable network of welfare and charitable services (such as schools, orphanages, and soup kitchens) for the Muslim population, and income for the maintenance of mosques and famous tombs, water supplies, and bridges. Large and influential bureaucracies developed to administer waqfs. This network of services and administrations has been designated by the Islamic legal scholar, J.N.D. Anderson, as "the waqf system."[2] The phrase, which has been adopted in this book, accurately describes the interconnections, duplications, and complementariness of different waqfs that gradually coalesced and cohered into a system.

The waqf system's social, economic, and political role became increasingly important during the late Ottoman period. Because the responsibilities and holdings of the waqf system in the areas under Ottoman control were so extensive, they required the establishment of a ministerial department and codified administrative procedures. In Palestine specifically, the waqf system developed into an important institution that controlled significant areas of agricultural land and urban property. It provided wealth and political influence to a class of scholars, clerics, and notables. During the British Mandate period, parts of the waqf system took on quasi-state functions and its administrators and managers assumed important political roles. It was in this form that the waqf system became part of the Palestinian national movement and part of the resistance to British colonialism, Zionism, and Jewish settlement.

The waqf system continued to exercise a political role after the creation of the State of Israel in 1948—both in Israel itself, and in the remnant of Palestine occupied by Israel in 1967. After the disintegration of the Ottoman Empire in 1917, the greater proportion of the Ottoman waqf system was absorbed into the new bureaucracies of the successor Arab states, such as Syria, Jordan, and Lebanon. Indeed, some reforms even led to the complete abolition of privately-managed waqfs. While waqfs continued to have a communal and religious role in these countries, they constituted neither a threat to the integrity of the state nor a focus of dissident minority agitation. By contrast, the historic functions of the Palestinian waqf system were and are considered by Israeli officials and politicians as a threat simultaneously to the physical integrity of the Israeli state, to its political stability, and to the institutional dominance of the Jewish majority. This perception remains despite complete Israeli-Jewish political and legal control and despite overwhelming Israeli military dominance over the Palestinian community. This book sets out to explain why, and in what ways, the remnant of the Ottoman and Mandate waqf system in Palestine is seen as still constituting a threat to the Israeli state.

A second, more important question, is why, assuming that the waqf system does constitute a threat, the system survives at all. Does its survival mean that the Israeli state permits its continued existence? Does it in fact serve the interests of the Israeli state in some way? If so, what are these interests? Or does the continued existence of the waqf system imply that there are limits to the coercive power of the Israeli state in the areas under its control—that, in effect, Israel has not had the means to eradicate the waqf system? If so, what does this indicate concerning the strength and durability of a well-established and religious Palestinian institution?

In examining the development of the relationship between the waqf system as a Muslim institution and the Israeli state, this book identifies three key linkages: the state's co-optation of the religious leadership supported by the waqf system; its integration of the administration of the system itself; and its control over the waqf system's resources (i.e., the endowed property and land that produce the revenue to support the waqf system's activities).[3] The first linkage—the co-optation of leadership—is between the state and the waqf system and is a function of varying degrees of control exerted by the state.[4] The crucial indicators here include which body makes the senior appointments, who pays the salaries, what vetting and approval are given, what demonstrations of loyalty must be made, and what legal and jurisdictional parameters are accepted.

The second linkage—the state's integration of the waqf system's administration—is also a matter of degree. The indicators here range from symbolic ones, such as the state's use of headed notepaper or the physical location of offices in government buildings, to more substantive indicators, such as how much freedom the waqf system has to develop areas of responsibility and new functions, or the locus of executive management and direction. Here the issue of the independence of funding also comes into play, suggesting an overlap with the third linkage—the control of waqf resources.

The control of the waqf system's resources is perhaps the most crucial linkage between the waqf system and the state. Here the indicators are the forms of control by the waqf administration and leadership over income from waqf land and property, from fees, from interest accruing from monetary endowments, and so on. The extent to which these resources are independent from state control gives a strong indication as to the degree of the waqf system's integration into state structures.

These three linkages can be seen in all the areas of the waqf system under Israeli control and during all the periods starting from 1948. In order to understand the context in which this relationship developed after 1948, it is necessary to appreciate the history of the relationship between the Palestinian waqf system and the Ottoman and British states prior to 1948. Chapter One sets the scene for the development of the waqf system to act to some extent as a mediating institution. Chapter Two focuses on the period up to 1965, at which point new legislation was passed that affected the administration of the Palestinian Muslim waqf system in Israel. Chapter Three considers these linkages in the light of the new legislation and analyzes its impact through case studies of the waqf system in three cities: Acre, Jaffa, and Haifa. Chapter Four examines the linkages established in the West Bank and the Gaza Strip as a result of the Israeli occupation. Chapter Five explores the political and legal anomaly established by the Israeli annexation of East Jerusalem, where greater emphasis is placed upon the question of the control over waqf resources, as the annexation makes the independent funding of any waqf administration particularly pertinent to our concerns here.

A Note on Sources

The primary sources for this research fall into three categories: internal documents and reports from government and waqf administration sources; English, Arabic, and Hebrew newspapers; and personal interviews. Due to the highly sensitive nature of the subject, some of the existing material has remained inaccessible. This applies to material from Israeli as well as Palestinian and Jordanian sources. Senior officials showed great reluctance to be interviewed on the record. This was partly a result of government restrictions on them, but also because of the continuing controversy surrounding the fate of the waqf system's assets, both in Israel and the occupied Palestinian territories. Many hours were spent sitting in corridors in the relevant departments trying to gain access to key officials, only eventually to receive bland statements bereft of figures and serious documentation to back them up. Similar difficulties were experienced in obtaining official reports and documents. Most of the important decisions concerning the waqf system in Israel are made by the Office of the Advisor on Arab Affairs to the Prime Minister. The discussions and decisions of this office remain classified. The lack of publicly available documentation also pertains to many of the decisions of the Awqaf Administration in East Jerusalem and the West Bank, and to the office of the *ma'mur al-awqaf*, the manager of public waqfs, in the Gaza Strip.

It is important to note that the waqf system in Israel does not figure high on the priorities of Israeli government officials, although it is important to the Palestinian Muslim community there. It is regarded as a time-consuming nuisance rather than an urgent issue and is frequently overlooked or shelved when budgets and strategies are planned.[5] Indeed, it is this very lack of attention that has created the conditions that have led to this study. Given that so little official documentation was available from either Israeli, Palestinian, or Jordanian sources, and that the subject itself constitutes a new, insufficiently researched field, it was often necessary to make deductions from what is publicly available. Policy decisions by waqf officials are similarly unavailable, and again I was obliged to piece together information from a number of sources. While research on the Islamic court records, the *sijill*s, is starting to reveal vast quantities of information on waqfs, much of it relates to historical periods largely beyond the scope of this study.

A number of steps have been taken to compensate for the limitations the political situation places upon the access to relevant source material. Interviews with senior government and waqf officials have been of particular use in gathering undocumented material, and this has frequently placed the other primary sources in their proper perspective. Special attention was paid in maintaining a consistent framework of preparation, questioning, recording, and referencing. These interviews provided an excellent source of data, and an additional step was taken in the course of this research to establish the reliability of key interviews. Notes were made during the interviews and subsequently transcribed and submitted to the interviewee to check for any inaccuracies or for off-the-record remarks. In this way most of the cited interviews have been acknowledged and accepted by the interviewees as an accurate reflection of their views. Relevant but nonattributable remarks that could be cross-checked with other interviews or documented material have been included. Where face-to-face interviews were denied, written questions were submitted and their answers formally acknowledged and recorded.

Since this study examines Israeli policy towards the waqf system fairly critically, care was taken to emphasize the use of data from Israeli sources and Israeli scholars. Some of the latter have been in government service and are regularly consulted on the waqf issue. I refer in particular to Professor Aharon Layish and Dr. Yitzhak Reiter of the Hebrew University, both of whom worked in the Office of the Advisor on Arab Affairs and both of whom encouraged my work by providing introductions and by suggesting useful references. Although the thrust of this book may not be entirely compatible with their views, it nevertheless seeks to present an accurate and even-handed description of the dilemma facing the Israeli government in its policies toward the waqf system. The investigation also reveals a network of nefarious activities carried out by individual Palestinians, particularly those appointed to boards of trustees in Israel. Although it is not the purpose of this book to dramatize the bribes, violent extortion, and corruption that have been a feature of waqf politics in the Palestinian community, some description has been unavoidable. It is hoped that this more sensational part of the material also is presented as accurately and fairly as possible. In any case, it should certainly not overshadow the author's attempt to understand the political relationship between an important Muslim institution and a modern non-Muslim state.

CHAPTER 1

The Palestinian Muslim Waqf System during the Late Ottoman Empire and the British Mandate

How was the waqf system created, and what was its purpose? This chapter presents a picture of the role of waqfs in Islamic society and the Arab world, particularly during the period under the Ottoman Empire (1516–1918). Understanding the nature of the waqf system and its relation to state power during the Ottoman and British periods provides a valuable perspective on the developments that have taken place during the Israeli period of control.

It is also revealing to contrast the Ottoman period with the British period. During most of the Ottoman period the state apparatus was weak, manifesting itself mainly through military coercion. Control over local resources, revenues, and administrative structures was exercised primarily through the agency of the local religious and social elites, and the legitimacy of state rule depended heavily upon its association with the judicial and religious consensus represented by these elites. In these circumstances, the waqf system operated primarily as the personal and communal fiefdoms of these elites.[1]

In contrast, the British Mandate period heralded a political context (to be repeated in 1948 and 1967) in which the ruling power was not only situated outside the judicial and religious consensus, by virtue of the fact that it was a non-Muslim power, but also created highly centralized state structures to govern the population and nonstate institutions directly. The British period marked the first time that the Palestinian Muslim waqf system acted—if only briefly—as a mediating institution between the state and the population.

The Waqf System in Islam and the Arab World

Waqfs were not explicitly mentioned in the Quran, but their creation was inspired by certain Quranic passages and from precedents, set by the Prophet Muhammad and the Caliph 'Umar and found in the *hadith*.[2] The absence of clear-cut provisions gave rise to disputes among Muslim jurisprudential scholars, yet over time a number of rules establishing the character of waqf and the conditions for its creation were agreed upon by the different schools of Muslim law. The rules were designed to safeguard the pious and holy nature of a waqf and to ensure that those who endowed land or property were *bona fide* benefactors. For example, it was specified that a founder of a waqf, the *waqif*, should be of sound mind and have attained his majority.[3] Similarly, in order to prevent the creation of endowments simply as a means of avoiding creditors, a *waqif* was required to be financially solvent.[4] In the Muslim legal system that prevailed during the Ottoman Empire, waqfs could also be created by Christians and Jews.[5] Neither was there any restriction against women creating waqfs, and many did so.[6]

It was not only because of their charitable purposes that waqf land and property differed from other holdings. Three critical restrictions were placed upon endowed land, which gave it its distinctive legal and holy character. First, once endowed, the land in question was inalienable. It could not be sold, mortgaged, bequeathed, or altered in any way.[7] Second, waqf land and property were endowed for perpetuity. This was to ensure that the charitable purpose on which the income was to be spent—for example, a mosque or orphanage—was guaranteed a regular and lasting income.[8] Third, a waqf endowment was irrevocable. Once a waqf was established, a *waqif* or his or her descendants could not change their minds.[9] These restrictions were designed to ensure that waqfs were created for altruistic purposes. Consequently, they gave the *waqif* a high moral position in the community. As a "blessing" or "gift" (*sadaqa*), the endowed land or property itself acquired holy and reverent connotations.

The waqf system was neither finite or static.[10] New methods of administration were continually developed that improved the efficiency of collecting revenue, maintaining structure, and providing services. At the same time, corruption and mismanagement led to the conversion of some waqfs to private property and to their dismemberment. Significantly, the late Ottoman period saw a trend towards greater state control, with centralized budgeting and accountability; this transition converted the waqf system from a collection of independent and overlapping charitable institutions into an embryonic social welfare arm of a government bureaucracy. Amid these changes, one feature remained constant: the waqf continued to be perceived as a holy institution serving the needs of the Muslim community and bringing religious blessings to founders, administrators, and beneficiaries alike.

The religious nature of the waqf, irrespective of whether its purpose was religious or secular, was underlined by the supervisory role given to the qadis, or religious judges. The creation of a waqf usually took the form of a written declaration, a *waqfiyya*, which was approved by a qadi and registered in the records of the shari'a court.[11] The *waqif* usually appointed a manager, or *mutawalli*, to direct the maintenance of the waqf property, the collection of rents or tithes, and the allocation of income. In particularly large waqfs, a team of secretaries, rent-collectors, and repairers could be employed.[12] The *mutawalli* held a key position in the good management of a waqf, and his or her position and activities had to be confirmed and monitored by a qadi.[13] In practice, the *waqif*, *mutawalli*, and qadi could all be related, and the scope for mismanagement, corruption, and embezzlement was large.

The purposes for which waqfs were created (which were spelled out in the *waqfiyya*) ranged from the very specific to the communal and general. For example, waqfs were created to furnish orphaned girls with dowries so that they could attract husbands; to provide income for the payment of fines of destitute prisoners; to buy clothes for aged villagers; or to arm soldiers.[14] On a grander scale, the Hijaz railway, running through Syria and Jordan on its way to Mecca, was funded by subscriptions from the Muslim public and came to be regarded as a waqf.[15] In this way waqfs played an important role in the daily lives of many Muslims.

Because waqfs have undergone complex transformations over the years, they have been described and defined in numerous ways, not all of which are relevant here. For our purposes, the most important are those definitions that refer to their legal status in land law, to the nature of their administration, and to the purposes for which they were founded. For the most part, waqfs consist of immovable land and property.[16] In the strict sense of shari'a law, only *mulk* land—that is, land that is privately owned—can be endowed. This restriction was meant to prevent the conversion of tenanted (*miri*) land that ultimately belonged to the state into waqf. (*Miri* comes from the Arabic word *amiriyya*, meaning "of the state.") Waqfs created from *mulk* land were called *waqf sahih*, or "true" waqf. But since *miri* land could be inherited and sold and was generally regarded by tenants as their own, in practice much *miri* land *was* converted into waqf.[17] Consequently, such waqf became known as *waqf ghayr sahih*, or "untrue" waqf.

While *waqf sahih* and *waqf ghayr sahih* are determined by the legal status of land or property ownership, two categories—*madbut* and *mulhaq*—are determined by the waqf's relationship to the state bureaucracy. As will be discussed later in this chapter, the Ottoman state increasingly began to interfere in the administration and control of waqfs, particularly those that had lapsed or been neglected or mismanaged, or those whose beneficiaries no longer existed. Those waqfs that came under the direct control of the state were known as *madbut* waqfs.[18] In contrast, *mulhaq* waqfs were privately administered, although by the end of the Ottoman period, the state had asserted a supervisory role over *mulhaq* waqfs through its increasing control over the shari'a courts to which they were accountable.[19]

The final set of categories relates to the purposes for which a waqf was established. One of the main motivations attributed to the creation of waqfs was the circumvention of Islamic inheritance laws. Shari'a law specified that all property was to be passed on to all the children of the deceased. This meant that houses and estates were continually divided and that the wealth of the family could be dissipated through fragmentation. By endowing portions of that wealth and by appointing, say, the eldest son and his descendants as *mutawalli*, a family could avoid the division of the property and keep its wealth intact. These endowments became known as waqf *dhurri* or *ahli*, literally meaning "family" waqfs, and while they were permitted in shari'a law, their status was a source of dispute.[20] The absence of a clear-cut prohibition in shari'a law led to the rapid proliferation of *dhurri* waqfs; in fact, Avraham Granott, a well-known scholar of the land tenure system of Palestine, estimates that 75 percent of all waqfs in Syria and Egypt during the Ottoman period were waqf *dhurri*.[21]

The popularity of waqf *dhurri* among the religious and political elite in the Arab world highlights the manner in which the elite made use of the waqf system to maintain its economic base and extend its influence. In this way, waqfs also had a bearing on the relationship between the religious and political elite and the state. For wealthy landowners with extensive estates, the threat of confiscation by the state was a constant source of concern.[22] Granott writes:

> Anyone who wished to protect his property against plots of the powerful or against confiscation for the benefit of the state—a common practice in the Ottoman empire—had no other way open to him except to proclaim his immovable property—houses or shops or factories, such as flour mills, soapworks, limekilns, and oil or sugar factories—as waqf foundations for the benefit of mosques or schools, and so to ensure to his descendants the income from the property, or at least part of it.[23]

Although endowing property did not guarantee its preservation, it did act as a deterrent as long as the state wished to operate within the religious and judicial consensus.

In contrast to waqf *dhurri*, waqf *khayri*, or public waqf (literally "charitable" waqf) were waqfs whose incomes were used to provide services to the community at large, be it schools, mosques, fountains, hospices, and so on.[24] They could be any size and were administered by a range of people not necessarily related to the *waqif*. Indeed, in many cases the distinction between the two is blurred, as endowments were often created for both public and family purposes, and the property and land were divided between the two.[25]

State officials were well aware that the waqf system benefitted the state as well. Bearing in mind the weakness of the centralized state apparatus, the waqf system was used to encourage immigration to certain regions, to stimulate trade, and to strengthen central control over particular provinces. Following his conquest of Jerusalem from the Crusaders, Salah al-Din, for example, created a number of endowments, which attracted builders, craftsmen, pilgrims, and scholars, thereby helping to reestablish the Islamic character of the city. The state also used waqfs as a vehicle by which it could provide services to the community. The Khaski Sultan waqf was a huge endowment created from the land given by Sultan Sulayman the Magnificent to his wife, Roxelana, to support a large soup kitchen for the poor in Jerusalem. Drinking water was supplied to Jerusalem from the Birkat Sulayman through aqueducts maintained by waqf funds.[26] The opportunities provided by the waqf system became more evident during the latter part of Ottoman rule, as we shall note later in this chapter.

An illuminating example of how waqfs could serve as a magnet and affect the life of a Palestinian city is provided by the waqf of Ahmad Pasha al-Jazzar.[27] The al-Jazzar waqf, established in 1784 by the governor of Acre and wali of Sidon, became the basis for the commercial and economic expansion of Acre in the late eighteenth and early nineteenth centuries. The stipulations of the *waqfiyya* included the construction of khans, public baths, market places, a mosque, a school, and shops; these were designed to encourage faith, trade, industry, and hygiene. The khans in particular attracted and encouraged the flow of trade through Acre's harbor. The Khan al-'Umdan, for example, was constructed close to the port with one wall adjoining the quay itself so as to allow the easy transfer and storage of goods. Grain warehouses were built into the walls of the ground floor, with sleeping and living quarters on the upper floors. The income from the waqf al-Jazzar permitted the building of two other similar khans.

In addition to the khans, markets and bazaars were built around the mosque. Their rents maintained the structure of the mosque and supported the religious and cleaning staff. Two public baths, the Pasha and the Sha'abi, were built in accordance with the Quranic injunction concerning cleanliness and attracted traders and travelers seeking refreshment and relaxation after a long journey through the mountains and deserts of the Syrian hinterland. The baths themselves were made profitable by tendering their management commercially.[28] As a result of these practical and commercially shrewd endowments, Ottoman Acre flourished; local legend boasted that "each day one thousand camels entered the city."

With its large dome and tall spires dominating the coastal landscape, the mosque al-Jazzar became the biggest and most prestigious mosque in the north of Palestine.[29] The *waqfiyya* laid down that income should be set aside for the support of an imam, a *khatib* (preacher), five muezzin, and a chief muezzin. (In an interview, the qadi of Acre referred to eight, but the *waqfiyya* specifies that only six muezzin were to be employed.) Doorkeepers, lamplighters, cleaners, and maintenance men were also employed. At a later date, the offices of the qadi of Acre as well as waqf administrators and the shari'a court for the region were housed in rooms around the mosque courtyard. Water from a stream outside Acre was channelled along a specially constructed aqueduct to a fountain outside the mosque for the benefit of the residents of the quarter.[30] Another stipulation of the *waqfiyya* was the establishment of a school, which occupied small rooms in the mosque courtyard. It contained a library and was the only school that was recognized by the al-Azhar University in Cairo, which provided automatic admission for the school's graduates.[31]

The Extent and Nature of Waqf Land and Property in Palestine

The waqf system played an important part in the political, economic, social, and religious life of the Islamic world. One way of observing that role in Palestine is to examine the extent of waqf land in what became Mandated Palestine after 1918. In this regard, it is important to note that the estimates of waqf holdings that have been made often are contradictory, causing confusion about the impact and political importance of the waqf system. Thus, before attempting to assess the extent of waqf land and property in Palestine, one must first address the absence of accurate figures on the subject.

For a number of reasons, the figures provided by scholars are deductions and calculations based on insufficient data. The Ottoman bureaucracy was not sufficiently developed to maintain complete records of all land registration and transactions. Of those records that were made, many have been lost. The British, who embarked upon a land registration program for taxation purposes, had not been able to complete it by the end of the Mandate period.[32] One might reasonably expect waqf holdings to be registered in the *sijill*s of the shari'a courts, but tallying all the waqfs recorded there is an ambitious task, and research into the *sijill*s has only just begun.[33] Writing in the 1930s, S.B. Himadeh tersely commented that "There is no record of the extent of waqf land and there are no reliable estimates."[34] This, however, would appear to be an exaggeration.

A second issue that complicates discussions of waqf land holdings is that the units of measure in which the available data are recorded are not always compatible. Information about waqfs is given in dunums (approximately four dunums make one acre), in monetary terms (Palestinian, Turkish, or Egyptian pounds, which will be referred to as P£, T£ and E£ respectively), and in percentages of waqf income, whether urban rents or rural tithes. Furthermore, distinctions between waqf *sahih* and waqf *ghayr sahih* are not always made clear, and the two are often lumped together when it does not make sense to do so. Most waqf *sahih* constituted urban waqfs whose income from rents may have been large, but whose actual land area was much smaller than the waqf *ghayr sahih*, which tended to comprise larger areas of (agricultural) land but produced less income. G. Baer contends that because there was much less *mulk* or freehold land in Palestine, there was not much waqf *sahih*.[35] Finally, it is not always clear what year is being referred to when estimates are given. The sources date from various times during the Ottoman administration and the British period, and the extent of waqf property varied over the 150 years in review.

The available data for waqf *sahih* (waqf created from *mulk*) are very sparse. The British government's "Report on Immigration, Land Settlement and Development," compiled by Sir John Hope-Simpson and known as the Hope-Simpson Report, claimed that waqf *sahih* on agricultural land amounted to no more than 100,000 dunums:

> The area of agricultural land dedicated as "true Waqf" is comparatively insignificant. In the whole of Palestine it is not claimed to extend to 100,000 dunams, and, in fact, the extent is probably much smaller.[36]

Since Hope-Simpson offers no sources for his figure, it is difficult to know how much credence may be given to this estimate. Nonetheless, given that most waqf *sahih* were urban, he was probably correct that the area was "insignificant" in terms of agricultural land in Palestine, which amounted to 8,044,000 dunums.[37] According to Hope-Simpson, then, 1.25 percent of the agricultural land in Palestine was waqf *sahih*. (It must be remembered that this is not the total urban and rural dunums that may be considered waqf *sahih*.)

The extent of urban waqf *sahih* is provided by J.B. Barron, the director of Revenue and Customs of the Mandatory government, who compiled an estimate of waqf income in 1922. For his estimate, he used income figures of the Supreme Muslim Council, a body created by the Mandate authorities that assumed, among other responsibilities, the direction of the public waqf in Palestine. Barron estimated that P£ 11,013 (or approximately 25 percent) of the Supreme Muslim Council's total income of P£ 43,297 would be derived from urban rents.[38] This figure must be qualified on two counts. First, as has already been mentioned, although urban waqf property tended to be waqf *sahih*, not all of it was, so the figure includes some *ghayr sahih*. Second, the figure refers only to waqf administered by the Supreme Muslim Council, and not to urban waqf that was *dhurri*, or private family waqf (which was also usually waqf *sahih*). Thus Barron tells us less about the extent or percentages of waqf *sahih* in urban areas than about its importance to the Supreme Muslim Council.

A third source for waqf *sahih* calculations is Y. Shimoni, who states that between 40 and 50 percent of waqf land is waqf *sahih*.[39] He does not explain the basis for his estimate, and his figure hardly corresponds with Hope-Simpson's, since it would make the total waqf of both types only 200,000 dunums, which is much too low. Shimoni also asserts, without explanation, that 40,000 dunums of waqf *sahih* was *dhurri* waqf. This may well be true, but it does not further our calculations much. A final source is Y. Vashitz, who wrote in 1947 that 33 percent of Ramla and 70 percent of the shops in towns such as Jaffa and Acre were waqf—probably, in our view, waqf *sahih*.[40] Like Shimoni, he does not provide evidence to support his estimate.

Figures for waqf *ghayr sahih* (which include subgroups such as *miri mawqufa* and waqf *tahsisat*) are more plentiful and more reliable. Granott calculates that waqf *ghayr sahih* comprises 600,000 dunums.[41] This calculation is based on the tithe collected by the Mandatory government for the Supreme Muslim Council, which amounted to P£ 30,000.[42] By comparing this income to other non-waqf tithes, Granott arrives at a figure of 550,000 dunums for *ghayr sahih*, but adds 50,000 dunums to make 600,000; he argues, correctly, that their area should be greater because "...the dedicated properties are neglected in comparison with other land, (therefore) it is presumed that their revenue is less."[43]

Shimoni also estimates that 720,000–1,000,000 dunums were waqf *ghayr sahih*;[44] he does not provide a source for this estimate. Abrahamovitch likewise gives no sources, and his estimate of waqf comes to 15 percent of agricultural land or 7 percent of the total land area, most of which was presumably waqf *ghayr sahih*.[45] Without the sources, it is difficult to establish the accuracy of these figures, but they do provide useful markers. Another important figure for making deductions for waqf *ghayr sahih* is that given by Barron, who states that the Supreme Muslim Council receives 12.75 percent of the total tithes of the country.[46] This figure allows us to check Granott's assessment. Following Granott's method of comparing waqf and non-waqf tithe income to reach an estimate of land area, Kupferschmidt increases the estimate to 700,000 dunums, and on this basis he concludes that waqf *ghayr sahih* amounted to 8.7 percent of agricultural land, or 2.7 percent of the total land area of Palestine.[47] Unfortunately, he does not explain why he increased Granott's figure, but one can assume that, like Granott, he wished to account for the unproductivity of the land. Since Granott's method of calculation seems to be the only one available to us, it is worth taking these calculations a little further.

If the agricultural land area of Palestine under the Mandate came to approximately 8,044,000 dunums, Granott's figure of 600,000 dunums for waqf *ghayr sahih* comes to only 7.5 percent of that land.[48] But Barron, who should know by virtue of his position within the Mandate government, claims that 12.75 percent of agricultural tithes come from waqf tithes, which, translated into area, comes to 1,025,610 dunums. Granott's calculations, therefore, appear to be conservative. If, instead, one takes Barron's figure as a starting point and adds, as Granott did, 50,000 dunums to compensate for the fact that waqf land tended to be unproductive, one arrives at the sum of 1,075,610 dunums. Thus, waqf *ghayr sahih* amounted to an estimated 13.4 percent of agricultural land in Palestine. One can fairly safely assume this to be a conservative estimate; if one added another 100,000 dunums, as Kupferschmidt does, for the unproductiveness of waqf land (instead of Granott's 50,000 dunums), the final figure could be closer to 15 percent. Furthermore, to arrive at the total amount of agricultural land that was waqf, Granott adds the 100,000 dunums of waqf *sahih* mentioned in Hope-Simpson to the final estimate of 1,175,610 dunums of waqf *ghayr sahih*.[49] This would bring the percentage closer to 16 percent. This estimate should be viewed with caution, because Hope-Simpson's estimate is uncorroborated. A more cautious estimate for agricultural waqf land in Palestine at the turn of the century, then, would range between 13 and 15 percent of the total agricultural area.

Waqf Administration in Palestine during the Late Ottoman Period

During the late Ottoman period, which stretched from the turn of the eighteenth century to the beginning of World War I in 1914, the waqf system was transformed from a system dominated by the religious and political elite in Palestine into one over which the state had considerable influence and control. Nevertheless, while the legal and administrative structures created by the state during this period permitted the incremental extension of its authority over significant parts of the waqf system, the state failed to achieve a complete monopoly over the waqf system. Thus, the elite families were able to retain, to a large extent, their influence over areas of waqf administration and a large number of waqfs.

As has already been observed, both family and public waqfs had become the administrative preserve of wealthy notable families. These families used the power and influence given to them through their control of the waqfs to act independently and at times contrary to the wishes of the central Ottoman authorities in Istanbul. In Palestine, established and influential families such as the Nusaybehs, the Khalidis, the Husaynis, the Abd' al-Hadis, the Tamimis, and the Jarallahs, all held important posts in the administration of both *khayri* and *dhurri* waqfs: it has been estimated that 40 percent of all waqf *sahih* property in Palestine belonged to these families.[50] But they had many more thousands of dunums of waqf *ghayr sahih*, which technically belonged to the state. Moreover, the failure to ensure proper cultivation in older and badly managed waqfs meant the immobilization or underutilization of valuable land.

In sum, from the perspective of Ottoman officials in Istanbul, the waqf system contributed to the regular and various assertions of regional autonomy against their central control (see Map 1). Thus, in order to consolidate the state's power and to bolster declining revenues, the Ottoman authorities set about centralizing and rationalizing the waqf system. The *tanzimat* reforms initiated by the Ottoman government during the middle of the nineteenth century were in part an attempt to deal with this issue. Focusing generally on land ownership, the administration of shari'a courts, and the extension of the jurisdiction of the state-run *nizamiyya* (civil) courts, the government also introduced important reforms that curtailed the authority of the local ulema and notables over the waqf system.[51]

This process of rationalization and centralization was not achieved in a single stroke. The reforms were introduced during the course of a century, and in fact were never completed. In many areas the code was ignored or only partially implemented, and the authority of the ulema and the shari'a courts continued to be respected. In many cases the same religious officials presided over both the shari'a and *nizamiyya* courts. However partial the implementation of these reforms, they did mark the gradual divergence of the state from the religious and judicial consensus. They also caused the first appearance of waqf-supported opposition to the state. As will be seen when we turn to the British Mandate period, the potential for the waqf system to be used as part of the resistance to reform would become more apparent with time.

During this same period, the Ottoman government set up administrative structures for the parts of the waqf system under its control, making them correspond to its provincial administrative structures. For example, the management of *madbut* waqfs in Palestine was divided between the *vilayet* (province) of Beirut and the *mutasarrif* (district) of Jerusalem. A position of *mudir* (administrator) was established in Jerusalem, and the person who held this position supervised the work of three *ma'murs* in the Gaza, Hebron, and Jaffa subdistricts. Their task was to examine receipts and expenditures and to approve repairs and improvements on waqf property in their charge.[52] Furthermore, in 1840 the Ottoman government set up a local administrative council, or *majlis*, in the *mutasarrif* of Jerusalem, on which Ottoman waqf officials were given seats. These initiatives showed how the Ottoman state was prepared to use its control over part of the waqf system to curb the power of the local religious and political elite. The government, by agreeing to the establishment of the *majlis*, simultaneously recognized the autonomous power of the elite and limited the effectiveness of that autonomy by placing its own officials

Map 1. Palestine during the Ottoman Period

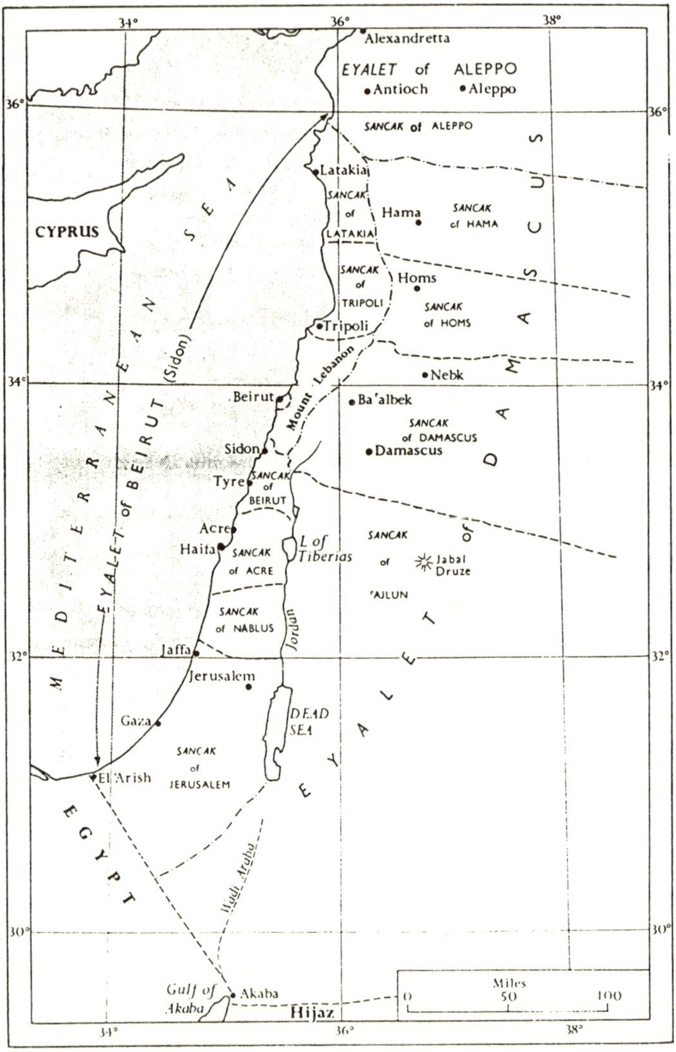

Source: Ma'oz, *Ottoman Reforms* (London: Oxford University Press, 1968).

on the *majlis*.[53] These Ottoman structures, therefore, constituted a form of co-optation of the elite.

By the second half of the nineteenth century, the Ottoman state involvement in waqf administration had developed to such an extent that a Ministry of Waqfs had been established. In 1883, the new ministry took over additional waqfs on the grounds that they were being mismanaged or that their status as waqf property was questionable. This step also reflected the government's desire to exercise greater authority over the provision of education and social welfare: the waqfs expropriated in this way were often those supporting mosques, Sufi *takiya*s (hospices), and religious schools. The income from these waqfs was redirected toward establishing a state educational system.[54] In the same way, the ministry also continued to take over *dhurri* waqfs whose beneficiaries had died or which in some way had lapsed. By 1914 some seventy *dhurri* waqfs in Palestine had been taken over by the Ministry of Waqfs.[55] These latter moves confirmed the centralizing and modernizing policies of the Ottoman state and constituted a clear extension of its power into the waqf system.

During the twilight of the Ottoman Empire, the pace of this kind of reform accelerated under the direction of the Young Turks, who substantially altered the administration of the waqf system in Palestine. The Young Turks attempted to limit further the waste and inefficiencies in the system by selling off derelict and unproductive buildings and lands and by transferring the profits to the State Treasury. They also continued the confiscation of waqfs said to be in public interest, and they abolished some *imaret*s, or soup kitchens, whose services were taken over by the state.[56] They speeded up the transfer of the lapsed waqfs from the *mutawalli*s who had managed them to the Ministry of Waqfs.[57] In addition, an arrangement whereby waqf tithes were collected by the state and allocated to the waqf beneficiaries on behalf of the waqf administrators, known as commutation, was extended from the Khaski Sultan waqf to include four other large family waqfs in the *sanjaq* of Jerusalem—the Nabi Da'ud, Nabi Musa, Shaykh Ahmad Dajani, and Abu Madyan waqfs.[58]

The implementation of these latter reforms marked a clear break from the religious and judicial consensus, and led to strong opposition. The influential notable families and ulema resisted the diminution of their powers and sought to influence the decisions of the *majalis* that affected their control over the waqf system. As a result of this opposition, not all the reforms were applied uniformly across the empire. A particularly contentious issue proved to be the transfer of the lapsed waqfs to the Ministry of Waqfs. These had been a lucrative source of income, property, and privileges for the notables and ulema.[59] The resistance of these elites did not take the form of open revolt, but was expressed instead in cumulative acts of noncompliance and obstruction.

These developments triggered the evolution of the waqf system from an autonomous and amorphous network of disparate endowments into a social welfare arm of the Ottoman state, albeit in embryonic form. The state sought to achieve this transformation by asserting its control in a number of ways: it centralized the administration of *madbut* waqfs; it legislated restrictions on the types of land that could be made into waqfs, thus checking the spiraling proliferation of waqfs; it appropriated mismanaged and lapsed waqfs to increase the proportion of the waqf system under its direct control and to accelerate their productivity; and it curbed the authority of the ulema and the notables over waqfs. In these ways one can see how the state used the waqf system as a vehicle through which it extended its own authority. This brief survey sets the scene for the next stage in the development of the waqf system, when, under the British Mandate it became both a mediating institution between the state and the Palestinian population and a vehicle for Palestinian nationalism and opposition to colonialism and Zionism.

The British Occupation of Palestine and the Mandate Period

Following the collapse of the Ottoman Empire and the establishment of the British Mandate for Palestine, the Muslim waqf system in Palestine was separated from the wider Muslim world by the creation of a new administrative structure, the Supreme Muslim Council, which oversaw the public waqf strictly within the borders of Mandatory Palestine. Although created by the British, the Council was dominated by the Palestinian religious elite and notables, and faced with British support for a Jewish "national home" policy and the activities of the Zionist movement, it soon appropriated additional roles. These developments all combined to give the Muslim waqf system in Palestine a "national" character that deepened as the Mandate progressed. Moreover, the Supreme Muslim Council's control of the waqf provided the Muslim elite with a clearly-demarcated organizational and resource base.

The British Mandate government's co-optation of the waqf system's leadership, and the degree of control it exercised over waqf system resources, reveal the nature of the waqf system's relationship with the state and the extent to which it came to constitute a mediating institution. By examining these matters, we can more clearly see why the waqf system was denied this mediating role after 1948 and 1967 by the Israeli state.

In 1917, the British forces occupying Palestine set up the Occupied Enemy Territory Administration, pending the capitulation of Turkey. When the League of Nations granted the British a "mandate" over Palestine in 1922, British government control over Palestine was confirmed. Prior to this, a Palestinian boycott of elections to a proposed legislative council had led the British government to try to obtain the cooperation of the local population by preserving the status quo as it related to religious affairs. As a result of the collapse of the Ottoman Empire, certain adjustments were required with regard to the Muslim community in Palestine and the legal separation of the shari'a courts from Istanbul. In order to examine these issues, a Committee for Moslem Religious Affairs was set up with the participation of Palestinian ulema and notables on one hand and British officials on the other. The most important issue to be considered was the transfer of powers of the *shaykh ul-*

islam, the highest religious authority in the Ottoman Empire, to a Jerusalem court of appeal. The court would be under the jurisdiction of the new body that had been specially created, the Supreme Muslim Council.[60] This was a highly symbolic and significant transfer; for the first time it established a single integrated shari'a court and waqf system within the borders of Palestine. Together with the establishment of the Supreme Muslim Council itself, it was probably the key event in the history and politics of the waqf system in Palestine.

The Supreme Muslim Council consisted of five members: a president, two representatives from the former *sanjaq*s of Acre and Nablus, and two representatives from the *sanjaq* (formerly *mutasarrif*) of Jerusalem, which included Jaffa, Hebron, and Gaza. These members were elected for four years by an electoral college in accordance with the former Ottoman electoral system.[61] The Supreme Muslim Council was empowered to appoint all shari'a court officers and any official or administrator financed from waqf funds, such as qadis and imams, and to administer the waqf system.[62] It was also given the power to approve the annual waqf budget, which it was routinely to transmit to the British Mandatory government "for information."[63]

The responsibility for day-to-day management of the waqf system was to be carried out by a newly established General Waqf Committee, to be chaired by the president of the Supreme Muslim Council. The waqf system itself was divided into six districts: Gaza, Jaffa, Acre, Nablus, Jerusalem, and Hebron. Local Waqf Committees supervised the work of waqf officials in their areas and oversaw the collection and distribution of waqf income. Each committee consisted of a mufti or the eldest *'alim* in the district, the local *ma'mur*, and two notables who were elected to serve for two years. The *ma'mur* from each local Waqf Committee sat on the General Waqf Committee, which was led by a director-general of the Waqf Administration.

By virtue of its structure and its relationship with the British Mandate government, the Supreme Muslim Council played the role of a mediating institution for a significant period of time. On the one hand there was a limited co-optation of the leadership in the sense that appointments required the approval of the British High Commissioner.[64] On the other hand, except for the funding of some teachers in waqf schools, in practice little state intervention took place since salaries and the creation of new posts were the responsibility of the Supreme Muslim Council itself. That the members of the Supreme Muslim Council were elected further increased its independence from state authorities. In the absence of a secular alternative recognized by the state, the Council was not only the key body representing the interests of the Muslim community in Palestine, but also the only institution that could directly represent the national aspirations of the Palestinians as a whole to the British government, despite the opposition the Council faced from a number of Palestinian quarters.[65]

The integration of the waqf system's administration into the state structures was similarly limited. Indeed, the high political profile that the Council later enjoyed and its wide-ranging powers and responsibilities raise the question of the extent to which it was a government institution at all. The original intention was clearly that it be so. As Kupferschmidt observes, the position of the *ra'is al-'ulama'*, or head of the ulema, was originally intended to be on the same footing as a "senior official" in the Mandatory government. The names of Council members appear in the government Blue Book and Civil Service List. Moreover, an office in Government House was allocated to the *ra'is al-'ulama'*, although it was only occupied for a few days before the Council decided to locate itself in the Madrassa Manjakiyya beside the Haram al-Sharif.[66] But while the Mandatory government retained formal control over the Council through a number of approval procedures, in practice the Council's separate administrative structure, which functioned in an entirely different location, points to a highly independent status.

A similar situation prevailed in the area of state. The Mandatory government agreed to continue the Ottoman practice of commuting the agricultural tithes that were due to the waqf system. As already noted, these were waqf tithes that the Ottoman government had collected along with other rural taxes, but which had been transferred to the Ministry of Waqfs as a means of improving efficiency. By continuing this practice, the Mandatory government provided a regular yearly income of P£ 30,000 to the Council, which amounted to about 50 percent of its income.[67] The commutation of waqf tithes, therefore, was of great practical assistance to the Council, enabling it to plan and budget ahead with a certain confidence. As noted, the government also continued to pay the salaries of certain types of teachers in waqf schools.[68]

Aware that such practices placed the waqf system in a position of dependency on the state, the Council made strenuous efforts to broaden its financial base. Researchers were sent to Istanbul to obtain documents and proofs aimed at security control over waqfs whose exact nature was in doubt. The Council pressed the government to take control over large waqfs (such as the Khaski Sultan), which had been taken over by the Ottoman government.[69] During the height of its struggle in the 1930s against British government policies and Zionist immigration, the Council also embarked upon extensive land reclamation schemes, draining and irrigating desert and swampland to increase their productivity. One such scheme involved the marshes of Wadi Rubin, south of Jaffa, which were cleared, drained, and planted with orange trees. Later, following further archival researches by the Supreme Muslim Council, an area north of Tel Aviv near Netanya, known as Birkat Ramadan, was discovered to be part of the Khalil al-Rahman waqf and, in 1936, a drainage scheme was constructed to cover approximately 25,000 dunums.[70]

The Council's efforts to ensure independent financing conflicted with the British commitment to a Jewish national home. The question of landownership was, and still is, the crux of the conflict between Zionist and Palestinian aspirations. During the Mandate period, the steady immigration of Jews and the growing land purchases through such institutions as the Jewish National Fund brought the issue to the forefront of the international political arena. As the leading Palestinian institution, the Supreme Muslim Council did not hesitate to frame the land issue in religious terms. Accordingly, it involved the waqf system in a campaign to obstruct further land sales and to extend the area of waqf land as a method of preventing land purchases by the Zionists.

Initially the Council sought to build up the social and religious pressure against sales to the Jews. It persuaded the leading Muslim scholar of the time, Rashid Rida, to issue a *fatwa* (religious dispensation) forbidding the sale of land to Jews.[71] The mufti of Jerusalem and president of the Supreme Muslim Council, Haj Amin al-Husayni, and other leading religious figures toured the country castigating sellers and brokers, and the theme was taken up by imams and *khatib*s in local mosques who preached on the "holiness" of Palestine.[72] As part of this campaign, public ceremonies were held in which Palestinians pledged not to sell land to Jews. Many leading landowners took part.[73]

A measure of the Supreme Muslim Council's determination to prevent sales was its attempt to compete with the Jewish National Fund over land purchases. The purchasing power of the Supreme Muslim Council was extremely limited, however, and it was not able to make even a fraction of the large-scale purchases it originally had envisaged. Instead, it attempted to frustrate Jewish purchasing strategies by scattering its purchases over a wide area, as the Jewish National Fund tended to buy only in regions where there was a possibility of expanding the size of the purchase later.[74] Similarly, the Supreme Muslim Council tried to persuade Palestinian Muslims to convert their *mulk* properties to waqf *dhurri* as a way of rendering land and property unsalable. This latter also had limited success, since, as we have noted, most agricultural land in Palestine is *miri*, and the Mandatory government observed the Ottoman land laws. It did not grant the Council's request to allow the conversion of *miri* into waqf, and as a consequence only small quantities of *mulk* were endowed in response to the Council's campaign.[75]

Despite the state's restrictions, the waqf system as represented by the Supreme Muslim Council was able to operate in a relatively autonomous manner. By the late 1920s, some British officials were expressing their concern at the latitude afforded to the Council. Luke, the chief secretary of the Mandatory government in the 1920s, observed that:

> The constitution....involved a delegation to the Supreme Muslim Council of jurisdiction so extensive and powers so wide as to be to some extent almost an abdication to the Administration of Palestine of responsibilities normally incumbent upon a Government![76]

Even though it had retained coercive administrative and financial powers to restrict the activities of the Council, the Mandatory government was loath to use them. One explanation lay in the changing political configuration in Palestine as a result of the Mandatory government's commitment to the Jewish national home policy. In view of the increase in Jewish immigration, settlement, and land acquisition, the government was reluctant to antagonize the Muslim community further. Granting the Muslims a degree of autonomous action in their religious affairs was seen as an important concession to the religious elite. As the head of the Middle East

Department of the Colonial Office, Sir John Shuckburgh, wrote in 1926:

> The institution of a Supreme Muslim Council in 1921 has, on the whole, been one of the most successful moves in Palestine. It practically gave the Mohammedans self-government in regard to Moslem affairs. This has worked smoothly and has no doubt done much to reconcile Mohammedans to the Mandatory regime with its unpopular Zionist flavor.[77]

The Mandatory government's reluctance to intervene allowed the Council to use the financial resources of the waqf system to mobilize opposition to the government. As we have noted, the funds were used to campaign against land sales to Zionist purchasers and to encourage the conversion of *mulk* land to waqf. The Council's control over a large number of educational institutions also allowed it to rally opinion against the government and Zionist organizations by introducing new curricula that drew attention to the current situation.[78]

Although the Council would not act in open defiance of the British until the mid-1930s, by the late 1920s there were indications that the British commitment to Jewish immigration would lead the Council into more overt opposition. For example, in what has become known as the Wailing Wall incident of 1929, Haj Amin al-Husayni, the mufti of Jerusalem and president of the Council's central committee, played a leading role in Palestinian reaction to what was perceived as Zionist attempts to encroach on the Muslim holy places.[79] During this period, a narrow, paved courtyard beside the western wall of the Haram al-Sharif—holy to Muslims and Jews alike—became the focus of intense intercommunal and interreligious conflict that erupted into riots and killings.

Muslim tradition holds that the Prophet Muhammad tethered his steed Buraq to this wall before his mystical flight to heaven. During the Ottoman period, Jews were given permission to use the area in front of the wall for prayers, provided no fixed religious appurtenances were used that would block the pavement. In general, an uneasy equilibrium between devout Jews and passing Muslims was maintained. The Mandatory government was at pains to maintain this status quo. However, given their increasing numbers, Jews began to assert themselves more forcefully along the wall, hampering the free passage of Muslim residents in the area. The news of discussion in Zionist circles regarding the possibility of buying the wall and adjoining pavement was alarming to Muslims; they were further provoked by the placement of a screen on the pavement to separate male and female Jewish worshippers. In response to this disruption, the Council reasserted the Muslim presence by practicing Sufi prayer rituals in the adjoining *zawiya*, which involved the banging of cymbals and gongs. This in turn precipitated a large Jewish demonstration to protest government inaction. The incident became a test of wills between religious communities in Palestine. The Council organized a nationwide campaign and established a committee to rally support from the international Muslim community. Thus, a general Islamic dimension, purporting to prevent the desecration of Muslim holy sites by Jews, was added to the nationalist dimension that reflected Palestinian Muslim fears of Jewish immigration and colonization.

In August 1929, riots broke out, Jewish settlements were attacked, and nearly 100 Jews were killed. The Mandatory government, aware of the sensitivities of Muslim communities in the other British colonies, saw the risk of a major conflagration and acted swiftly. It brought in the British navy from Egypt and sought to quell the Palestinian interior with the army. The government also persuaded the Palestinian religious elite to denounce the killings. The Wailing Wall incident reflected the Council's commitment to the Palestinian national struggle, and the ensuing conflict projected Haj Amin al-Husayni, the *ra'is al-'ulama'* and head of the Supreme Muslim Council, to the forefront of the national political leaders.[80] It also demonstrated the willingness of the Council to support this struggle with the funds of the waqf system. The Council's participation in the Great Revolt of 1936–39 and the general strike merely confirmed this support.[81]

These events show the extent to which the Council as a representative body was obliged to part company with the British state authorities over the Jewish national home policy. Indeed, it was the Council's independent administrative structure, its relatively autonomous control over its resources, its ability to resist co-optation, and its representational functions that enabled it to take an oppositionist position. To regain control over the Council and the resources of the waqf system, the Mandatory government was forced to exercise its coercive powers. In both these ways the mediating role of the Council was confirmed and exemplified; the freedom to act independently existed, but the state retained ultimate authority. In 1937, at the height of the Arab Revolt, the Mandatory government's Defense (Muslim Waqf) Regulations[82] suspended the five-person central committee of the Council, and replaced it by a government-appointed commission. Haj Amin, the *ra'is al-'ulama'*, sought sanctuary in the Haram al-Sharif but finally fled to Lebanon. Other members and employees of the Council and ulema were either arrested or deported, or fled into exile.[83]

During the following eleven years of the British Mandate, the waqf system, the shari'a court, the related educational institutions, and the entire Supreme Muslim Council structure country-wide were run by the British-appointed commission. The government's control of the commission was underlined by the appointment of two British officials; the third member was Dr. Yusuf Maykal, a Palestinian lawyer.[84] The land campaigns ceased, as did the confrontations with Jews that had been supported by the Supreme Muslim Council. Repairs, support for educational and charitable work, and the smooth running of the shari'a courts continued. Removed from its participation in the national struggle going on around it, the post-1937 Council effectively became part of the bureaucracy of the Mandatory government.

The Mandatory government's imposition of the 1937 Defense Regulations marked the failure of its policy towards the waqf system as a mediating institution. One can posit three possible reasons for this failure. First, the state was an alien non-Muslim power that lacked any strong moral or religious sanction to justify its coercive powers; it lay outside the Muslim religious and judicial consensus, and its relations with a strong Islamic institution always required a difficult balancing act.

Second, in an attempt to redress its commitment to Jewish immigration and settlement, the Mandatory government ceded administrative and financial control over the allocation of significant resources to the religious elite administering the waqf system. As a result, it could not prevent these funds from being used to oppose its policies. Finally, by adhering to the policy of establishing a Jewish national home, the government could neither obtain the loyalty of that elite by offering them sufficient guarantees as to the continuity of their positions and privileges, nor could it credibly add to their legitimacy in the eyes of their community. Once the state failed to co-opt the religious elite and had no control over the administrative structure or resources that the elite commanded, the waqf system ceased to be a mediating institution and became instead a vehicle for nationalist opposition. To protect its own policy objectives, the state was obliged to take full control.

* * * * *

On the whole, under the political circumstances of the British Mandate for Palestine, the conditions that permitted the waqf system to play a mediating role had improved considerably. The establishment of a single centralized administration had created a coherent and more rational system, while the legal, political, and geographical separation from the rest of the Muslim world gave it a Palestinian and national character. Furthermore, the state recognized both the waqf system's right to organize the Muslim community as well as its representational role. Owning property and land, serving the population, managed by a religious elite, held together by an ideological purpose, the waqf system was, in the absence of any credible alternative, in a strong position to reflect the aspirations of its constituency and to mediate with the British state authorities. One could almost say that after long gestation during the Ottoman period, the waqf system had finally come into its own as a mediating institution.

For a time there is no doubt that the mediating role worked. For its own purposes the Mandatory government was at pains to respect the waqf system's jurisdiction and to ensure that it was able to function. The breakdown of the relationship and the absorption of the system into the state occurred when the policies of the state undermined the future of the system itself, causing the Supreme Muslim Council to abandon its mediating role in favor of outright opposition, a position the state could not sustain.

After 1948 and again after 1967, the Israeli state would be forced to confront the power and influence of the waqf system. It chose a number of different options to deal with the various geographical regions of historical Palestine under its sovereignty. These options reflected the relative strengths and weaknesses of the state and of the waqf system in those regions.

CHAPTER 2

The Muslim Waqf System in Israel, 1948–1964

1948 and Its Aftermath

By the start of the 1940s, the British government realized that its commitment to a Jewish national home had created a dilemma it could not solve and decided to hand the problem to the United Nations. The United Nations partition plan was passed by the General Assembly in November 1947; it divided Mandatory Palestine into two states, one Jewish and one Arab, with an enclave around Jerusalem under international supervision.[1] Although Jews formed about one-third of the population of Palestine at the time, the plan specified that the Jewish state was to receive approximately 60 percent of the land.[2] Thus the UN partition plan was perceived by Palestinians as a victory for the Zionist immigrants; consequently, they rejected it.

The partition plan also provided for the termination of the British Mandate on 14 May 1948, but before that date Jewish and Palestinian irregulars fought to gain control over as much of the land of Palestine as possible. On 15 May, Zionist leaders declared the establishment of the State of Israel, and set up a provisional government to administer all the areas occupied by the Jewish forces (see Map 2). The combined armies of Syria, Iraq, Transjordan, and Egypt had intervened on behalf of the Palestinians but were defeated, and the parties agreed to a series of armistice accords that were finally signed in 1949. The agreements left the new State of Israel in possession of over three-quarters of Mandatory Palestine. What remained were the West Bank (which was incorporated into the Hashemite Kingdom of Jordan) and the Gaza Strip (which was administered by Egypt).

Due to the new borders set out in the armistice agreements and Israel's refusal to allow the Palestinians who had fled the hostilities to return, the Palestinian population that remained in Israel was rendered a minority. In 1946, for example, there were 600,000 Jews and 1,230,000 Palestinians living in the whole of Palestine. On the eve of the 1948 war, 700,000 Jews and 900,000 Palestinians lived in those areas that were to become Israel.[3] Of the 900,000 Palestinians, 770,000 were made refugees during the hostilities, leaving only 130,000, which amounted to 14 percent of the population of Israel in 1948. By 1965, following a program of rapid Jewish immigration, this percentage dropped to 11.5 percent, despite the large natural increase of Palestinians that had meanwhile taken place.[4] Of this new Palestinian minority in Israel, Palestinian Muslims constituted the largest religious community, comprising 69 percent of Palestinians in Israel in 1950 and 71 percent in 1965.[5]

The political landscape of this severely reduced community changed dramatically during the years following the 1948 war, and the impact of the new situation upon the waqf system was similarly great. Even before the declaration of the State of Israel, Muslim communal organization in Palestine had been on the verge of collapse. Religious leaders, preachers, waqf officials, and mosque attendants fled the hostilities and subsequently found themselves unable to return to their homes. As a consequence, by the end of 1948 many mosques were closed and religious buildings abandoned, and services and burials were unable to take place.[6] Some mosques, such as the Jarayna mosque in Haifa and the Nabi 'Ukashah mosque in Jerusalem, were severely damaged by the fighting; the *zawiya* Nabi Da'ud and the adjacent Dajani cemetery in Jerusalem were damaged as well.[7] In some cases, Palestinians made homeless as a result of the fighting had taken refuge inside mosques and continued to live there.[8] Moreover, with only one qadi, Shaykh Tahir al-Tabari, remaining in Israel, the shari'a courts were unable to operate, leading to a suspension of marriages, divorces, the execution of wills, and other matters of personal status.[9] Of the nine Sufi orders in Palestine during the Mandate, only two were left in Israel.[10]

Immediately following the establishment of the state, mosques and mosque officials received grants from the newly established Israeli Ministry for Religious Affairs to carry out some religious services.[11] But without the majority of its officials, the waqf system ceased to function. The Supreme Muslim Council *ma'murs*, in whose name the waqf *madbut* were registered, had fled, and rents, repairs and general management were left unsupervised.[12] The local Waqf Committees disappeared and the health and welfare services they had provided were discontinued.[13] Waqf buildings that had been extensively damaged during the fighting often were not repaired. The waqf schools in Jaffa, Haifa, and Acre were closed.

Communal organization was disrupted in other ways. As one of its first steps following the declaration of the state on 14 May, the Israeli government resolved that British Mandatory law would continue to apply until Israeli legislation was introduced to replace it.[14] This implied that the state would not tamper with the rights and legal status of Muslim and Christian communities. In fact, however, the imposition of military rule and the expulsion and flight of hundreds of thousands of Palestinians therefore entailed a dramatic loss of political power and of civil liberties. Military rule, based on the British Defense (Emergency) Regulations of 1945, was imposed on all areas under the control of the Israeli armed forces in which substantial numbers of Palestinians lived. These included Galilee, the area known

Map 2. The UN Partition Plan and Israel

Source: D. McDowall, *Palestine and Israel* (London: I.B. Tauris, 1989), p. 27.

as the Triangle, parts of the Negev desert around Beersheba, and parts of Jaffa, Lydda, Ramla, and Acre.[15] Military governors were made responsible for freedom of expression, publications, property, and all forms of transport. In addition, Palestinian areas could be turned into "closed areas" where entry or exit was forbidden without securing permission from the military governor. This meant that all communication and coordination between different Palestinian groups and individuals could be closely monitored. Moreover, military governors were given powers to impose house and town restrictions and detention orders. To preside over this system, military courts were established, which provided no recourse for appeal except to a higher military authority. These regulations were annually renewed by successive Israeli governments until 1966. In this way the Palestinian Muslim community was given no opportunity to reestablish its Waqf Committees, appoint new personnel, or vote in new elections for a representative Muslim body (such as the Supreme Muslim Council).

The armistice agreement had a profound impact on the waqf system; it fragmented the single territorial and administrative unit that had existed under the Council. Under the armistice agreement boundaries, finalized in 1949, waqf land and properties were separated from the religious properties or institutions they were supporting. The greater proportion of the lands of the Khaski Sultan and Tamimi waqfs, for example, were situated inside Israel, while the institutions they supported were inside the West Bank. Of the 313 large mosques in Palestine, 200 mosques or religious buildings were located in the area that became Israel. The area inside Israel contained important mosques and institutions, including the Great Mosque and the Muslim Library in Jaffa, the Haram Sayyidna 'Ali near Herzliyya, the al-Jazzar mosque in Acre, the Great Mosques in Ramla and Lydda, and the well-known Mamilla and Dajani cemeteries in Jerusalem as well as the cemeteries in Acre and Afula.[16] But virtually all the waqfs in the Old City of Jerusalem, the Haram al-Sharif, the administrative offices of the Supreme Muslim Council, the Ibrahimi mosque in Hebron, the waqf bazaars and suqs in Nablus, and the Great Mosque and the burial place of the Prophet Muhammed's grandfather in Gaza were located on the Jordanian and Egyptian sides of the armistice lines.

Following the 1948 war, Palestinian Muslims inside Israel faced a demoralizing and bleak situation. Their political aspirations had been completely squashed, their numbers depleted, their homes and localities occupied by armed troops, their mosques abandoned, their communal organizations and structures destroyed, and their contacts with the wider Arab and Muslim world cut. Leaderless and powerless, they were unable to muster the resistance and the strength to assert themselves. An official Israeli government summary confirms these conclusions:

> Upon the termination of Mandatory rule and the outbreak of the War of Independence the religious institutions of the Moslem Community in the country collapsed. Senior religious personnel, muftis and qadis....fled from the country. The system of religious jurisdiction broke down completely. Most of the officials concerned in religious services fled. The communal educational system and the

> social welfare and health institutions ceased to exist. Among those who left the country were also members of the Supreme Muslim Council and its Wakf Committee...and the members of the Governmental Awqaf Commission, appointed by the High Commissioner by virtue of the Palestine (Defense) Order in Council, 1937. Israeli Moslems thus remained without religious organization and religious leadership.[17]

Evidence suggests that the new Israeli government was uncertain about what to do with the administration of the Palestinian Muslim community and its waqf land. Prior to the establishment of the state, the Zionist Commission proposed the internationalization of the "holy places," a proposal that was later echoed by Chaim Weizmann, the first president of Israel. However, several drafts of the constitution proposed the maintenance of the status quo with regard to the holy places.[18] Furthermore, the UN partition resolution of 1947, which had been accepted by the Zionist leaders, stated that: "the family law and personal status of the various minorities, and other religious interests, *including endowments*, shall be respected."[19] In addition, the head of the Division of Muslim and Druze Affairs of the Israeli Ministry of Religious Affairs initially advocated a continuation of the Mandate system with some modifications.[20]

It appears that the Zionist leaders had not planned to alter the waqf system to any great extent, although it would be safe to assume that the state intended to maintain strict political control, similar to that imposed in 1937 by the British over the Supreme Muslim Council. The first hint that the Israeli government was beginning to take a harder line appeared in May 1949, when the first prime minister, David Ben-Gurion, was asked the government's intention with regard to the waqf system. He replied that the government was studying "how to settle these matters according to the Islamic laws of the waqf, and current....circumstances in Israel."[21] Only after the passing of the Absentee Property Law of 1950 did a clearer policy become evident.

Despite its clear military and political superiority, the new Israeli government was faced with a difficult political problem with regard to the waqf system. Although Israeli armed forces militarily controlled 75 percent of the land of Mandatory Palestine, only approximately 10 percent of that land was actually owned by Jews.[22] In order to establish a viable and credible state, the government had not only to inhibit Palestinian political aspirations but also to gain ownership of the land already under its military control. This had obvious repercussions for the waqf system, given the land area under its management. Indeed, to have left the waqf system intact would have resulted in a series of Muslim, and therefore Palestinian, enclaves inside the new state's territory that would have amounted to at least 10 and possibly 20 percent of the cultivated area of Israel. Because of their religious status, these waqf enclaves would have fallen outside the political and legal jurisdiction of the new Israeli state. If the waqf system were to function in the same autonomous semi-independent manner as it had under the Mandate, it would undermine the physical integrity of the embryonic state as well as its control over the waqf resources and administrative structure. This would give the controlling Muslim religious elite considerable independence and allow it to act as a mediating institution, if not a representative body. The Israeli government prevented the waqf system from regaining its mediating role because the state needed a territorial base to give substance to its claims to statehood, and because conferring a mediating role on the waqf system, let alone any other Palestinian institution, would undermine its political claims to a "Jewish" state on the territory under its control. Such an outcome would constantly call into question the legitimacy of the Israeli state in the eyes of its Muslim citizens. This explains why the Israeli government did not envision reconstituting the Supreme Muslim Council to govern the waqf system.

But the Israeli state could not simply liquidate the waqf system and its administrative structure. Given the continued presence of some 130,000 Palestinians, the majority of whom were Muslims, some structure had to be established to represent their concerns and to win, if not their loyalty to, at least their acquiescence in, the new state. This required a recognition of their separate and particular interests, be it the continued application of shari'a law in questions of personal status, or in the upkeep of mosques, cemeteries, and other religious properties. The new state had to concede this recognition in a tightly-restricted manner; it could not surrender control over the waqf system's resources or administration.

At this point, a methodological problem needs to be mentioned. Because the Israeli occupation of the West Bank, Gaza Strip, Sinai, and the Golan Heights brought dramatic changes in the economic, military, and political balance of forces in the area, 1967 is the date generally used to mark the beginning of the new period of Palestinian and Israeli affairs. As far as the waqf system is concerned, the more important date is 1965, when the Third Amendment to the Absentee Property Law of 1950 was passed. This legislation led to further dismemberment of the waqf system and to a far-reaching administrative reorganization. Consequently, and despite the risk of decoupling developments in the waqf system from the general political situation, this chapter will focus on events up to 1965. (The post-1965 period is considered in the following chapter.)

Israeli State Control over Waqf Resources

Because Jews owned relatively little land in Palestine, the new Israeli state sought to acquire land abandoned by Palestinian landowners, including waqf land. With the departure of the leaders of the Supreme Muslim Council and local *ma'mur*s, the Israeli state expropriated much of the waqf system's land. Such acquisitions also served to remove the waqf system's independent financial base and complemented the state's policies with regard to integrating the system's administration and co-optating its leadership. Soon the administration of the waqf system became totally integrated into the Israeli state.

The Absentee Property Law of 1950 was the single most important piece of legislation affecting waqf and other Palestinian property. It was part of a network of laws that transferred the resources of the Muslim waqf system established for the benefit of the Muslim community to Israeli Jews in the form of Israeli state lands, or land owned by the Jewish National Fund. Under the provisions of these laws, 80 percent of the total land area of Israel was acquired from Palestinians. According to Don Peretz, this land, categorized by the Israeli state as "abandoned property," "was one of the greatest contributions towards making Israel a viable state".[23]

Passed by the Israeli Knesset (Parliament) on 14 May 1950, the Absentee Property Law was ostensibly intended to protect the property of Palestinian refugees residing abroad. The law created the office of a "Custodian of Absentee Property" who was made responsible for the maintenance of refugee property, rentals, the collection of rents, and other matters related to the property's management until a settlement of the refugee question could be reached. In reality, however, the office was used to legitimize the dispossession of refugees of their land and property, without which the state would have had only a small territorial basis.

The Absentee Property Law gave the Custodian two wide-ranging powers: he could decide who was an absentee, and he could transfer property under his management to any other body without accountability. Article 1 specified dates and circumstances within which a person was defined as "absentee":

> (b) "absentee" means—
> 1) any person who, at any time during the period between the 29th November, 1947 and the day on which a declaration is published....[that the state of emergency declared by the Provisional Council of State on the 19th May has ceased to exist,] was the legal owner of any property situated in the area of Israel or enjoyed or held it...and who at any time during the said period—
>
> i) was a national or citizen of Lebanon, Egypt, Syria, Saudi Arabia, Transjordan, Iraq or the Yemen, or,
> ii) was a Palestinian citizen and left his ordinary place of residence in Palestine a) for a place outside Palestine before the 1st September, 1948, or b) for a place in Palestine held at the time by forces which sought to prevent the establishing of the State of Israel or which fought against it after its establishment.[24]

The dates specified include some six months before the end of the Mandate and, therefore, defined a very large number of Palestinians as "absentee." This included not only those who had avoided the fighting by going abroad, but those who had taken holidays or had made business trips. As Peretz writes:

> Every Arab in Palestine who had left his town or village after November 29th, 1947 was liable to be classified as an absentee under the regulations. All Arabs who held property in the New City of Acre, regardless of the fact that they may never have travelled further than the few metres to the Old City, were classified as absentees. The thirty thousand Arabs who fled from one place to another within Israel, but who never left the country, were also liable to have their property declared absentee. Any individual who may have gone to Beirut or Bethlehem for a one-day visit during the latter days of the Mandate was automatically an absentee.[25]

Article 30 of the Law allowed the Custodian to decide which Palestinians were absentee, and Article 17 made this decision irrevocable. This meant that once Palestinian property had been passed on by the Custodian to another institution, it could not be returned, even if the Custodian was found to have been in error.

The specific applicability of the Absentee Property Law to waqf property is ambiguous. Indeed, the term "waqf" is not expressly mentioned in the law at all. Article 1 defined absentee property as:

> immovable and movable property, moneys, any vested or contingent right in property, goodwill and any right in a body of persons or in the management thereof, of which an absentee was the legal owner or which the absentee enjoyed or held, himself or through another.[26]

Article 9(d) refers to absentee property as "vested property, being an endowment," which seems to indicate some attempt to include waqf as absentee. Other than this, there is reference to the law's relation to waqf property. Eisenman, a leading scholar of shari'a law in Palestine and Israel, writes that the law was "deemed to cover all waqf and *mevkufe*," but the basis of this interpretation of the law is unclear.[27]

Given the salient political role played by the Supreme Muslim Council and its control over the waqf system during the Mandate period, the absence of an explicit reference to waqf property is surprising. Since a Muslim community (i.e., a potential beneficiary of the waqf system) still existed in the new Israeli state, there was nothing in the law's definition of absentee property per se that would prevent the continuation of that system. Nonetheless, the Israeli government accomplished its acquisition of waqf land and property under the law by classifying the Supreme Muslim Council, which had managed public waqf until its dissolution in 1937, as absentee. It made this designation on the grounds that most of the Council's senior officers (in whose name land and property had been registered) had fled or been expelled. Supreme Muslim Council property was therefore placed in the hands of the Custodian, and in this way the Israeli government was able to avoid the accusation of directly acquiring the religious property of the Muslim community.

The only waqfs that escaped the provisions of the Absentee Property Law were *mulhaq* and *dhurri* waqfs whose *mutawalli*s still resided in Israel and who did not fall under the conditions that would have classified them as absentee.[28] All other property that the Supreme Muslim Council had administered was classified as absentee property and appropriated by the Custodian. Palestinians in Israel expressed considerable resentment over this interpretation of the Absentee Property Law and insofar as was possible given the conditions of martial law, mounted strong opposition to it.

Although the law stopped short of classifying waqf property as absentee, the Custodian proceeded to dispose of large amounts of waqf property through a network of laws, of which the Absentee Property Law was only part. A lot of property was transferred, in particular to the Jewish National Fund. An examination of the stages by which this transformation took place reveals three important aspects in the interaction between the Israeli state and the waqf system: the lengths to which the Israeli state was prepared to go to gain control over the waqf system's resources; the manner in which the state sought to legitimize that control; and the extent to which the Jewish National Fund was the final recipient of the resources of the Muslim community. This third aspect, in fact representing the transfer of the resources of the Muslim community to the Jewish community, was to have specific political repercussions, which are described later.

In the first step of the process, the Custodian was empowered to sell property under his jurisdiction to a "Development Authority" that the Knesset created in 1950 especially for this purpose.[29] The Development Authority was not permitted, in turn, to sell property received from the Custodian to any body other than the state, the Jewish National Fund, or a local authority.[30] In this way the Israeli government ensured that the property it had obtained through the Absentee Property Law remained in Jewish hands. The Development Authority thus acted as means of "laundering" confiscated Palestinian property. In the words of one historian, "By this legal fiction the state avoided, amongst other things, the censure which might have accrued on direct confiscation."[31] A former chairman of the Jewish National Fund, Granott, noted that

> The Development Authority was based upon a sort of legal fiction. It was not desired to transfer abandoned property to government ownership, as this would be interpreted as confiscation of the abandoned property. The government was disinclined to take such a step, which had been unfavourably regarded abroad, and no doubt opposed....It was necessary to find the means of disposing of the property legally.[32]

The transformation of Muslim waqf property into exclusively Jewish property was completed in the next stage of the process. The Jewish National Fund was given the first choice on all land purchases offered by the Development Authority.[33]

It is difficult to determine the exact quantities of Palestinian property and land transferred in this way. Peretz observed that the Fund acquired 2.5 million dunums from the Israeli government, and that most of it "must have been absentee property."[34] Neither has it been revealed what proportion of that absentee property acquired by the Fund was waqf, but there is no doubt that most waqf land, if not virtually all of it, was transferred to the Fund and its subsidiaries. The principle of Jewish exclusivity laid out in the Fund's charter is estimated to apply to 92.6 percent of the land in Israel.[35] It is significant that the executive structures of the Jewish National Fund and the Israel Lands Administration, the land-owning body of the Israeli government, overlap, and that they frequently coordinate their purchasing, development, and settlement policies.[36] It was by these routes, then, that waqf land (which had been endowed for the benefit of the Palestinian Muslim community) was incorporated into an institution that served the interests of the Israeli Jewish community exclusively.

Another law that affected waqf property controlled by the Custodian was the Land Acquisition (Validation of Act and Compensation) Law of 1953.[37] This law confirmed and ratified retrospectively the sale of waqf property by the Custodian to Development authorities; it also established procedures for offering compensation, by which the Israeli government sought to make the confiscation and transfer of their land more acceptable to Muslims. The compensation from sales of waqf property did not, however, go to the Muslim community in Israel, but to Israel's Ministry of Religious Affairs. As a result, no evidence exists of a correlation between the compensation and sales income, and such expenditure by the Ministry of Religious Affairs on Muslim affairs.[38] (Indeed, one Palestinian lawyer and legal researcher, Sabri Jiryis, goes so far as to claim that the sales did not exist.[39]) If the sales did take place, it is quite probable that the income received by the ministry may have been dispersed among the full range of its activities, including Jewish activities. In reply to a written question submitted to Nissam Dana, director of the Muslim and Druze division of the ministry, the director revealed that the division kept no figures, but that what was described as "large amounts" were made available by the Custodian to advisory committees that recommended projects for which the funds could be spent.[40]

Without knowing the exact amount of waqf land or property that existed prior to 1948, it is virtually impossible to make any accurate estimate of the property and land acquired by the Israeli state and the Jewish National Fund. The Muslim and Druze division does not have official figures, and those in the Custodian's office are neither collated or publicly available.[41] Lustick claims that 75 percent of waqf land and property transferred through a combination of the Absentee Property Law and other laws by the mid-1970s, but gives no sources.[42] Furthermore, one needs to distinguish between the waqf property and land that was lost through legislation and through the activities of the government-appointed Muslim advisory committees empowered to sell such assets, matters to be examined later.

A very approximate estimate of the losses brought about as a result of legislation can be deduced by considering the following factors. First, the greater proportion of waqf land and property of the Mandate period was located in Israel after 1948. Apart from Jerusalem, Hebron, and Nablus, most urban waqf property was to be found in Jaffa, Lydda, Ramla, Haifa, and Acre. Similarly, much of the cultivated land of Palestine was located on the coastal plain between Gaza and Haifa, and on the plains of Acre, Esdraelon, and Huleh, which fell to Israel.[43] It is reasonable to assume, therefore, that many of the waqfs based on *miri* land (*mawquf* and *tahsisat* waqfs) were found there. (Using the figures arrived at in Chapter One, as much as 15 percent of these areas would be waqf.) Since the land reclamation scheme initiated by the Supreme Muslim Council, the Sayyidna 'Ali waqf near Herzliyya had become one of the largest and most productive waqfs and was now also in Israel. These deductions are partially confirmed by a report in the Israeli newspaper *Ha'Aretz*, based upon an interview with a former Advisor on Arab Affairs in the Prime Minister's Office. There it was estimated that up to half of the waqf of Palestine was located in Israel after 1948.[44]

The Israeli government distinguished between "religious" waqf property (such as mosques, shrines, and cemeteries) and "secular" waqf property (which comprised agricultural land and commercial and residential property).[45] Although both were held by the Custodian, "secular" property was disposed of through the laws outlined earlier. Some former "religious" property was also disposed of. No records are available from the Palestinian villages that were destroyed by the Israeli government during and in the immediate aftermath of the 1948 war; these contained small cemeteries, shrines, and mosques, many of which were waqf.

From these factors we may tentatively conclude that Lustick's estimate of 75 percent may in fact be conservative. A more accurate figure may be in the neighborhood of 80 or 85 percent. Taking into account activities of the advisory committees, which are described in the next section, the figure almost certainly could be closer to 90 percent. Until 1965, all waqf property deemed as absentee, both "religious" and "secular," was held by the Custodian, with the Minister of Religious Affairs acting merely as "agent." Therefore, there was ample opportunity for waqf property to be transferred to Israeli Jewish institutions.

If one accepts that approximately 1,075,610 dunums was waqf land during Mandatory Palestine (see Chapter One) and that half of this was located in Israel, this would amount to 537,805 dunums. Assuming that Lustick's figure of 75 percent for the amount of waqf land transferred to Israeli Jewish institutions is a conservative estimate, and that 80 percent would be more accurate, we can deduce that approximately 430,244 dunums (or approximately 107,560 acres) were transferred through the workings of the Absentee Property Law and associated laws. It must be borne in mind that this figure refers mostly to agricultural land and does not take into account the bulk of urban waqf properties, which would be much harder to deduce.

The Integration of Waqf Administration

The goal of Israeli government policy toward the administrative structure of the waqf system was to reduce the management of Muslim communal affairs in Israel to a bureaucratic arm of the Israeli state. This is particularly evident in the absence of any autonomous representative Muslim body and in the government's control over the provision of funds for communal services. This policy, clearly complements the policies that removed the financial base of the waqf system from the administrators and religious elite.

Although the new Israeli government did not announce a clear policy, the Ministry of Religious Affairs unilaterally assumed responsibility for the affairs of the Muslim community. The reestablishment of shari'a courts began as early as 1948. Initially, one was set up in Acre and another in Nazareth; by the end of 1950 two more were constituted, in Jaffa and Taybe. The jurisdiction of the Jaffa court was extended to the Bedouin of the Negev in the south of the country. A court of appeal, consisting of three qadis, was also established, to replace the Jerusalem court of appeal that had existed under the Mandate.[46] The ministry also conducted an emergency survey of the Muslim holy places, making recommendations for repairs and steps to prevent the dilapidation of mosques, shrines, and cemeteries.[47] A number of stipends were also paid out to mosque attendants. Although the Muslim community obviously welcomed grants and salaries as an interim measure, it viewed the Israeli government's assumption of responsibility in this way as direct state intervention in Muslim communal affairs, and as a precedent that the state later made permanent. It should be noted that many of these steps were taken while peace and armistice negotiations were being discussed and before the new borders of the state had been agreed.

After the State of Israel was established, the new government announced that, pending legislation, British Mandate law would continue to be applied. However, the decision was made not to reconstitute the Supreme Muslim Council. Instead, the Council's jurisdiction was taken over by Israel's Ministry of Religious Affairs. In reply to a question in the Knesset on this issue, Prime Minister Ben-Gurion explained:

> In the wake of the war forced on us by some Arab states, members of the Central Waqf Committee and of the Supreme Muslim Council left the territory of Israel. Thus there is no committee to control waqf. To ensure that waqf property should not be neglected, the Ministry of Religions [*sic*] took over the care of the holy places, and the Custodian of Abandoned Property took over lands and buildings, as far as possible.[48]

Accordingly, the Ministry for Religious Affairs created two departments concerned with Palestinian religious communities: the Division of Muslim and Druze Affairs, and the Division of Christian Affairs.

The Muslim and Druze division was given responsibility for the administration of Muslim waqf property. It was here that the Israeli government introduced a distinction between "religious" and "secular" property. Such a distinction does not exist in shari'a law, where endowed commercial property is regarded as religious in the same sense as a mosque is religious. For the Israeli government, however, "religious" property comprised mosques, cemeteries, tombs, and shrines, while "secular" property comprised all the remaining shops, houses, fields, wells, and so on. At this early stage, "religious" waqf property was still in the hands of the Custodian of Absentee Property, but following an agreement signed in 1951 between the Custodian and the Ministry of Religious Affairs, the Muslim and Druze division was given the responsibility of administering all property so defined. This responsibility was further formalized in 1954 when the Custodian appointed the Division as the "agent" in administering waqf property. The Muslim and Druze division was also made responsible for the administration of small proportions of waqf property through appointed committees. These committees oversaw the maintenance of the buildings, the collection of rents, and any sales that took place. In contrast, "secular" waqf property continued to be held by the Custodian, and in 1953 it was sold to Israel's Development Authority.[49]

Thus, the resources of the waqf system were divided into two parts and their administration was fully incorporated into the state's bureaucracy, albeit in two separate ministries. It is important to note that under this new structure, qadis and other appointed Muslim officials had no legal authority over the administration of the waqf system. Although some were given an *ad hoc* advisory role, but essentially they were left as bystanders in the administration of the remnant of the waqf properties. The government's direct involvement illustrates the extent to which the waqf system of the Supreme Muslim Council was being dismantled and reconstructed.

Funds for the budget of the Muslim and Druze division came from two sources. One was the income produced by the Custodian-held waqf property designated as secular, which was passed on to the Ministry for Religious Affairs; the other was the income from the "religious" property that the Ministry for Religious Affairs administered as the "agent" of the Custodian.[50] No complete figures are publicly available for income and expenditure during this period, but certain deductions can be made. In 1964–65, the Custodian allocated 120,000 Israeli *lira* (IL) to the Ministry of Religious Affairs from the income of waqf property still in its possession (the first source); the ministry itself is said to have derived IL 50,000 from waqf property it administered (the second source).[51] This amounts to a total from both sources of IL 170,000.[52] Aharon Layish, an Israeli scholar who was formerly the Assistant Advisor on Arab Affairs at the Prime Minister's Office and who worked alongside the Muslim and Druze division between 1963 and 1966, has estimated that the expenditure "on the requirements of the Muslim community" came to approximately IL 1,500,000 by 1965.[53] Of this, some IL 900,000 came from allocations made by the Custodian, and the remainder from waqf property held by the Ministry of Religious Affairs.

There were also funds available to the Muslim and Druze division from the sales of "secular" waqf property by the Custodian to the Israel Development Authority. These were spent on what could be termed "capital" projects. By 1955 three projects had been completed: a health center in al-Tira and Baq'a al-Gharbiyya, an orphanage and home for the aged in Jaffa, and a large orphanage in Acre. (A seminary for the training of qadis in al-Jazzar has been repeatedly promised but has not to this date been implemented.)[54] According to Layish, IL 3 million from the sales of waqf property by the Custodian had been spent on these projects by 1965.[55]

Although the Israeli government was able to absorb the administration of the waqf system into its own bureaucracy, and to keep tight control over the use of funds and the allocation of resources, it also needed to secure the support of the Muslim religious leadership to minimize the disaffection amongst the Palestinian population. The majority of this leadership had departed, however, which neces-sitated the partial creation of a new religious leadership.

The Co-optation of Muslim Leadership

To help create a new religious leadership, the Division of Muslim and Druze Affairs was made responsible for the appointments and salaries of religious officials. It appointed qadis and mosque officials such as imams, muezzin, and *khatib*s, as well as cleaners, guards, and caretakers.[56] By 1950, 67 imams and 24 muezzin had been appointed, and by 1956 this had increased to 205 people working in 100 mosques.[57] Many Palestinian Muslims objected to this interference in their communal affairs, but their protests were rejected by the government, which went on to confirm the appointments and structural innovations in a new law, the Shari'a Courts (Validation of Appointments) Law, 5714-1953.[58] The government would achieve further control over the Muslim leadership in 1961, when it passed the Qadis Law.

The Qadis Law established a governmental committee to oversee future appointments. The committee comprised nine persons, all of whom were appointed by the state. Of the nine, only five were required to be Muslim. This meant that government-selected Jewish or Christian civil servants were permitted to influence the appointment of the religious leaders of the Muslim community. Qadis were also obliged to swear an oath of allegiance to the president of Israel, and the salaries of all shari'a court and mosque personnel were paid by the government.[59] The most public example of the successful co-optation of the Palestinian qadis in Israel is their participation in the festivities commemorating Israeli "Independence Day."

The Israeli government refused to appoint a mufti for the Palestinian community in Israel, a refusal that had two effects. From a political standpoint, the absence of a mufti greatly diminished the possibility of a leader uniting the qadis in their separate geographical districts against the secular Israeli authorities. From a religious standpoint, the lack of an eminent religious personage to overrule minority views within the Muslim community has made it difficult for the qadis to speak as a coherent body on questions of communal importance, religious or political. Moreover, under shari'a law, only a mufti is eligible to interpret and conduct exegesis on the law; qadis cannot do this. The absence of a mufti in Israel has therefore led to the very real possibility that Muslim law relating to personal status will ossify.[60]

The waqf-funded schools (Ahmadiyya in Acre, Dar al-'Ulum in Jaffa, and two waqf schools in Haifa) had been closed as a result of the fighting in 1948 and were not allowed to reopen.[61] The government also rejected repeated requests that an Islamic seminary be permitted to set up in the al-Jazzar mosque courtyard. This meant that the essential role such institutions provide in passing on the values of the community were not replaced, and that the community could not train its leaders. Religious scholars are obliged to study abroad, and the cost of such an undertaking dissuades a great number of potential religious leaders (thereby lowering the level of shari'a education in Israel) or makes them dependent upon state bursaries. These changes helped to weaken the role of Islam in Palestinian society and provided the government with another means of weakening the independence of the Muslim community.

Nevertheless, the Israeli government was not successful in quelling the dissent among religious Muslims. In response to persistent objections by Palestinian Muslims regarding their lack of influence over waqf property, in 1952 the government began to appoint a number of advisory committees to supervise the management of "religious" property. Their tasks were to oversee the maintenance and repair of mosques, shrines, and cemeteries as well as the distribution of funds to small charitable projects (limited to grants for students, bursaries for the training of religious officials, and repairs for religious properties).[62]

Advisory committees were set up in Haifa, Jaffa, Acre, Lydda, and Ramla. In 1955 the annual budget for all the committees was IL 70,000.[63] Their link with the administration of waqf property was through an interministerial committee that had the actual responsibility of disbursing the funds.[64] This committee comprised representatives from the Ministry of Finance and the Ministry for Religious Affairs, and it acted in accordance with the recommendations of the advisory committees.[65]

The advisory committees were weak and had very little legitimacy in the eyes of the Palestinian Muslim community. They were not authorized to supervise any large expenditure or to appoint mosque officials and other waqf personnel. They were not permitted to form a nationwide liaison body or to coordinate their activities, with the result that they remained fragmented and isolated from each other.[66] Furthermore, they had no legal jurisdiction over waqf property, and acted merely as executors of decisions made by the Custodian and the Ministry of Religious Affairs. They were often government employees, and given the continued existence of martial law, it is almost certain that their appointments were screened by the Israeli military and intelligence services. In contrast to the role of the Supreme Muslim Council or the Awqaf Administration in Jerusalem, the advisory committees had a minimal role as representatives of the Muslim community. Indeed, their primary function appeared to be to provide the Israeli government with a veneer of Muslim participation in its acquisition of waqf property and the administration of Muslim affairs.

Opposition to Israeli Policies

Muslims had three broad objections to the Israeli state's handling of the waqf system. First, they objected to the inclusion of waqf land under the Absentee Property Law, which they saw as an attack on their Islamic faith: by being leased and sold off by the Custodian, the waqf's sacred inalienability was violated, and the last vestiges of the waqf system and its holy places were being administered by civil servants of a Zionist and Jewish state. Second, the Muslims believed that Israeli government control over waqf income and appointments constituted an interference in their communal affairs; they found it unacceptable that their traditions and customs should be subjected to government approval. Finally, Palestinian Muslims were concerned that their community was being discriminated against, contrasting the minimum of control the government accorded them over waqf property, schools, and religious courts to the relative latitude that the state granted to the Christian, Druze, and Bahai communities. This last objection is worth studying in greater detail, for it demonstrates how the Israeli state singled out the Muslim community for special treatment, in an attempt to constrain the political aspirations of the Palestinians inside Israel.

The chief contrast that can be drawn between the various Christian communities and the Muslim community is that, for the most part, the land and properties of the former were exempted from the provisions of the Absentee Property Law.[67] The Israeli government argued that the presence of an organized church structure within the recognized Christian communities permitted it to release church property and Christian waqf held by the Custodian.[68] In fact, the property of the Greek Orthodox Patriarchate inside Israel was still registered in the name of the Patriarchate located in Jordanian Jerusalem and was therefore absentee as defined by the legislation.[69] However, as Layish noted, the government perceived "no legal bar to the Custodian's releasing it to the Patriarchate."[70]

Similarly, the Greek Catholic community was registered in the name of an archdiocese comprising Acre, Haifa, Nazareth, and Galilee. The archbishop, Archbishop Hakim, had left Palestine during the 1948 war and resided temporarily in Lebanon. Although he was allowed to return soon after the establishment of the State of Israel, he was technically an absentee according to the provisions of the Absentee Property Law. In this case, also, the Custodian was able to exercise discretion and release Greek Catholic property.[71] Such examples give credence to Muslim claims that they were the targets of discrimination. The preferential treatment for the Christians was also extended to the education system and the ecclesiastical courts: Christians were permitted to run their own schools and appoint their own judges to independently constituted ecclesiastical courts.[72]

The Druze community was given relative latitude as well. The Druze population has never been more than 10 percent of the Palestinian population in Israel, yet during this period five Druze qadis were appointed, as opposed to six Muslim qadis. The Druze community also was given relative independence over its endowment system. The Druze Religious Courts Law, passed on 25 December 1962, gave the Druze religious courts authority over personal status and endowed property.[73]

Initially, Palestinian Muslims in Israel expressed their objections to the government's policies toward their communal affairs through verbal protests and attempts at persuasion. Newspaper articles protesting state control carried titles such as "Allah is not an Absentee," "God is a refugee," and so on.[74] An attempt was made to establish a national committee that would coordinate efforts to free waqf property, and a conference was held in Acre in November 1954.[75] Questions were asked in the Knesset, and the cabinet was pressed to consider the issue of allowing the Muslim community to manage its own affairs.[76] Support for the Muslim demands also came from Christians and Jews.[77] In 1958, for example, the Ihud party of Martin Buber urged the government to restore the waqf system to the Muslim community.[78] But in the main, these efforts had no effect.

The failure of these peaceful attempts led to popular demonstrations against the policies. The protests were frequently triggered by news of the sales of waqf property by the Custodian to Israeli Jewish enterprises, and by activities of the Advisory Committees in general. For example, the sale of the Abu Nabi cemetery in Jaffa (authorized by the local advisory committee) to an Israeli Jewish development company led to violent protests at the cemetery, but to no avail. The Abu Nabi cemetery is now the site of the Tel Aviv Hilton.[79]

More challenging to the government were the legal efforts undertaken by Palestinian Muslims to regain control over waqf property. Two cases were taken as far as the Supreme Court; in each case, the argument was made that it was within the jurisdiction of the shari'a courts to appoint new *mutawalli*s to replace absentees, thus removing a particular waqf from the Custodian. The second of these two cases was successful.[80] However, the judgment applied only to *mulhaq* waqfs held by the Custodian; the government maintained that Custodian control over *madbut* waqfs could not be challenged, since government jurisdiction over them had been passed on from the High Commissioner by the 1937 Defense (Muslim Waqf) Regulations.

In response to this position, a group of Muslim lawyers in 1961 mounted what was the most serious legal challenge to the power of the Custodian since the passing of the Absentee Property Law. They argued that since the Qadis Law of 1961 cancelled the 1921 Order-in-Council, the 1937 Regulations that were based on that Order-in-Council were also canceled. Therefore, they asserted, jurisdiction of the shari'a courts over *madbut* waqfs was revived and new *mutawalli*s could be appointed in the place of the Custodian. The Supreme Court ruled that the 1937 Defense Regulations existed independent of the 1921 Order-in-Council, and that the Custodian thus maintained its possession over the Muslim waqf.[81] However, the persistence of these legal claims was disturbing for the government; the whole process of the transferring of waqf property to Jewish settlements and enterprises would have unravelled had the courts ruled in favor of the litigants. The government's determination to finalize the dismantling of the Muslim waqf system and to make any transaction irrevocable led to the passing of the Third Amendment to the Absentee Property Law, to be explored later.

One further indication of Palestinian Muslims' refusal to legitimize the actions of the Israeli state can be seen in their reluctance to create new waqfs. Very few endowments were created under the new regime. Between 1948 and 1965, only three cases of newly created waqfs are known to have been recorded.[82] In 1963, out of 2,921 cases in the Israeli shari'a courts dealing with matters of personal status, only 13 were related to waqf affairs. In 1964 there were 10 out of 3,126 court cases. As Layish points out, most of these were not new endowments, but had to do with the appointment of new *mutawalli*s to prevent waqf *dhurri* property passing to an heir who had been classified as an absentee in Israeli law.[83]

The presence of a substantial Muslim minority with claims to the land, property, and administration of the waqf system, and with nationalist political aspirations, continued to pose an acute problem for the state. During the period that followed, the government would introduce further changes in its control over the waqf system.

Chapter 3

The Muslim Waqf System in Israel, 1965–1988

During the period from 1948 to 1965, the political and legal steps taken by the Israeli government toward the waqf system should be viewed primarily in light of the new state's urgent need to secure control over as much land as possible. In order to develop economically, to settle new immigrants, and to survive as a state, it needed to consolidate its precarious hold on the land it acquired. During the 1950s, the government's acquisition of waqf land and property and its assumption of the role of the Supreme Muslim Council served these territorial requirements well. Consequently, resolving the question of Muslim control over the waqf system and management over its communal affairs became a secondary issue. This set of priorities, however, led to serious anomalies in the legal status of waqf property which in turn contributed to political tensions between the Jewish majority and the Palestinian minority.

This chapter examines the Israeli government's attempt to ameliorate the tensions and problems created by its handling of the waqf system. The state recognized that greater Muslim representation was required in the management of the community's affairs, but the structures it established only succeeded in alienating Palestinians further.

The 1965 establishment of a new form of waqf administration in accordance with the Third Amendment to the Absentee Property Law coincided with two fundamental changes in the position of Palestinian Muslims in Israel. First, military rule for the Arabs inside the 1949 armistice lines—which had become the internationally recognized borders of Israel—was terminated. Second, during the 1967 war Israel conquered the remaining parts of Mandatory Palestine—the West Bank and the Gaza Strip—together with the Sinai peninsula and the Golan Heights. The termination of military rule in 1966 allowed Palestinian Muslims greater freedom of movement, greater opportunities for education and economic prosperity, and greater participation in the political processes in Israel. The occupation of the West

Bank and Gaza Strip a year later allowed Palestinians in Israel for the first time in nineteen years to meet their families, their compatriots, and their coreligionists in the areas occupied by Israel. Reunions, weddings, and holiday visits all promoted the reestablishment of family ties and communal bonds and led to a growing awareness of a Palestinian identity (as opposed to the state-formulated "Israeli Arab" identity).[1] In a confidential report, compiled by the District Commissioner of the Northern District of Israel, Israel Koenig acknowledged these developments:

> The Israeli Arab population has received a nationalistic momentum since the Six Day War. The policy of free contact with the West Bank and the open bridges [across the Jordan river] has renewed the contact with the Arabs of Judea and Samaria [West Bank] and the Palestinians East of the River Jordan, and this has created a basis for a show of determination and slogans for a nationalistic struggle in Israel.[2]

These two important changes were accompanied by a significant increase in the proportion of Palestinians (Muslim, Christian, and Druze) in the total population of Israel. In 1965, they constituted 11.5 percent of all Israeli citizens. In 1985, they comprised 17 percent.[3] These changes resulted in the growing radicalization of the Palestinian minority in Israel and a substantial raising of their political profile. This has been reflected in the transformation of the Muslim community from a subdued and largely acquiescent minority on the margin of political life in 1948 to an increasingly significant force, conducting a number of vociferous campaigns against state policy. In this chapter Israeli policies toward the waqf system are examined in this political, social, and demographic context.

The Third Amendment to the Absentee Property Law

The Third Amendment to the Absentee Property Law, which was passed by the Knesset on 2 February 1965, was designed specifically to deal with Muslim waqfs (which had not been mentioned in the parent law), and it brought about a major legal reform of the waqf system in Israel.[4] An earlier attempt to get a similar, though generally milder, bill through the Knesset in 1959 was thwarted by the calling of elections.[5]

The Third Amendment, which applied only to the waqf property under jurisdiction of the Custodian of Absentee Property, had two important features. First, it authorized full and retroactive transfer of ownership from the "absentee" to the Custodian.[6] Whereas previously there had been some doubt as to the legality of the Custodian's management rights over *mulhaq* and *madbut* waqf, the amendment established that both management and full ownership of these properties lay with the Custodian.

Second, section 29A (b) of the amendment provided for the "release" of waqf property held by the Custodian to beneficiaries of the waqf. Under the terms of the law, "beneficiaries" were defined as either the family concerned (in the case of *mulhaq* waqfs) or an appointed board of trustees (in the case of *madbut* waqfs). This "release" was legislated regardless of whether "absentee" *mutawallis* wished a release of this sort to take place or whether it was in the interests of Muslim community. The most significant provision of this section was that waqf property was to be released without "any restriction, qualification or any similar limitation prescribed by or under any law or any document relating to the endowment."[7] In effect, this specification abolished the waqf character of the property held by the Custodian, the essence of a waqf being its "restrictions" and "qualifications" on the use of the property endowed and over the distribution of income. This clause, then, amounted to the alienation of all the property released by the Custodian property. Only mosques were to remain inalienable.

The amendment did not mean that the beneficiaries of *mulhaq* waqfs (usually a family) could receive the property. More often than not, agreements between the Custodian and the Israel Development Authority had already been concluded and the properties concerned already sold. Instead, the beneficiaries were to receive compensation as stipulated under the Land Acquisition Act of 1953.[8] In these cases, compensation was paid at 1950 land values, which took no account of the high inflation since that date, and therefore was based on a figure that was substantially lower than actual current value.[9]

For *madbut* waqfs, the Custodian released land and property to government-appointed boards of trustees established in Jaffa, Ramla, Lydda, Haifa, Acre, Nazareth, and Shefa'amr. Significantly, not all waqfs were released, but only those in certain localities that had not yet been disposed of by the Custodian.[10] The boards of trustees were entrusted with much wider powers than the advisory committees set up in the pre-1965 period. They were entrusted with both the management and the authority to sell and dispose of waqf property as they saw fit. Section 29C of the amendment gave the following definition: "A Board of Trustees shall be a body competent to acquire and transfer any right, enter into any obligation and be a party to any legal proceedings and to any contract."

At first glance, the granting of such wide-ranging powers to the boards of trustees appeared to satisfy many of the demands of the Muslim community for control over the waqf system. Even though the waqf system by then had been emasculated by the Absentee Property Law and the sales of the Custodian, the principle that it should be administered by the Muslim community appeared to have been belatedly conceded. This aspect of the amendment shows the Israeli state's attempt to establish an institution through which its relations with the Muslim community could be mediated. However, the powers granted to the boards of trustees were more apparent than real. In practice, the Israeli government made use of its legal prerogative by appointing recognized government supporters as members of the boards, so the apparent concession was effectively negated. In the years following the passing of this amendment, the boards were responsible for the sale of large quantities of the waqf property they administered to Israeli Jewish entrepreneurs.[11] One may conclude that by giving such powers to the boards of trustees, the government was in reality seeking to dispose of waqf property by more palatable legal means than those vested in the Custodian.

Two further sections in the amendment require attention. A distinction was made between two kinds of funds available to the boards: funds derived from regular income such as rents, and funds available though the sales of waqf property. In addition, clear regulations were laid down regarding what could be spent from which funds. Funds from regular income could be spent on "relief of the poor, scholarships to pupils at schools, vocational training, health, religious instruction and religious worship or custom."[12] These funds were to be spent only within the area in which the board operated. For example, income from the shops belonging to a waqf in Acre could not be spent on an educational project in Jaffa. The second category, funds from the sales of waqf properties (called "consideration" in the amendment) could only be spent on the establishment of "orphanages, schools, including schools for vocational training, clinics, mosques."[13] The expenditure of the "consideration" was not restricted to the locality of the board.

Through these detailed specifications, the Israeli government ensured that their boards of trustees, who were government appointees, could not spend waqf income in any way that might resemble political activity. No doubt the government was mindful of the precedent set by the Supreme Muslim Council during the Mandate period and was concerned that the boards should not form the nucleus of any similar body. Restricting the spending of the regular income of the boards to their immediate locality resulted in the fragmentation of the remnant of the Muslim waqf system into separate localities and prevented the building up of a single waqf treasury. Moreover, it ensured that the boards could undertake only piecemeal projects and that the Muslim community would continue to depend upon the state for its general administrative expenses. That there is still no Muslim school in Israel is a direct result of the amendment.

The Third Amendment to the Absentee Property Law effectively implemented the government's priorities. While on the one hand it freed the remaining waqf properties from the restrictions of shari'a law, such as sale, it limited the political use to which those funds could be put by placing restrictions upon them. In essence, the amendment allowed the state to continue its policy of transferring the resources of the Muslim community to the Jewish community under the ostensible aegis of Muslim bodies confined to specific responsibilities. However, the amendment failed to give the boards of trustees sufficient independence and credibility.

Despite the controversy and resistance elicited by the Third Amendment and its policies with regard to the waqf system, some Israeli scholars persist in interpreting these policies in a positive light. In assessing the impact of the 1965 amendment, Eisenman, for example, argues that the waqf system "emerged much the same as it had been in the later days of the Mandate and not very different from that in the Ottoman Empire."[14] He argues further that the 1965 amendment did little to interfere with waqf law itself, an indication of the Israeli government's sensitivity to the needs of the Muslim community:

> There is very little in the reforms that can be said to be inimical to their [the Muslim community's] interests by comparison with the previous state of affairs. Though

> interference has occurred in the law applicable to property fallen under the control of the secular government...unlike neighboring Muslim states, no interference was made in the law of waqf itself, in effect in the Muslim community. In this regard Israel turned out to be one of the most conservative countries in the Middle East.[15]

Another scholar, Aharon Layish, took the comparison between Israel and the Arab states even further. He regarded the 1965 amendment as part of a spectrum of "waqf reforms" implemented throughout the Arab world and contends that

> The Israeli legislator adapted, *mutatis mutandis*, several principles laid down by the Arab States in introducing reforms in the waqf....In empowering the Custodian to transfer full ownership of family waqf property to the beneficiaries, lifting all restrictions hitherto applying to it, the Knesset followed the example of several Arab states, especially Syria and Egypt.[16]

Writing in the mid-1960s, Layish compared the abolition in Egypt of the *ahli* waqf (the Egyptian version of the *dhurri* waqf) to the Israeli Custodian's release of *mulhaq* and *dhurri* waqfs to their beneficiaries. Like Eisenman, he argues that the 1965 amendment did not in fact go as far as the reforms promulgated in Syria and Egypt, since it dealt only with waqf property in the possession of the Custodian and not all waqf property.[17] The implication is that the 1965 amendment was a liberal and progressive reform.

The arguments of these commentators can be summarized as follows: a) Israeli legislation gave the Muslim community a significant degree of control over the waqf system through the boards of trustees, which presumably administered it in Muslim interests, thereby creating a structure similar to that during the Ottoman Empire and the British Mandate; b) Israeli legislation did not transgress the shari'a to any significant degree; and c) Israeli legislation can be favorably compared with the reforms carried out in Arab states.

With regard to the first argument, Eisenman is correct in noting similarities between the role of the local waqf committees of the British period and the role of the Israeli-appointed boards of trustees: both were localized, both had limited managerial responsibilities, and both were accountable to a central authority for finance and appointments. It is also true that the 1965 amendment continued the exclusion, begun under the Ottomans, of *madbut* waqfs from the legal jurisdiction of the shari'a courts, and that it extended the practice developed during the Ottoman and Mandate periods of permitting the waqf administrators to ignore the terms of the *waqfiyya* for *madbut* waqfs.[18] Yet such similarities are insignificant in light of one crucial distinction between the two: The Israeli government-appointed boards of trustees and the administration of *madbut* waqfs were all part of a state bureaucracy with a guiding Zionist ideology intent on minimizing, preferably permanently, the social and political profile of the Muslim community in Israel. Although the waqf administration of the Mandate period was not totally autonomous, it did, at least, form part of a structure designed to promote, serve, and represent the interests of the Muslim community.

To compare the pre-1948 structures to the post-1965 structures is greatly to underestimate the strength and independence of the waqf system under the Mandate. Such a comparison also fails to recognize the political motivations that led the British authorities to take control over the waqf system in the first place. Indeed, Eisenman overlooks the fundamental change in the waqf system brought about by the creation of the State of Israel. *Madbut* and *mulhaq* waqfs were initially defined as absentee property and disposed of at the discretion of the Custodian of Absentee Property. Following the passing of the 1965 amendment, the Custodian was also able to "release" waqf properties to beneficiaries or to the board of trustees, provided they were first stripped of their waqf character. Thus, property that was to have any semblance of Muslim participation in its administration was not to be waqf at all. This was certainly not the situation during the Ottoman or British periods. It is also relevant to note that the areas of jurisdiction of the appointed boards of trustees were restricted to municipal locales, and as such, were much smaller than those of the British Mandate. The large rural waqf properties, for example, were outside their jurisdiction. In light of this, Eisenman's comparison of waqf Israeli legislation with the system under Ottoman and British Mandate rule is without substance.

Concerning the second argument, Israeli scholars Eisenman and Layish are again correct in arguing that the Absentee Property Law and the 1965 amendment did not alter the shari'a law as it concerned the waqf, but that the legislation dealt solely with the management and ownership of waqf property under the jurisdiction of the Custodian of Absentee Property. When one considers the impact of Israeli secular legislation on the Muslim waqf, however, their emphasis is excessively legalistic. Vesting ownership rights of Muslim waqf property in the Custodian constituted an alienation of waqf, which in itself transgresses shari'a law. There was, it is true, no alteration in shari'a, but the overriding secular law rendered an inviolate law of waqf essentially meaningless. The argument fails to acknowledge that there is little point in an inviolate law of waqf when waqf property can be arbitrarily expropriated. Indeed, there was no need for the Knesset to interfere with the shari'a law since it could easily be overridden by secular law. The same approach was used when the Israeli government addressed the issues of polygamy and divorce in the Muslim community in Israel; shari'a law itself was not interfered with, but the customs of the Muslim community were made subordinate to Israeli secular law.[19]

The third argument, which favorably compares Israeli legislation with the waqf reforms of Arab states, also erroneously interprets uncontroversial facts. Some Arab countries have reformed the Muslim waqf institution. For example, in 1949, the post-French Mandate republican government in Syria incorporated waqf *khayri* into the state and abolished waqf *dhurri* and waqf *mushtarak* (mixed *khayri-dhurri* waqf).[20] It also forbade the creation of new *dhurri* waqfs. Similar changes took place in Lebanon. In Jordan no attempt was made to abolish *dhurri* waqf, but the state progressively asserted a greater supervisory control over its administration.[21]

But the best known example of twentieth-century reforms in the waqf institution took place in Egypt. Immediately after the military coup d'etat in 1952, the new

Egyptian government abolished the waqf *ahli*.[22] Under this legislation waqf properties were divided among the beneficiaries, or returned to the *waqif* when possible. In the same year the Egyptian Ministry of Waqfs took over *khayri* waqfs, over which King Faruq presided as *nazir* or *mutawalli*. These waqfs amounted to approximately 100,000 *feddans* of land (about 105,800 acres).[23] A second law in 1953 extended the jurisdiction of the Ministry of Waqfs to all other remaining *khayri* waqfs except those still administered by *waqifs*.[24] In addition, the law permitted the Ministry of Waqfs to ignore the provisions of the *waqfiyyas* so that the income of *khayri* waqfs could be gathered into a central treasury.

These reforms of the *khayri* waqf amounted to the complete nationalization of the Egyptian waqf system and were characteristic of the thorough overhaul of the ancien regime undertaken by Egypt's new rulers. The most striking feature of the waqf reforms, however, was their implementation in the context of the land distribution program of the populist government. As Baer writes, they were

> the direct result of the establishment of the new military regime whose agrarian reform was one of the main pillars of its socio-economic policy. The abolition of all kinds of mortmain, entail and other forms of tying up property has been a corollary of agrarian reforms in many countries, and the Egyptian agrarian reform, too, would have forfeited many of its potential gains had it left the waqf untouched.[25]

Indeed, a third law passed in 1957 also involved the waqf system and confirms the context in which these reforms took place. All agricultural land that was waqf was placed in the hands of a Land Reform Committee, which redistributed it according to the Land Reform Law.[26]

The Israeli government, on the other hand, neither redistributed waqf land, which may have been of some benefit to Palestinian Muslims, nor did it fully incorporate waqf *khayri* into the state structures as in Egypt and Syria. Instead, Israel administered waqf land as "absentee" property under the jurisdiction of a secular ministry; it did not abolish waqf *dhurri* but merely released waqf *mulhaq* under the control of the Custodian.[27] The comparison with Egypt and Syria is, therefore, quite superficial. The "nationalization" of waqf property took the form of the Israeli state acquiring waqf land and property through the Custodian and selling or leasing it to enterprises which, as we have seen, followed the Jewish exclusivity clauses of the Jewish National Fund.

Israeli scholars' positive interpretation of the Israeli government's policies towards the waqf system does not fully correspond with the wider context in which the policies were implemented. First, the fundamental requirement of the new state was its quest for land, and this quest lay behind all its dealings with Palestinian property. The dismemberment of the waqf system merely formed a part of that policy. As Jiryis writes: "The Israeli government acted no differently with regard to waqf properties than it had in handling the rest of the property of Arabs inside Israel. In both cases it aimed to annex it permanently."[28] Second, Israel's acquisition of waqf land was intended to neutralize the political power of the Muslim leadership; without an independent financial base it was dependent upon government salaries and grants. Finally, the Third Amendment was at least partially designed to provide legitimacy to these policies. It is to this aspect that we now turn.

The Boards of Trustees

Following the passing of the 1965 amendment, boards of trustees were set up gradually by the Israeli government in areas in which the Palestinian minority in Israel was concentrated. The scandals, the corruption, and the violence that accompanied the operations of the boards allowed the continued transfer of the waqf system's resources to the Israeli state. They also discredited and weakened the status of the new Muslim elite associated with the boards.

The first three were set up between March 1966 and November 1967 in Jaffa, Haifa, and Acre. As we have noted, their areas of jurisdiction did not correspond to the previous Mandate boundaries of the local waqf committees, but were limited to the geographical areas of the local authority where they were located, such as Tel Aviv–Jaffa, Lydda, and so on. This meant that a large number of waqfs lay outside the area of jurisdiction of any board of trustees, and that therefore Palestinian Muslims were not given the opportunity to have a say in their management. For example, half the properties claimed by the Jaffa Board of Trustees as waqfs of the Jaffa district of the Mandate period were not released by the Custodian, since they fell outside the municipal boundaries of Tel Aviv–Jaffa.[29]

The same situation existed in other areas, and many important and prestigious waqfs, such as the Sayyidna 'Ali waqf, remained outside the jurisdiction of the boards. The system also made it possible to prevent large waqfs with extensive agricultural holdings from being transferred from the Custodian to the boards. Instead, the boards were left with dilapidated and urban waqf properties that were expensive to maintain. The concern over which waqfs would be released was taken by the prime minister's Advisor on Arab Affairs, who chaired a committee for releasing property.[30] It is also important to note that not all waqf properties were released to the boards of trustees. Before the amendment was passed, the Custodian already disposed of significant amounts to various Israeli Jewish bodies, and the Ministry of Religious Affairs held other properties as "agent" for the Custodian.

The 1965 amendment did not specify the procedures by which the boards would be established, other than that they were to be appointed by the government. Section 29 (b) of the law states only that the government "shall, by notice in *Reshumot* [Official Gazette], appoint boards of trustees for the area of each of the following local authorities: Tel-Aviv–Jaffa, Ramla, Lod, Haifa, Acre, Nazareth, Shefa'amr." Consultations with members of the local Muslim community were not required. This allowed the government to appoint those who would implement its policies without dissent. It appears that board members were selected and appointed by the prime minister's Advisor on Arab Affairs, although this was not required by the terms of the 1965 amendment.[31] The result was the appointment of Palestinian

Muslims who did not command the respect of their compatriots; often they were government employees and almost certainly screened by the Israeli intelligence services.[32] Indeed, it became the practice in some areas for board members to be nominated by various political parties, which in turn involved the boards in local council political battles, to the detriment of the real responsibilities under their care.[33] Consequently, the government's intention to use the 1965 amendment to assuage Palestinian Muslim public opinion was severely compromised from the outset. Boards members were either of insufficient stature or closely associated with the Israeli state, and therefore the boards could hardly be considered as a mediating institution.

Muslim fears were borne out by the corrupt and incompetent conduct of the boards. Members of the boards were variously accused of embezzling waqf funds, selling off waqf property under their control for personal gain, leasing it to Israeli Jewish entrepreneurs to the detriment of the Palestinian Muslim community, and allowing the property in their care to become dilapidated.[34]

The functions of the boards of trustees were extremely limited and this, too, compromised their potential role as a mediating institution. As already noted, the specifications laid out in the 1965 amendment appeared designed to prevent any coordination among the boards regarding the disbursement of waqf funds that could be reminiscent of Supreme Muslim Council control over the "income" and the "consideration" of waqf property. The boards were further restricted by the limited income at their disposal. The 1965 amendment did not specify what kind of budget should be made available to the boards, with the result that they have been seriously underfinanced while at the same time they were made responsible for additional properties requiring maintenance.[35] For example, in 1983 the Jaffa Board received from the Office of the Prime Minister's Advisor of Arab Affairs the monthly sum of 5,000 Israeli shekels (IS; approximately $500) when its minimum administrative and running costs came to IS 27,000.[36] The underfinancing of the boards has meant that they have remained dependent upon government approval for their activities, further diminishing their status in the eyes of the Muslim community.

Continuing Muslim concern about the boards, stretching from their inception to the present day, illustrates the crucial role they have played in the Muslim waqf system in Israel. The remainder of this chapter will examine the activities of the three main boards, in Jaffa, Haifa, and Acre, as well as the controversies surrounding them and the fate of waqf properties within their jurisdictions.

Acre

The city of Acre is on the northern coast of Israel, fifteen miles from the Lebanese border. The old walled city of Acre has ancient origins, and the present Ottoman structures are built upon Crusader and Mamluk foundations. During the period of the British Mandate the area outside the walls of Acre underwent a planned urban development that became the basis of the Israeli New Town after 1948. Many

Palestinian inhabitants of the Old City and the New Town fled the hostilities, only to be replaced by refugees from the surrounding villages and Haifa.[37] Although some (mostly middle class) Palestinians live in the New Town, most live in the Old City, which suffers from poor housing, neglect, and a lack of adequate services and civic facilities. Thus the geographical division between the two parts of Acre, dramatized by the huge Ottoman walls, is heightened by ethnic and social divisions that often lead to political tensions between the two.[38] It should be remembered that the 1947 UN partition plan placed Acre in the area that was to have become the Arab state—a fact often resuscitated by Palestinians during moments of intercommunal tension.

As an ancient seaport and wealthy trading center, Acre was the location of many endowments. It has been estimated that between 80 and 90 percent of the Old City of Acre was once endowed.[39] Waqf land in the immediate vicinity of Acre includes 80 dunums along the sea just outside the walls, 350 dunums in the Mansi area, and approximately 350 dunums in the Abu Atabi area.[40] The most noteworthy endowment in Acre was the extensive Ahmad Pasha al-Jazzar waqf, created in the late eighteenth century. The founder of this waqf, al-Jazzar, was the highly independent Ottoman governor of the north of Palestine and southern Lebanon. Partly in order to stimulate trade and industry, he established a large waqf based mainly on income from the productive agricultural land in the vicinity of Acre. Markets, shops, khans, and public baths were all constructed and endowed to attract commerce and to provide an income for the large mosque and other charitable institutions. More than one-third of the Old City of Acre belonged to the al-Jazzar waqf, and it included shops, residences, workshops, warehouses, and two soap factories.[41] By the end of the nineteenth century the al-Jazzar waqf had been absorbed into the Ottoman Ministry of Waqfs and thus became a *madbut* waqf. In addition to the al-Jazzar waqf there were four *dhurri* waqfs in Acre, which had extensive holdings including khans; these, too, supported mosques and other charitable institutions.[42]

Despite the large quantities of waqf in the Old City and despite the reforms instituted by the Supreme Muslim Council, much of the waqf property in Acre was in poor condition. A guide to Acre, written in 1946 by two members of the Mandate's Department of Antiquities, contains some photographs that reveal the dilapidated Suq al-Abyad, a major property belonging to the waqf al-Jazzar.[43] A survey carried out in 1962 by Israel's Planning Office recommended that many waqf properties attached to the al-Jazzar mosque should be "excavated."[44] The use of the term "excavated," rather than "cleared" or "restored," suggests that the neglect of the waqf properties in Acre dates back much further than the Mandate period.

The waqf issue in Acre and the activities of the Acre board of trustees are closely tied up with the future of the Old City as a predominantly Palestinian residential and commercial area. The Israeli government views the Old City as a Palestinian nationalist enclave with severe crime and social problems, and has attempted to reduce its population and alter its character. As a result of the government's control over waqf property in the Old City, a number of proposals have been introduced and partially implemented.

As in other areas of Israel, the establishment of the state led to the transfer of most of Acre's waqf property to the Custodian of Absentee Property, particularly the al-Jazzar waqf, which was *madbut*. As we have seen, the Custodian sold much of this property to the Israeli Development Authority. In the case of Acre, the Development Authority formed the Old Acre Development Company to refurbish sites of historical interest and to develop the Old City's tourist potential. Waqf properties, such as the Khan al-'Umdan or the "Turkish bazaar" (an arcade of shops forming the southern and eastern walls of the al-Jazzar mosque) were regarded as particularly suitable for this purpose. Furthermore, in conjunction with the Acre municipality, the company planned to recreate the Old City as a "museum-city," with tickets on sale at the City's main entrances.[45] Palestinians in the Old City feared that in practice this would entail the drastic reduction of their population and their resettlement elsewhere.

Such fears were heightened by other factors. Much of the rest of the property in the Old City was transferred from the Israel Development Authority to Amidar—the Israeli National Housing Corporation for Immigrants Ltd.[46] Amidar, which means "our people" (i.e., the Jewish people) in Hebrew, showed little interest in restoring the property under its control, and indeed, it has imposed strict conditions on the repairs it permits its Palestinian tenants to carry out.[47] This fact, combined with poor services and the policy of encouraging Israeli Jewish entrepreneurs to take over businesses in the Old City, convinced Palestinian residents that the Acre municipality, the Old Acre Development Company, and Amidar were intent on encouraging them to leave the Old City. These fears proved to have some foundation: for example, in 1980, the municipality began constructing new housing units for Palestinians of the Old City in Makr, a village just outside the municipal boundaries. One of the conditions of residence in these units is the surrender of all claims to residence in the Old City. Despite the area's overcrowding and shortages, the houses thus vacated are then sealed and left empty.[48]

Given the political sensitivity of these issues, the plans proceeded at a very slow pace. Then, in the mid-1970s, it was discovered that the Acre Board of Trustees had cooperated in the implementation of these plans. Not long after its establishment in 1966, the board had agreed to the release of a number of waqf properties that had already been earmarked for development by the Old Acre Development Board.[49] The terms of the agreements did not come to light, but they apparently allowed the Old Acre Development Company to refurbish Muslim property for profit, with little gain for the impoverished and neglected Palestinians inside the Old City. The agreements are believed to have included 99-year leases on a number of important Islamic properties and scores of shops. Rents had been fixed at a given level with the stipulation that they would be increased by 30 percent every seven years to account for inflation.[50] Even so, given the actual rate of inflation in Israel since the mid-1970s, the rents collected by the board were soon nominal.

Although most Palestinians had reservations about the government-appointed board, they were nevertheless shocked by the government's choice of board members, and accused the appointees of personal gain. The outrage was such that by 1978 the government was forced to ask the board to resign, but Palestinians in the Old City were not satisfied since the agreement with the Old Acre Development Company remained in place. The issue continued to aggravate tensions between the Palestinians of the Old City and the Israeli state institutions, and between the two parts of Acre, new and old. Finally, under the more sympathetic policies pursued by Ezer Weizman, who became minister without portfolio but with special responsibility for Arab affairs in the mid-1980s, the agreement was renegotiated. All but fifteen unused properties were returned to the board; for the fifteen, the rents were increased to market levels. A retroactive payment was made for the losses incurred on the other properties.[51]

However, criticism of the board remains. The new board appointed to replace the disbanded one is no better than its predecessor. As in Jaffa, the board lacks sufficient funds to maintain cemeteries and to cover its operating costs. It remains dependent upon government favors for extra funds to carry out needed repairs on waqf properties. Furthermore, the issue of the board's accountability to the Muslim community in Acre is yet to be addressed.

What is striking in this case study of Acre is the relatively low level of popular organized resistance to the operations of the Acre board. Above and beyond the extremely adverse public opinion, there were some protests from the Acre branch of the Israeli Communist Party and from a local Palestinian union of university graduates, but there was no sustained alternative leadership for the Muslim community. For most of the period under discussion, the qadi of the Acre-based shari'a court represented the new and co-opted elite. Despite his claims to be pursuing the interests of the Muslim community, he operated within the parameters laid down by his position as a state appointee. Given the relative passivity of the local Muslim community, and state pressures over the questions of land sales and transfers, the boards of trustees and the co-opted leadership had a free and largely unimpeded rein in Acre.

Jaffa

In the case of Jaffa, resistance to the activities of the boards, however disorganized and disunited, resulted in frequent state intervention to ensure that the state changes remained in place. The city of Jaffa is one of the oldest in Palestine and served for centuries as the chief port of the region. In the Middle Ages it was the point of arrival and departure for Christian pilgrims to Jerusalem.[52] Although Jaffa itself had few monuments of great religious significance, such as burial places of holy men or renowned scholars, it was, nevertheless, a wealthy and important trading center, and many waqfs had been created by prosperous families in and around the city. According to Mandate records, up to 33 percent of the shops in Jaffa were endowed by 1921.[53] In addition, the famous mosques at Sayyidna 'Ali and Nabi Rubin, north and south of Jaffa respectively, were supported by wealthy waqfs and became popular sites of annual festivals.

On the eve of the 1948 war, the Palestinian Arab population of Jaffa numbered approximately 75,000. The Jewish population lived in the newly constructed settlement on its northern fringes, Tel Aviv. The majority of the Palestinian inhabitants were either driven out or fled during the hostilities; by the end of the war, only 3,000 remained. Over the past forty years, however, the number of Palestinians in Jaffa has steadily increased to approximately 15,000, although no accurate figures are available.[54]

After the establishment of the State of Israel in 1948, almost all of Jaffa (with the exception of some church property) was taken over by the Custodian of Absentee Property and subsequently passed on either to the Israel Development Authority or to the Jewish National Fund. The ensuing development work along the coast has led to the creation of an Israeli Jewish tourist center and an artists colony in the central area of Old Jaffa. The old winding streets and alleys that had offered privacy and seclusion to the Palestinian inhabitants now sport cafeterias, restaurants, bars, nightclubs, galleries, and souvenir shops. The atmosphere is Western and modern rather than Islamic and conservative. The residential areas still occupied by Palestinians consist mainly of dilapidated slums awaiting a clearance and redevelopment program. Due to political problems associated with the relocation of the Palestinian inhabitants, the program has not yet been fully implemented.[55]

Under the Absentee Property Law, most of the waqf property in the area was placed in the hands of the Custodian and leased out to Israeli Jewish entrepreneurs as souvenir shops, restaurants, and cafes.[56] Some mosques were converted into other uses. Al-Wihda mosque was converted into a synagogue, al-Siksik mosque became a Bulgarian restaurant and nightclub, and al-Nuzha was left abandoned and used for prostitution.[57] A similar fate befell the cemeteries in the Jaffa area: part of the Abu Nabi cemetery became a park and the site of the Tel Aviv Hilton has already been cited. Similarly, part of the Taso cemetery on the outskirts of Jaffa was also expropriated for an urban expressway.[58]

It was expected that after the establishment of the Jaffa Board of Trustees legislated in the 1965 amendment, such misuse of waqf property would be stopped or curtailed. The Jaffa board was set up in 1966 and its members were appointed by Shmuel Toledano, then the prime minister's Advisor on Arab Affairs. The board was discredited from its very creation. The chairman, Nazmi Jabali, was a known alcoholic who "spends his time in the bars trying to get someone to buy him a drink."[59] In 1973, he was accused of demanding bribes from a number of Israeli Jewish entrepreneurs in exchange for selling the remainder of the Abu Nabi cemetery.[60] Another leading board member was a convicted criminal who obtained his release through plea bargaining.[61] Other members also have admitted to accepting bribes for approving the sale of waqf property of which they were trustees. From the outset, then, the potential of the Jaffa Board to act as a representative or mediating institution for Jaffa's Muslim population was seriously compromised.[62]

The absence of credibility resulting from the appointment of such people to the Jaffa board was compounded by a number of other factors. First, it was unclear how much authority the board held. Second, the extent of the properties released to the board was insignificant. According to a report in the daily Israeli *Ha'Aretz*, a list of

150 waqf properties that should fall under the Jaffa board's jurisdiction was submitted by the board to the Office of the Prime Minister's Advisor on Arab Affairs. Eighty of these properties were discounted by the advisor on the grounds either that the waqf claims could not be proven or that they were outside the boundaries of the Tel Aviv–Jaffa municipality and therefore outside the board's area of jurisdiction. Of the remaining seventy, thirty were discounted either because they were regarded as having no specific religious purpose, or because their educational, charitable, and welfare functions had been superseded by the state. A further twenty had already been disposed of by the Israel Lands Administration and the Custodian of Absentee Property. A mere seventeen properties remained, most of them mosques and cemeteries that produced no income for the board. Three of the seventeen properties—two old houses and a complex of some fifty small shops and workshops—produced income amounting to IS 500,000 in 1981.[63]

A third factor limiting the board's effectiveness was the inadequacy of the budget at its disposal. The Jaffa board had very little property to manage; moreover it produced little income and required extensive maintenance. As has already been noted, in 1983 the Jaffa board received from the Office of the Prime Minister's Advisor on Arab Affairs the monthly sum of IS 5,000 (approximately $500), when its minimum administrative and running costs came to IS 27,000.[64] As a result of these factors and the nefarious activities of the trustees, the board was regarded as no more than a means by which the government could continue to dispossess the community of its property and throw Islam into disrepute.

In turning to the specific activities of the Jaffa board, it is important to note that not all its illicit sales and financial dealings have yet come to light. The full extent to which the board members collaborated in the further disposal of waqf property in Jaffa may never be known. In the early 1980s, one particularly controversial agreement attracted a great deal of public attention and highlighted the nature of the government-appointed boards, bringing the waqf issue to prominence on the Israeli political agenda. This agreement concerned the Hasan Bek mosque, close to the center of Jaffa and just south of some major commercial development in Tel Aviv.

The Hasan Bek controversy first became public in 1978 when complaints against the original board had reached such a pitch that the government was forced to replace the existing board members with more respected individuals, including, briefly, the popular imam of the Mahmudiyya mosque in Jaffa, Shaykh Bassam.[65] The new board discovered that the old board had leased the Hasan Bek mosque to a Jewish enterprise, the Edgar Company, directed by Gershon Peres, the brother of former Prime Minister Shimon Peres. The lease had been concluded directly after the mosque had been released to the board by the Custodian of Absentee Property.[66] The former board had agreed that the lease should last for forty-nine years to permit the construction of a tourist and shopping center in the mosque, leaving a small area for prayers.[67] Also significant was the disclosure that the lease was signed in the Office of the Prime Minister's Advisor on Arab Affairs.[68]

The new board's initial request that the lease be annulled was opposed by the Tel Aviv municipality, and the board embarked upon a vociferous and highly-publicized campaign to put pressure upon the municipality. The campaign culminated in 1981 in a mass Friday prayer meeting in the mosque, which received considerable international media attention and attracted substantial funds for the mosque's restoration.[69] The issue threatened to cause great embarrassment for the Israeli government, highlighting the nature of the appointed boards and the fate of the waqf system in particular, and the discriminatory policies of the government towards the Palestinians in general. A serious escalation of the dispute was avoided when the government belatedly "discovered" that the Hasan Bek mosque had in fact been expropriated some years previous to the disclosure, and that the lease was therefore void.[70] Some bureaucratic sleight of hand saved the day for the government, now spared both embarrassment and the appearance of intervening on behalf of the Muslims. The threat to the mosque from developers had been lifted, and the rising tensions began to die down.

Still, although the acquisition of the mosque by the government removed the mosque from the responsibility of the board, the issue did not completely fade away. State funds for restoration work promised by the Office of the Prime Minister's Advisor on Arab Affairs were to be supplemented by contributions from the board.[71] These did not materialize, however, until after the collapse of the mosques's minaret, allegedly by saboteurs, thus rekindling some of the earlier passions. Renovation work began in 1985 and was overseen by a board that had been constituted for the third time, and that was said to be more amenable to the government than the one that had replaced the original board in the late 1970s. Funds in the amount of $200,000 were made available from the Israeli Ministry of Religious Affairs, and another $100,000 was donated by the Amman-based Muslim Unity Organization.[72] The Awqaf Administration in Jerusalem also contributed JD 70,000.[73] At present the mosque renovation work has been stalled due to lack of funds.

It was during this contentious period that Shaykh Bassam resigned from the board on the grounds that it was being manipulated by the government.[74] The former chairman, Abed Kabub, was dismissed in 1985, accused by the government of financial irregularities. Their replacements soon became embroiled in controversial financial transactions. One such transaction involved a Muslim cemetery in north Tel Aviv and resulted in investigations by both the Israeli State Comptroller (attorney-general) and the Ministry of Religious Affairs.[75] This affair and other illegal agreements have been linked to the murder of the chairman of the new board, Ahmed Fanjari, on 9 September 1988.[76]

These events demonstrate that the Jaffa Board of Trustees served the interests of the Israeli state in two ways. First, by collaborating in the sales of waqf property to Israeli Jewish entrepreneurs, the board helped facilitate the state's policy of transferring the resources of the Muslim community to the Israeli Jewish community. Second, the existence of the board and its ostensible representative nature prevented the emergence of a clear and united leadership in Jaffa. As illustrated in the cases of Shaykh Bassam and Abed Kabub, when representative leaders were co-opted they either were obliged to resign in protest over the government's actions or were dismissed when they showed too much independence. This further added to the dissension and disunity in the community. In contrast to the Acre case, the Jaffa events show how the operations of the board provoked considerable opposition. This suggests that the attempt by the state to create a new elite to legitimize its policies and to contain Muslim opposition to the transfer of waqf resources was not entirely successful. On a number of occasions direct state intervention was required.

Haifa

The opposition to the activities of the board of trustees can be even more clearly seen in the case of Haifa, where the opposition was more united and had a surer understanding of the implications of the 1965 amendment. Haifa is an important harbor city in the north of Israel whose main development took place during the late nineteenth and early twentieth centuries, largely at the expense of the neighboring port of Acre. (This was due primarily to the introduction of deep-draught vessels requiring a deeper anchorage than Acre could provide, and to the construction of an oil refinery and related industries on its outskirts.) During the British Mandate period Haifa was a vibrant commercial and intellectual center with a mixed Palestinian Arab and Jewish population; Jews only slightly outnumbered Arabs. Palestinian newspapers and political parties were based there. Following the 1948 war, the Palestinian population was dramatically reduced to no more than 8 percent of the city's population. By 1966 it had increased to approximately 19 percent.[77]

Because Haifa was a relatively modern city, waqf property there was not nearly as extensive as in Jaffa and Acre. Nevertheless, the city contained some significant Islamic sites, such as the al-Nasr mosque, built in the eighteenth century.[78] During the British Mandate period two other sites were established that would become important symbols Palestinian resistance to colonialism and Zionism. The first was the grave and mosque named after Shaykh 'Izz al-Din al-Qassim, a guerrilla leader killed by the British in 1935 and considered by Palestinian nationalists as one of their first martyrs. The second site was the Istiqlal mosque and cemetery, which was supported by a large *dhurri* endowment established in 1938. By 1948 this large waqf comprised 59 properties and land in and around Haifa, including many of the properties close to the city's center and its docks and railway station.[79] The remainder of waqf property in Haifa was mostly managed by the Supreme Muslim Council, which also supported a number of schools there.[80]

After 1948, the *madbut* waqfs of Haifa fell under the jurisdiction of the Custodian of Absentee Property. The management of the Istiqlal waqf, which was *dhurri* (and therefore not a priori taken over by the Custodian provided the administrators remained in Israel), lapsed after disagreements over who was entitled to be *mutawalli*. In 1958, the qadi of Acre (the highest authority in the entire shari'a system in Israel) appointed a committee to manage the Istiqlal waqf, and only then was any active supervision of the affairs of the waqf undertaken.[81] One major problem in documenting the activities of the Haifa Board of Trustees is that the Istiqlal Committee played a prominent role and its chairman, Suhil Shukri, was also chairman of the government-appointed Board of Trustees.[82] Thus, some of the charges of which he is accused refer to his capacity as chairman of the board and others as chairman of the Istiqlal Committee. To the extent that his dual role led to the further dismemberment of the waqf system in Haifa, without any gains for the Muslim community, the distinction may be irrelevant; it becomes important, however, when trying to trace accountability. Corruption and embezzlement by the chairman of the Istiqlal Committee is ultimately the responsibility of the qadi of Acre, who can dismiss him. That Suhil Shukri was permitted to negotiate secret land sales of waqf properties and accept bribes as chairman of the board of trustees without any censure indicates a measure of connivance and endorsement on the part of the government as well. In dealing with the waqf issue, it is difficult to disentangle the two.

As chairman of the Istiqlal Committee, Shukri had only limited success in prizing the properties belonging to the waqf from the government. In 1979 the committee had obtained compensation for ten of the sites and a promise of IS 50,000 for the income accruing to the waqf, but having failed to secure the release of another forty-six sites, it took the government to court.[83] The committee's attempts to free waqf properties from the Israeli government did not reflect any nationalist zeal or undue concern for fellow Palestinians. Although some grants were made to assist needy Palestinian Arabs in Israel, the nature of these grants indicate a complete acceptance of the Israeli status quo. For example, in 1969 the Istiqlal Committee established a fund from waqf income to provide grants to Palestinian Arab students at the Technion, a prestigious Israeli college of higher education. The fund was called the Levi Eshkol Fund after a former Israeli premier, reflecting a considerable desire both to gain respectability with the Israeli Jewish political establishment and to avoid controversy.[84] Similarly in 1972, the committee set aside another sum of money for the educational needs of a Palestinian family whose father had been killed while serving in the Israeli border guards, a unit of the Israeli army often used to suppress Palestinian demonstrations and composed partly of Palestinians approved by the Israeli secret services and regarded as collaborators and quislings by their compatriots.[85] Such public association of a waqf with the political establishment did not endear Shukri to Haifa Muslims, but it was the issue of land sales involving waqf property that caused the greatest outrage.

As chairman of both the Istiqlal Committee and of the Haifa Board of Trustees, Shukri was accused of a wide range of secret property deals. Although he may have been legally entitled to make such transactions, they were seen to run counter to the long-term interests of the Muslim community and indeed to cause further destruction of the Palestinian heritage. In this way his activities corresponded more closely to the interests of the state than of the Muslim community of Haifa. Shukri was accused of selling 31,346 dunums (nearly 8,000 acres) of land in the Haifa area in 1965.[86] This was clearly an Istiqlal waqf property, since the boards of trustees had not yet been created. He was also accused of selling the Small Mosque in the center of Haifa in 1968 and, in 1974, another forty dunums (ten acres) of real estate. Both these properties were under the jurisdiction of the boards of trustees. He has been accused of selling the Istiqlal cemetery in 1976 for IS 130,000.[87] Together with members of the Haifa board, he was accused of misappropriating the income from such sales and from rents of waqf property for personal gain.

In 1976 Shukri conducted secret negotiations with developers, who demolished the Shaykh 'Izz al-Din al-Qassim mosque and partially demolished the Small Mosque.[88] The following year the majority of the board resigned. Shukri was dismissed by the Israeli government and emigrated to the United States, reputedly a millionaire.[89] The new board, the identity of whose members remained secret for many years, continued to sell and dispose of waqf property in a controversial manner.[90]

Further controversy was created by the decision of the Istiqlal Committee to proceed with the negotiations over the Istiqlal cemetery. The Istiqlal cemetery is located between the commercial center of Haifa and the port area, and is therefore a prime site for development. As we have noted, the committee under Shukri had negotiated an undisclosed agreement with the municipality over the sale and use of the site in 1976. The municipality's proposals included removal of the buried remains and the construction of apartments, a kindergarten, and a shopping center for the Muslims of Haifa.[91] The *fatwa*, or legal opinion in shari'a law, which permitted the removal of the remains had already been issued by the qadi of Acre, Muhammad Hubayshi, as a prerequisite for the sale in 1976.[92] It was the issuance of this *fatwa* that alerted the Muslims of Haifa to what some saw as a threat to the cemetery. The most vocal opponents of the municipality's plans were represented by the Islamic Initiative Committee (*lujnet al-mubadara al-islamiyya*), which had been formed as a response to the destruction of the two mosques mentioned above. The Islamic Initiative Committee suspected that the municipality's proposals were a ploy to allay Muslim fears that the municipality would later plea lack of funds and build a profitable commercial property, and that the apartments, kindergarten, and shopping center would never be built. The Islamic Initiative Committee's counter-proposal was to preserve the Istiqlal cemetery as a site of the Palestinian national heritage and to construct much-needed housing units on specific alternative sites.[93] The Islamic Initiative Committee was also concerned that the municipality had offered the Istiqlal Committee IS 500,000 for vaguely defined "religious purposes," funds that could easily be misappropriated by Committee members.[94] The Islamic Initiative Committee's campaign to save the cemetery failed, however, and on 8 June 1981, bulldozers demolished the gravestones and plowed up the ground.[95]

By 1984 it was clear that the suspicions of the Islamic Initiative Committee had been justified. Instead of the promised housing, kindergarten, and shopping center for Palestinians, a commercial property was to be built upon the site of the Istiqlal cemetery.[96] (Some units for Palestinian families were to be made available elsewhere in the city.) The Islamic Initiative Committee is continuing its campaign, demanding that members of the board of trustees and the Istiqlal Committee be elected, that some of the past land deals be abrogated, and that more of the Haifa waqf property be released

This survey of the activities of the Haifa Board of Trustees reveals much the same pattern outlined in the Jaffa case. The Haifa board was similarly used as a vehicle for the transfer of resources of the Muslim community to the Israeli Jewish community, and key figures, such as the qadi of Acre and the head of a leading Palestinian family in Haifa, were successfully co-opted. What is of particular interest in the Haifa case, however, is the prominent role played by the Islamic Initiative Committee. While Jaffa Muslims had attempted to organize against the activities of the board, for the most part they were too fragmented to provide effective resistance. The Islamic Initiative Committee, on the other hand, was able (with the support of the Israeli Communist Party) to form a clear alternative to the board and the co-opted Muslim leadership.

* * * * *

The waqf issue—specifically the transfer of waqf resources and the administration of the remnant of the waqf system—has remained high on the political agenda of the Palestinians inside Israel. This is in part a consequence of the anger generated by the state's appointment of disreputable persons to the waqf boards of trustees, the underfinancing of their activities, and the restrictions placed on their jurisdiction and freedom of management—not to mention the state's seizure of waqf resources. But the endurance of the issue is also a consequence of organized resistance. Local groups such as the Islamic Initiative Committee in Haifa and the League of Jaffa Arabs exposed the operations of the boards through public meetings and publications. The First Islamic Conference in 1961 in Acre was unsuccessful, but a second conference held in 1985 in Nazareth issued demands for the release of all waqf properties to bodies of elected representatives of the Muslim community.[97] Community leaders and local council leaders have also taken up the issue. At a meeting organized in 1983, Muhammad Zaydan, chairman of the Kufr Manda local council, called for the release of waqf properties in the area, saying, "We have the talent to run our own affairs without the help of the Custodian and the Office of the Prime Minister's Advisor on Arab Affairs."[98] Reverend Shehadi Shehadi, chairman of the National Committee of the Defense of Arab Lands, also criticized the government's treatment of Muslim waqf.[99]

The New Communist Party of Israel, better known by its Hebrew acronym RAKAH, took up the issue seriously and through its Knesset members submitted a number of bills designed to secure the full release of waqf properties for the Muslim community.[100] The RAKAH-backed "Congress of Arab Masses," which was banned from meeting in 1980, included a paragraph on the waqf issue among nine specific demands. It reads:

> Releasing the Moslem religious Trust (Waqf) which have been arbitrarily seized by the authorities and handing them over to committees to be elected by the members of the Moslem community in every town and village where such Trusts do exist.[101]

The Labor-Mapam coalition (*Ma'arakh*) also pledged its support for a review of government policy concerning waqf properties as a result of pressure from its Palestinian members. In a newspaper interview, a prominent Palestinian Labor party member of the Knesset, Muhammad Watad, claimed to be preparing a bill to this end.[102] Similarly the radical Palestinian nationalist grouping, *abna' al-balad*, and its associates in the Progressive National Movement have organized work camps in cemeteries to restore damaged headstones and to clean up rubbish and undergrowth around the stones as a means of demonstrating their concern and interest in the waqf question.[103]

In the early 1980s, following the revival of Islamic fundamentalism throughout the Muslim world, the fundamentalist Islamic Associations in Israel have begun to add their voice to the criticisms of the boards of trustees and to call for the release of waqf properties.[104] A leader of one of the Islamic groups in Jaffa sat briefly on the Jaffa Board of Trustees between 1978 and 1980, but he resigned because he was convinced that the board was being manipulated by the government.[105]

Some former senior Israeli civil servants have also voiced criticism of Israeli policy since the establishment of the boards in 1965. They regard the present policy as an unnecessary impediment to the development of harmonious relations between the Israeli government and the Palestinian minority, and believe that the security concerns upon which much of the policy was based no longer apply. For example, Yitzhak Reiter, from 1979 to 1987 senior research officer in the Office of the Prime Minister's Advisor on Arab Affairs, argued in an Israeli academic journal that the 1965 amendment failed in its objective to assuage Muslim public opinion and, instead, introduced a fresh series of disputes between the government and the Muslim community.[106] Similarly, General Zvi Peleg, a former member of the military administration in the occupied territories, who has closely followed developments in the waqf issue in Jaffa, has been quoted as saying, "I am no Leftist and I believe we have rights over all this land, but what was done with the waqf property is simply a stupidity."[107] The government has yet to address convincingly the legitimate complaints of the Muslim community in Israel regarding the management of waqf properties.[108]

CHAPTER 4

The Muslim Waqf System in the Occupied Territories, 1967–1988

The Israeli occupation of the West Bank and Gaza Strip in 1967 brought the last remaining parts of the Palestinian waqf system under Israeli control (see Map 3). Yet instead of establishing complete command over the system's resources, administration, and leadership, as it had done in Israel itself, the government permitted the West Bank and Gaza "sub-systems" of the Palestinian waqf to operate independently of the state structures, albeit with differing degrees of autonomy. Does this relative independence indicate that despite the overwhelming military dominance of the Israeli state, there was a limit upon its coercive power in its relation with a traditional religious institution? Does it reveal hidden strengths in the waqf system in relation to state power? Or did the continuation of the waqf system serve the interests of the Israeli state in ways not possible inside Israel?

Clearly some of the answers to these questions lie in the very different situations that prevailed with regard to the remnant of the waqf system in Israel, and the systems in the West Bank and the Gaza Strip. In the West Bank, in particular, the presence of another major player in the drama, Jordan, affected the unfolding of events. Despite the state of belligerency that formally existed between Israel and Jordan, Jordan was still able to maintain strong administrative links with the West Bank. It continued the funding and management of health, agricultural, and education programs to an extent that paralleled the military administration of the Israeli state. Of special interest to this study is that Jordan also supported a department of waqfs known as the Awqaf Administration, which operated from offices throughout Jerusalem and the rest of the West Bank. Thus the waqf system in the West Bank and the Gaza Strip had an intergovernmental role as well as one that could act as a mediating institution between the Israeli state and the Muslim population. The presence of the Jordanian state as an additional player helped to maintain the waqf system in the West Bank as a functioning and evolving institution. Because it fell under the legal jurisdiction of the Jordanian shari'a laws, the waqf system was not accountable to the Israeli military government in the same way that the educational, charitable, and municipal institutions were. As a result, the waqf system provided both a vehicle for the implementation of Jordanian government policies in the West Bank and, through its operations in different regions and towns, a medium of cohesion for the population of the West Bank.[1]

The importance of this differentiating factor can be seen when one contrasts the role of the West Bank Awqaf Administration with that of the office of the *ma'mur al-awqaf* in the Gaza Strip. There, the waqf system had not been developed by any state authority, and lacking sufficient resources, it stagnated. Rather than integrating the Gaza Strip into Egypt, as Jordan had integrated the West Bank, the Egyptian government had sought to administer it on a temporary basis pending a peace settlement. Egypt appointed a governor of the Strip who was given general oversight over waqf affairs, and its general policy was to consolidate the status quo. Few funds were furnished by the Egyptian state to replace the income channeled by the Supreme Muslim Council to the Gaza waqf district, income that was now lost due to the establishment of the State of Israel. As a consequence, the office of the *ma'mur al-awqaf* in the Gaza Strip could not successfully respond to the new political environment and the problems facing the inhabitants of the Gaza Strip. Among the most serious of these problems concerned the absorption of the large influx of Palestinian refugees from what became Israel and the attempt to meet their material and political needs.

A second important factor that accounts for the Israeli state's separate approaches to the waqf system in the West Bank and Gaza Strip and the one operating in Israel itself is that the territories remained occupied rather than annexed. As noted earlier, the martial law imposed between 1948 and 1966 in certain areas of Israel with heavy Arab concentrations prevented any effective Palestinian political mobilization or resistance to the land acquisition policies of the Israeli state. While the same applied in the occupied territories for much of the period under review, Israel's imposition of a military administration in the territories rather than annexation meant that the administrative structures of the waqf system in the West Bank and Gaza Strip survived.

To a large extent, these two differentiating factors—Jordanian involvement and military government—account for the contrasting situations between the West Bank and Gaza Strip on the one hand, and between the territories and Israel on the other. In what follows, we consider the state's control over the system's resources in the occupied territories, the degree to which the system was administratively integrated into the governmental bureaucracy, and the degree of co-optation of the system's leadership. The next section gives a brief picture of the most salient features of the structures that were in place before 1967; these had an important bearing upon the developments after 1967.

Map 3. The West Bank and Gaza Strip

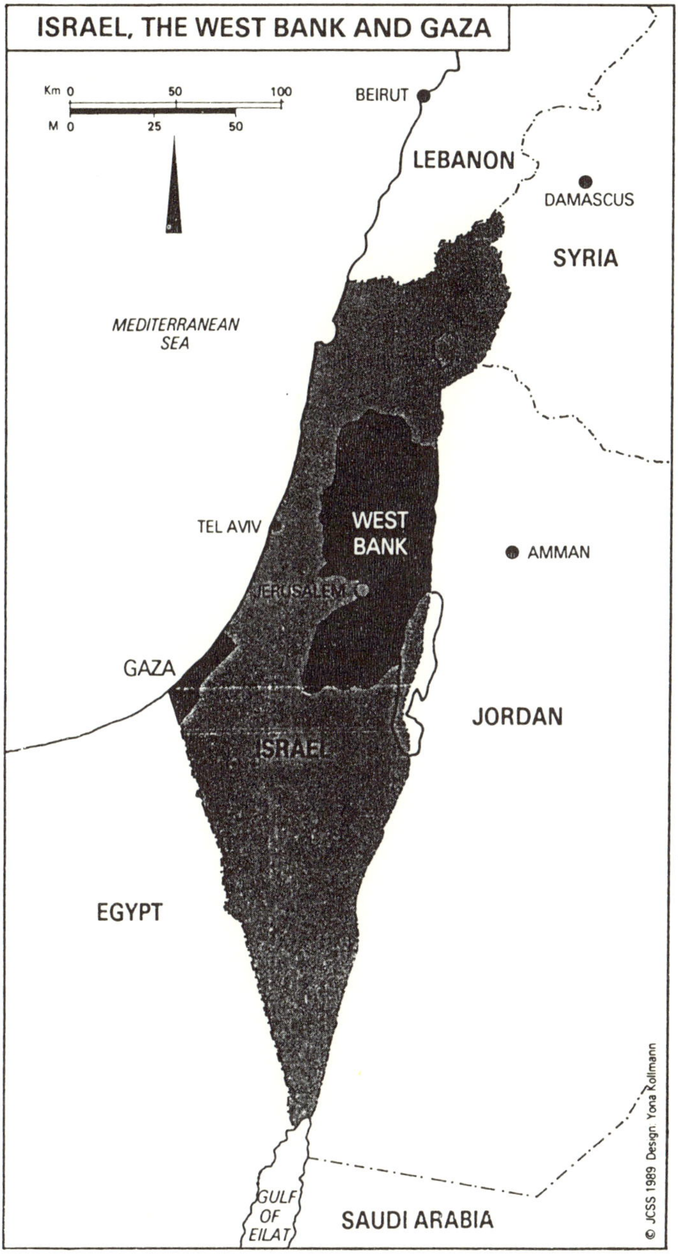

Source: Jaffee Centre for Strategic Studies, *The West Bank and Gaza* (Tel Aviv: JCSS, 1989), Appendix 3.

The Historical Background

The West Bank

Following the termination of the British Mandate over Palestine and the establishment of the State of Israel in 1948, war broke out between the Arab states and the new state. The Jordan valley and the highland areas of Palestine were occupied by the Transjordanian army, and after the hostilities ended with the armistice agreements of 1949, the kidney-shaped area popularly known as the West Bank remained under Transjordanian control.

The immediate post-1948 circumstances were extremely confusing for all concerned. Until the formal annexation of the West Bank in 1950 by what was by then called Jordan, the final status of the West Bank, and with it the fate of such Mandatory institutions as the Supreme Muslim Council, had been unclear. Prior to the Jordanian annexation, the military governor issued a proclamation declaring that all regulations and laws in force in Palestine up to the termination of the Mandate should remain in force unless they contradicted the Jordanian Defense Regulations.[2] This meant that the waqf system, as established by the Supreme Muslim Council, continued to function as well as possible given the abrupt disruption of the Mandate government services, the immense losses of lands and properties to the new Israeli state, and the additional burden on its services caused by the huge influx of refugees.[3]

Jordan's annexation of the West Bank introduced several important changes in the waqf administration there. In order to understand these changes, a brief survey of the Transjordanian system in effect at the time of annexation is in order.

The waqf system in Transjordan, which was closely based on Ottoman structures, was different from that established in Palestine under the Supreme Muslim Council. During the very early years of Transjordan, the administration of waqfs was rudimentary, being under the direct supervision of the qadis.[4] It was not until Transjordan's new constitution was approved in 1946 that a central waqf administration was created under the jurisdiction of the shari'a courts.[5]

Specifically, the December 1946 law and accompanying regulations establishing the Awqaf Administration stipulated that the new body was directly accountable to the Prime Minister's Council, or cabinet.[6] It was governed by a Higher Council of three members appointed by the king that met twice monthly to examine waqf budgets, expenses, appointments, and the activities of local waqf committees. A director-general appointed by the Higher Council was in charge of the administration and executed the Council's decisions. A central treasury, separate from that of the state, was also established under the control of the Higher Council for the Awqaf Administration's income and expenses.[7] Busson de Janssens notes that the major expenditure was the maintenance of religious property and the payment of employees' salaries.[8] Local committees of three members appointed from the local residents were established under the chairmanship of the local qadi; the number and location of these committees were not specified.[9] The Awqaf Administration also appointed the *mutawallis* of *dhurri* waqfs and approved their annual accounts, thus acquiring a limited supervisory role over these waqfs.[10] This more centralized structure contrasts with the structure established by the Mandatory government in Palestine and the Supreme Muslim Council prior to the Defence Regulations of 1937.[11] Jordan's Awqaf Administration was more vulnerable to direct government supervision and lacked an electoral procedure or a nominal representative base.

The Transjordanian government's first political step concerning the waqf system in the West Bank following the 1948 war was the appointment in December 1948 of a new Mufti of Jerusalem and *ra'is al-majlis*. The new mufti, Husam al-Din Jarallah, was a supporter of the Hashemite ruler[12] and his appointment was partly a preemptive move on Abdullah's part to prevent the former Mufti of Jerusalem, Haj Amin al-Husayni, from assuming the post.[13] A conference of West Bank notables met in Jericho in 1950 to confirm this step and the Jordanian annexation of the West Bank. The post of Mufti of Jerusalem was made subordinate to the Mufti of Jordan whose seat was in Amman.[14]

The Jordanian government's policy during this period was to integrate West Bank waqf administration with that of the East Bank. Consequently, many powers were centralized in Amman, establishing a unified system for the East and West Banks. In 1951 the Supreme Muslim Council was formally abolished and the powers of the *ra'is al-majlis* were transferred to the prime minister in Amman.[15] The *qadi al-quda'* (chief qadi) became responsible for the Awqaf Administration, including appointments and the payment of salaries. District offices were set up in Jerusalem, Hebron, Ramallah, Jenin, and Nablus. The district offices, accountable to an assistant head (*muraqeb*) in Jerusalem, were responsible for collecting rents; administering schools, orphanages, and shari'a schools; and maintaining waqf property. Waqf income hitherto accruing to the Supreme Muslim Council was sent to Amman to the central treasury for waqf and religious affairs, and expenditures were decided upon in Amman. In 1952 these changes became formalized, following the adoption of the new Jordanian constitution.

Despite this structure, the strong institutional base and organizational history of waqf administration on the West Bank led to the evolution of a system in which each department in Amman had a parallel department in Jerusalem. A department head in Jerusalem was accountable to a Jerusalem director-general for most day-to-day decisions and oversaw the running of the West Bank district offices.[16] The system was clearly a compromise between the demands for administrative efficiency and the Jordanian government's political concerns to recognize the status of the Jerusalem-based waqf administration, and it led to some confusion. In 1960 Hasan Tahbub became director-general of the Awqaf Administration for the West Bank based in Jerusalem.

Some Muslim bodies independent of the Awqaf Administration were established in Jerusalem during the Jordanian period and these were overseen by the *qadi al-quda'* in Amman. One of these bodies was a board of scholars, *hay'at al-'ulama'*, established in 1951 and made up of no more than ten officials appointed by the king for three-year terms. David Farhi, the Israeli military officer responsible for religious affairs in the early years of the occupation, who later became an academic, points out that this body was the only Jordanian state institution actually based in

Jerusalem. Other bodies centered in that city were either district offices or reported to the *qadi al-quda'* in Amman.[17] The board's offices were located at the old Supreme Muslim Council premises, the Madrassa Manjakiyya.[18] A Council for Preaching and Guidance, the *majlis al-wa'z wal-irshad*, was established in 1962 and supervised the administration of and preaching in mosques. Also following Supreme Muslim Council precedent, a Committee for the Restoration of al-Aqsa and the Dome of the Rock was set up.[19]

The establishment of these structures show that the Jordanian government attempted to follow the rationalizations in waqf administration that had been instituted by the Supreme Muslim Council. Many of the reforms were far-reaching and constituted a radical reform of the system. In 1960 Jordan introduced new regulations that permitted the Awqaf Administration to bypass the stipulations laid down in the *waqfiyya*s and systematized the procedures for renting waqf lands and properties. A further reform was the abolition of hereditary posts in the management of *khayri* waqfs as well as of other religious positions in the Awqaf Administration. In 1962 Jordan abolished the local waqf committees and hired employees to administer the regional waqfs.[20] Also in 1962, the Jordanian parliament passed a law stating that on the death of the incumbent, the position of *mutawalli* of the waqf would pass to the Awqaf Administration. This meant that over time waqfs that were not specifically *dhurri* eventually fell under the jurisdiction of the Awqaf Administration.

These laws added up to a considerable extension of Jordanian state power over the waqf system. The abolition of hereditary posts dealt a crushing blow to the influence of the Muslim religious elite, particularly in Jerusalem. All the leading notable families were affected, since these positions in the religious hierarchy—mufti, *shaykh al-haram*, qadi, *bashkatib*, and so on—were a major source of wealth and prestige. Moreover, the dissolution of local waqf committees curtailed the influence of regional families acting independently of the central waqf administration. There was a certain amount of opposition to these changes. Some families publicly objected to the loss of their *mutawalli* positions and attempted to challenge the Awqaf Administration's right to take this step. For example, the al-Disi family in Jerusalem refused to accept the loss of its management rights over the land near the Shaykh Jaraah mosque and tried (unsuccessfully) to prevent the Awqaf Administration from building on it by obtaining an injunction from the land settlement courts.[21] One should not conclude from these policies that the Jordanian government was entirely hostile to independent waqf management. As early as 1953, an important reform permitted the changing of *miri* land to *mulk*, a procedure the Supreme Muslim Council had long sought from the British.[22]

These reforms brought little change to the method of collecting waqf income. The Jordanian government continued the British policy of commuting the tithes (*'ushr*) collected from the *tahsisat* waqfs by awarding the Awqaf Administration an annual grant. The amount awarded, however, was much less than what the British had allocated.[23] During the 1960s farmers were often exempted from paying the *'ushr* tax, in line with the low taxation on land in general, but the government continued to pay an annual amount as a way of recognizing the waqf nature of the land and the Awqaf Administration's management of it. This annual grant averaged little more than JD 23,000 and was a very small percentage of the total income of the Awqaf Administration. In addition to this grant, 10 percent of the income taxes collected by the Jordanian government also went to the Awqaf Administration as the "social tax" (*al-daribat al-ijtima'iyya*).[24]

During the Jordanian period, attempts also were made to improve the use of waqf urban and agricultural land. Although these improvements depended largely on the efforts of local officers, some major redevelopment plans were supported by the central administration, particularly in the Jerusalem area. For example, in the late 1950s and the early 1960s much of Saladin Street in East Jerusalem was developed and built upon using waqf funds. Indeed, such reinvestment was the chief means by which the Awqaf Administration's income on the West Bank was increased from its own resources.[25]

It is significant that, in contrast to the situation prevailing inside Israel, new *khayri* waqfs were also created. One example of this is the Ritz Hotel in Jerusalem, part of which is dedicated to the Awqaf Administration's orphanage in Jerusalem, the Dar al-Aytam. Since these new waqfs were now under centralized control, special bank accounts (*amanat* accounts) were opened for them, so that their stipulations could be respected. Their management, however, was still retained by the Awqaf Administration.[26] The creation of new *khayri* waqfs represented a certain degree of confidence in the integrity and authenticity of the Awqaf Administration. They were also a sign of how the centralization and extension of state power over the waqf system was carried out within the religious and judicial consensus. As we have seen in the al-Disi case, some opposition was expressed against the Jordanian reforms. But in establishing these reforms on the West Bank, the Jordanian government no doubt benefitted from the fragmentation and scattering of the Palestinian religious elite after 1948. At the same time, Palestinian Muslims created new waqfs that were managed by a Jordanian government-funded department, which reveals broad Palestinian acceptance and support for these reforms.

Of all the reforms and changes introduced by the Jordanian government before 1967, the single most important measure affecting waqf administration on the West Bank was the 1966 Administration of Waqfs and Islamic Affairs Law.[27] Passed less than a year before the Israeli occupation of the West Bank, it was the culmination of the administrative procedures described above and established the framework of waqf administration that continued after the Israeli occupation.

Even though the Awqaf Administration already existed when the 1966 law came out, the new law did contain detailed regulations specifying the structure and authority of its diverse posts and bodies.[28] It established a *majlis al-awqaf w'al-shu'un al-islamiyya* (Council for Waqfs and Islamic Affairs), chaired by a president who was also the *qadi al-quda'*. The director-general of the Awqaf Administration, accountable to the Council, oversaw the work of the director of Awqaf, the administrative director, and the director of the Haram compound in Jerusalem. Article 3 established five departments of the Administration: General Administration, Haram compound in Jerusalem, Preaching and Guidance, Property and Finance, and Engineering and Maintenance. The authority of each department head was defined and included such matters as the upper limits of expenditure and the kinds of contractual relations permissible.[29] Great emphasis was laid on keeping records, collecting *waqfiyya* documents,[30] and recruiting trained and educated personnel.[31] It is interesting to note that the system whereby Jerusalem ran parallel departments coordinated by a director-general in that city remained in place, even though the law made no mention of it.

This brief description of the waqf system in the West Bank during the Jordanian period indicates how the system was integrated into the state apparatus. Waqf income was fed into a central treasury, and waqf management became part of a Jordanian department administered from Amman. The abolition of hereditary posts resulted in either the gradual replacement of some members of the Palestinian religious elite by paid employees of the Awqaf Administration, or the co-optation of others by putting them on the Jordanian state payroll. One striking aspect of these developments is that they were implemented without creating serious opposition in religious circles; such opposition as existed came largely from Palestinian nationalist and political circles.[32] On the whole, the Jordanian government did not alienate the religious establishment and was able to offer it sufficient inducements (salaries, status) to procure its support.[33]

The Gaza Strip

There is almost no academic study on the waqf system in the Gaza Strip.[34] None of the reports issued by the office of the *ma'mur al-awqaf* in the Gaza Strip is publicly available, there are few newspaper reports, and few people are willing to be interviewed on the subject.[35] What follows is therefore largely derived from interviews with people who have had some connection with the waqf system in the Gaza Strip, supplemented by personal observations and, where possible, by documentary material.

The West Bank waqf administration was incorporated into the Jordanian system and gradually modernized and improved in keeping with general Jordanian developments. In the Gaza Strip, however, the changes that were introduced resulted in the partial absorption of the waqf system into the Egyptian military administration, thus laying the groundwork for greater Israeli interference in waqf affairs in Gaza than was the case in the West Bank. In addition, the waqf system's inability to respond to the great influx of refugees in 1948 meant that it played little part in helping Palestinian society in Gaza meet the major challenges that faced it. The system's political role, therefore, was relatively small.

A brief review of the situation that prevailed in the Gaza Strip during the British Mandate, provides useful background information. The Supreme Muslim Council, established by the British Mandatory government, had set up six local waqf committees in various parts of Palestine to administer waqf affairs. One of these was in the Gaza district. The jurisdiction of the Gaza waqf committee stretched beyond the borders of the present area known as the Gaza Strip, northward towards Majdal

(Ashkelon), and eastward toward Beersheba.[36] The committee was empowered to administer local waqfs and audit the accounts of *mulhaq* or *dhurri* waqfs, and could carry out its activities without reference to the governing secular authorities in its district. Its activities were supervised by a General Waqf Committee, established by the Supreme Muslim Council. Gaza was represented on the General Waqf Committee by the *ma'mur al-awqaf* and a member of the local committee.[37]

The Gaza district contained a number of large waqfs made up of agricultural lands now lying inside Israel. These included the Masa'id waqf, comprising 280 dunums, and the Mughaqa waqf, whose rents provided an income for the Supreme Muslim Council. Another well-known *madbut* waqf, which supported the *zawiyat* al-Hunud in the Old City of Jerusalem and a mosque in Gaza City, was made up of between twenty and twenty-five shops in Gaza City. There were also Haramayn waqfs, which had properties scattered throughout the Gaza district. (These have now become *amanat* waqfs run by a committee of trustees.) The famous Khalil al-Rahman waqf of Hebron also received E£ 300,000 per year in tithes (*'ushr*), from the village of 'Abassan in the Gaza Strip. The Abu Khadr waqf, created in 1943, included more than 3,000 dunums of land in the Gaza, Isdud, and Bir Sab'a areas and P£ 30,000. The cash was for the construction of an Islamic hospital and the land was intended to produce income to maintain it. Any cash left over was to be invested in a special account and the interest used for maintenance.[38] The waqf was managed by a committee comprising the qadi of Gaza and officials of the Supreme Muslim Council. The Council also claimed that the village of Jdayda, now a suburb of Gaza City, was a waqf established by the Mamluk Sultan Qaytbay.[39]

There were also a number of *dhurri* and *mulhaq* waqfs in the Gaza district. The well-known Abu Madyan waqf had four shops in Gaza town, and Barron mentions the al-Huda waqf in Gaza.[40] Similarly, the al-Radwan, Husayni, Makhi, Murshid, and Faris families all had family waqfs in the district.[41]

Land belonging to the large Mughaqa waqf (registered by the British as waqf of the Mosque of Said Hashim) became the subject of a bitter court case between the Supreme Muslim Council and the tenant farmers. The case demonstrated the Supreme Muslim Council's wish to extend and rationalize the waqf holdings under its management. The land in question comprised 3,000 dunums near the Wadi Gaza; the farmers claimed ownership rights, which were contested by the Council. In 1946 the High Court ruled that the land was waqf *sahih* and therefore not owned by the farmers. The farmers subsequently appealed to the Supreme Court, which pronounced that the land was in fact *miri mawquf*, that is, *ghayr sahih*. Although this meant that the Supreme Muslim Council could evict the farmers, the Court expressed the hope that it would let them stay.[42] The dispute remains unresolved today.[43]

The figures that are available for the early part of the Mandate indicate that income from the waqf land and property of the Gaza district made a valuable contribution to the Supreme Muslim Council's annual budget. In 1922, for example, 23 percent of the total agricultural tithes and nearly 17 percent of the income from rents came from the Gaza district.[44] In turn this waqf income supported a number of charitable institutions, such as the al-Falah school, which provided a class for blind pupils. The Council also funded a library, which was established in the al-'Amari mosque in Gaza City, and which contained a number of ancient Qurans.[45] Intrinsic to the religious life in the Gaza district was the fact that Gaza town also contained two famous mosques: the Great Mosque, built on Byzantine foundations, and the Mosque of Said Hashim, the grandfather of Muhammad, who is buried inside the mosque. The presence of the latter provided a focal point for an annual religious festival (*mawsim*) in the area, during which time food (paid for with waqf funds) was distributed to the poor.[46]

The departure of the British in 1948 was followed by Egyptian military operations in the south of Palestine that were designed to prevent the forcible partition of Palestine. By the end of the year Egyptian armed forces and Palestinian irregulars were confined to a coastal stretch between a point just north of Gaza town and the Egyptian border-crossing at Rafah. The cease-fire lines were transformed into the armistice lines in 1949. An Egyptian military administration was set up, but Egypt did not annex or integrate the Gaza Strip into its administration. Some Egyptian laws were applied to the Strip, particularly after Nasser seized power in 1952, but in general, administrative, as opposed to political, intervention in the Strip was kept to a minimum.[47] Two notable exceptions, the abolition of the *dhurri* waqf and the financial oversight of waqf affairs, will be examined later.

Egyptian rule in the Gaza Strip preserved the waqf administration in Gaza as a district office subordinate to a higher authority. The widening of waqf administration functions and the strengthening of its powers developed only incrementally over a long period of time. Although waqf administration remained separate from the Egyptian state, it never achieved the full autonomy that such separateness implied. Following the introduction of the Egyptian General Administration in the Gaza Strip, the Supreme Muslim Council was reestablished in Gaza town on the assumption that a negotiated solution between the Arab states and Israel would return it to Jerusalem. This was done in accordance with an Egyptian military ordinance (Military Order No. 6) that stated that all the British Mandatory laws would continue unless they contradicted Egyptian military regulations. The former president of the Supreme Muslim Council, Haj Amin al-Husayni, also established the All Palestine Government in Gaza, but since he had been removed from office by the British in 1937, he had no formal connection with the Supreme Muslim Council. It is unclear what role or influence, if any, he had on waqf administration in the Gaza Strip during this early period.[48] Some years later, he was obliged to move his Palestine government offices to Cairo.

Under Egyptian rule, the military governor acted as the formal head of the Supreme Muslim Council, the *ra'is al-majlis*. He was thus responsible for the appointment of all qadis in the Strip and the appointment of the *ma'mur al-awqaf* of the Gaza committee. This relationship was to last until the reforms of 1957, and on paper it suggested Egypt's co-optation of the waqf leadership. In practice, the *ma'mur al-awqaf* was never appointed by the Egyptian governor, and the existing *ma'mur* appointed by the Supreme Muslim Council merely continued in his position into the Israeli period; thus, no precedent was set, and the appointment procedure was left unclear. Thus, the degree of co-optation that took place during this period has to be left undetermined.

The Gaza district waqf committee continued to function as a local body with limited functions. Nevertheless, it faced a vastly different situation. Much of the property under its jurisdiction was now located inside the new borders of Israel. Most of the lands of the large Masa'id waqf were now in Israel, to the north of the Strip, while the Mughraqa waqf lands straddled the border to the east.[49] The situation led to a sharp drop in income, which severely hampered the committee's activities. This was compounded by the influx of between 160,000 and 180,000 refugees from the Israeli-controlled parts of Palestine.[50] Some of these refugees took shelter in mosques, cemeteries, and on land managed by the local waqf committee. The organizational confusion, the decline in waqf income, the suddenness of the new situation, and the perception that the refugee crisis was a temporary situation pending a peace settlement, prevented the local committee from responding to the needs of the refugees and the community in a systematic way. When the United Nations Relief and Works Agency for Palestine Refugees (UNRWA) was established, the local committee began to lease some waqf land and property to it at nominal rents and to resume its management and charitable works. By 1950 the local waqf committee had arranged for the construction of eighteen mosques in the eight UNRWA-run refugee camps as well as the disbursement of financial grants.[51]

In general, Egyptian rule did not alter many aspects of waqf administration in the Gaza Strip, but two important changes carried out during the period were to have a considerable impact on waqf affairs and administration there. First, in 1954 Egypt abolished all waqf *dhurri* (or *ahli,* as it is called in Egypt). The Egyptian military order promulgated in the Gaza Strip was based closely on the measures introduced by President Nasser for the abolition of waqf *ahli* in Egypt.[52] Thus all waqfs that were not created for strictly charitable purposes were abolished. As compensation, beneficiaries were entitled to their proportional share in existing waqf *dhurri* either as one-off payments or as shares of property and from the *amwal al-badal* (the proceeds from the sale of waqf property that is in the care of the shari'a courts).[53]

Although there was little resistance to this order in the Gaza Strip, problems developed in its execution. In most cases the beneficiaries were numerous, and the portion of the waqf due to each was so small that few felt motivated to demand their compensatory share, either in the form of payment or in property shares. The controversy centered on the difficulties some beneficiaries found in obtaining compensation. As a result, several years passed before the order could be implemented fully.[54]

The second change introduced by the Egyptian administration was the formalization of the administrative relationship between the local waqf committee and the General Administration under the Egyptian governor. This legislation was promulgated after the four-month occupation of the Gaza Strip by Israel in 1956. The lack of an effective Egyptian or Arab response to the occupation led to growing nationalist fervor among Palestinians in the Gaza Strip. President Nasser allowed the creation of the Legislative Council in Gaza, in an attempt to co-opt and mollify radical nationalist opinion and to match his rhetoric with deeds. Half the Council was elected by members of branches of the Nasserite Arab Socialist Union in the Gaza Strip, and the other half was appointed by the Egyptian governor. The chairman, Dr. Haydar Abd al-Shafi, was a Palestinian and the Council was given powers to legislate new laws and amend existing ones. The Egyptian governor, however, reserved the right to veto any legislation unless it was passed in two successive years.[55]

With regard to the Gaza Strip waqf system, the failure of the Arab states to restore the Palestinians to their homeland increasingly made redundant the structures inherited from the preceding era. The Gaza Strip was too small an area to have the higher echelon of the Supreme Muslim Council located in the same place as the local waqf committee. A new relationship was required between the Egyptian General Administration, representing the Supreme Muslim Council, and the waqf system. Military Order 564, passed in 1957, was an attempt to balance the administrative control demanded by the political concerns of the Egyptian government and its unwillingness to tamper too drastically with the existing structures.[56]

In essence, Order 564 defined the new relationship by distributing the functions of the local committee among the governor, the General Administration, the higher shari'a court, and the local waqf committee. The local waqf committee was to be known henceforth as the Waqf Administration. Article 1 attached the Waqf Administration to the Finance Department and gave it responsibility for all waqf affairs, as well as for the care of mosques, *zawiyas*, and Muslim tombs and cemeteries. Article 2 confirmed it as a separate legal body with an independent budget and the authority to make its own appointments. However, the annual budget had to be approved and major items of expenditure had to be countersigned by the director of the Finance Department in the General Administration. By the late 1960s an annual grant of E£ 50,000 was made available to the Waqf Administration. The Legislative Council took no direct control over the Waqf Administration, but the governor was required to seek its approval for its activities.[57]

In practice, the legal autonomy accorded the Waqf Administration in Article 2 was seriously qualified by the financial oversight of the Finance Department. While the Waqf Administration could act relatively autonomously of the General Administration with regard to appointments, internal administration, and the use of mosques and other religious buildings, the approval of the governor was required in order to release funds required for any construction work, including even small repairs. There appear to have been few areas of major contention due mainly to the low political profile taken by the director and employees of the Waqf Administration. Rather than indicating a conjunction of interests, this may instead confirm the extent of Egyptian control over the waqf system. Indeed, the close relation between the General Administration and the Waqf Administration can be exemplified by the fact that the latter was exempted from paying civil court fees and the cost of enforcing civil court decisions. The Waqf Administration could also enforce evictions through administrative *diktat* and bypass the courts altogether.[58] On religious matters the *ma'mur al-awqaf* (renamed the *mudir* of the Waqf Administration) was obliged to consult with members of the shari'a court of appeal in Gaza. It is important to note that Order 564 did not amend the authority of the governor to appoint the *ma'mur al-awqaf*.

In summary, the waqf system in the Gaza Strip was transformed during the period of Egyptian administration. From a lower-echelon local administration accountable to a central authority in Jerusalem, it became a semi-autonomous but closely supervised extension of the Egyptian administrative structure. Its potential role as a mediating institution was greatly circumscribed and never fully developed. Although the waqf system retained nominal control over its resources, financial transactions were subject to the approval of the state. The administration remained independent of the state structures but its freedom of action was dependent upon the availability of funds. The degree of co-optation is obscured by the fact that while salaries and bursaries were dependent to some extent on state funds, senior appointments were not made during this period. Meanwhile, the responsibilities and the demands placed upon the waqf system greatly increased during this period, and it was not able to respond sufficiently. Without sufficient internal and independent resources and without a firm commitment by the state, as was the case in the West Bank, the waqf committee in the Gaza Strip could not influence social and political developments in any significant way. By 1967 its role had become increasingly marginalized. This trend was to continue during the Israeli occupation.

Political and Legal Aspects of the Israeli Occupation

Following the Arab defeat in 1967, Israeli troops occupied East Jerusalem, the West Bank, the Gaza Strip, Sinai, and the Golan Heights. (The Sinai peninsula and the Golan Heights are excluded from this discussion, since they did not form part of Mandatory Palestine.) Even while hostilities were continuing, the Israeli government set about establishing a military government in the territories it occupied. On 7 June, its Proclamation No. 2 gave the military commanders of the various occupied territories all powers of legislation, appointment, and administration. At the same time, the municipal boundaries of (Israeli) West Jerusalem were extended to include East Jerusalem and parts of the West Bank, which were annexed to Israel (see Map 3).

The period of Israeli occupation between 1967 and 1987—that is, until the beginning of the intifada—is often divided into two parts. During the first ten years of military government, the ruling Labor party showed interest in reaching a negotiated settlement with Jordan and retaining the strategic highlands and areas in the Jordan valley. From 1977 to 1987, the Likud-dominated government showed a more explicit commitment to a Greater Israel ideology. This is reflected in the increasing regulation of Palestinian society, the settlement of Jews in areas of dense Palestinian residency, and an unwillingness to enter into negotiations that might lead to an Israeli withdrawal from the West Bank and Gaza Strip.[59]

Although it is true that the change in government in 1977 marks changes in emphasis with regard to the occupied territories, it would be misleading to exaggerate the importance of policy changes that took place at that time. During the entire twenty-year period, the Israeli state consistently pursued its twin objectives: the acquisition of land and the constraining of Palestinian political aspirations. During the ten years of Labor party tenure, the acquisition of land was primarily instigated by the military. In the West Bank, for example, acquisition was guided by what was known as the Alon plan, in which the main centers of Palestinian population were avoided.

Nevertheless, it was during the Labor period that Israeli settler groups were permitted to take over properties in the center of Hebron and were given access to Palestinian historical and religious sites. These actions set critical precedents for the greater demands made by the settlers during the Likud period. Similarly, rural areas ostensibly closed for military purposes in the first period later became sites of Israeli civilian settlements under an expanded Likud program of settlement construction. The Labor government also carried out deportations, expulsions, and house demolitions, and imposed administrative detentions and curfews. In the first three years of the occupation, the refugee camps in the Gaza Strip, in particular, experienced a brutal and violent repression.[60] There was thus a continuity in Israeli policy throughout the twenty years covered in this chapter, despite the changes of emphasis by successive Israeli governments.

Initially, the Israeli government accepted the international perception of itself as occupiers of the West Bank and Gaza Strip.[61] By February 1968, however, it changed the designation "occupied territories" to "the administered territories of Judea, Samaria and Gaza." Subsequently, the Israeli government refused to acknowledge the "enemy territory" status of these lands as designated under international law, regarding itself as an "administrator" of the territories rather than as "belligerent occupier." With this legal interpretation, the Israeli government was able to declare the West Bank and Gaza Strip *terra nullus*.[62]

These interpretations have a direct bearing upon the Israeli government's approach to the waqf system and the "holy places" that the waqfs supported. In international law, the protection of legal sites is governed by a number of Hague and Geneva Conventions. Article 56 of the "Protection of Cultural Property in Time of War or Military Occupation," annexed as Regulations to both the 1899 Hague Convention II and the 1907 Hague Convention IV, treats all religious and charitable institutions as private property. Destruction and willful damage to such property is, therefore, forbidden. Both Jordan and Israel have signed and ratified the 1954 Hague Convention for the "Protection of Cultural Property in the Event of Armed Conflict," which covers both religious buildings and waqf land and property on the West Bank. Similarly, Article 53 of the 1977 Geneva Protocol I (Protection of Cultural Objects and Places of Worship) and Article 16 of the 1977 Geneva Protocol II (which has the same title) prohibit any act of hostility against cultural property or its use in any military effort or as an object of reprisal. This convention has been signed by Jordan but not by Israel.

While in theory Jordanian and Egyptian law or military regulations continued to apply in the occupied territories, the Israeli military government between 1967 and 1988 issued nearly 2,000 military orders that supplemented, overrode, or cancelled the existing laws. These orders have ranged from specifications of the agricultural products that can be grown to the banning of the Palestinian flag (as well as the colors of the flag) and nationalistic songs. Virtually all aspects of Palestinian life are governed by these military regulations.[63]

Some aspects of religious life are also subject to military regulations. These have usually been concerned with the question of access to sites regarded as antiquities, or religious sites closed by the military government. No specific regulations refer to the waqf system in either the West Bank or the Gaza Strip, which were treated separately. In the West Bank the military government set aside a section for religious affairs, but in practice no formal intervention or link was made. The 1985 Annual Report of the "Civil Administration of Judaea and Samaria" (the official title of the Israeli military government in the West Bank) simply notes, under a subheading "Muslims", the following:

> Despite the fact that the population of the area is comprised primarily of Sunni Moslems, the Civil Administration has minimal contact with this community. This is due to the fact that the Muslim religious hierarchy in the area is completely subservient to the Supreme Muslim Council, which is connected to the Jordanian Wakf Office.[64]

Leaving aside the text's misrepresentation of the Awqaf Administration as the Supreme Muslim Council, we nevertheless note that no administrative structure connected the military government with the waqf or shari'a court system. By contrast, in the Gaza Strip an officer of the military government has an undefined supervisory role over the budget and appointment procedures of both the waqf system and the shari'a courts.

The Awqaf Administration in the West Bank

It would be reasonable to assume that following the Israeli occupation of the West Bank and the establishment of a non-Muslim military government, the waqf system would again become politicized, as it had been under the British Mandate. Since there was no military takeover of the waqf system, the Awqaf Administration might have seized the opportunity to refocus its activities by asserting its independence and defending Palestinian interests. After all, it was one of the few Palestinian institutions that continued to exist after the occupation; it had offices in major towns and responsibilities in virtually every village and district. One might expect it to assume the role of mediator between the occupiers and the occupied. This did not happen. Was it because of the coercive power of the occupying state, or was it because the administration and leadership of the waqf system itself failed to exploit the new political circumstances?

Co-optation of the Leadership: The Higher Islamic Board

Set up shortly after the occupation of the West Bank by the Israeli army, the

Higher Islamic Board was a key body representing Muslim and Palestinian interests. It also assumed a supervisory role over the waqf system in the West Bank. The circumstances surrounding its establishment and its subsequent marginalization indicate the degree to which the Israeli military government was prepared to tolerate the independence of leadership and operations in Palestinian bodies. This case study also reveals the way in which Jordanian and Israeli state interests converged in depoliticizing the waqf system in the West Bank.

As has already been noted, the Israeli military administration established in the West Bank superseded the powers of the Jordanian government and its responsibilities in religious affairs. This meant that the shari'a courts and the Awqaf Administration in Jerusalem and the West Bank were technically to come under the control of the Israeli military government. But the administrative center of the waqf system and of the shari'a courts was located in Jerusalem, which had been annexed to Israel. This meant that the waqf system and the shari'a courts there should have been placed under the jurisdiction of the Ministry of Religious Affairs.[65]

Given the complexity of the situation, it is not surprising that Israeli policies were confused at the beginning. Immediately after the cessation of hostilities in June 1967, the Israeli Ministries of Defense and of Religious Affairs assumed responsibility for Muslim holy places and waqf property throughout the West Bank. In Jerusalem, the Ministry of Religious Affairs sought to absorb the Awqaf Administration into its own bureaucracy, as it had done with the Muslim religious courts and waqf inside Israel. To this end the Israeli government contacted the director-general of the Awqaf Administration in the West Bank, Hasan Tahbub, concerning the administration of waqfs in East Jerusalem. He and Shaykh Abd al-Hamid al-Sa'ih, the most senior qadi in the West Bank, insisted on a policy of total noninterference on the part of the Israeli government.[66]

Aware that insensitivity on this issue could antagonize the entire Muslim community on the West Bank, with consequent political and security implications, the Israeli government transferred the responsibility for Muslim religious affairs from the Ministry of Religious Affairs to the Ministry of Defense.[67] This represented the tacit concession by the Israeli government that Jerusalem remained part of the West Bank, at least as far as the waqf system was concerned. It also meant a de facto—though not a de jure—recognition of Awqaf Administration; the relationship between the Israeli government and the Administration in Jerusalem is described in Chapter Five.[68]

To counter the Israeli government's attempts to assume responsibility for Muslim religious affairs, Shaykh al-Sa'ih issued a *fatwa* stating that Muslims who live under a non-Muslim occupation must organize a body to represent them,[69] and convened a meeting to establish an organization to oversee the interests of the community in the occupied West Bank.[70] The meeting, held on 24 July 1967 in the shari'a court offices in East Jerusalem, was attended by twenty-three persons who constituted themselves as the Higher Islamic Board.[71] The representativity of the new body was confirmed by letters of support and recognition from municipalities, trade unions, cultural associations, and leading individuals across the West Bank that provided the legitimacy it required for its later actions. For example, prominent ulema from the Nablus region wrote:

> The residents and Qadis of the City of Nablus declare their support for your insistence on the Arab character of Jerusalem, which is an integral part of the West Bank of the Kingdom of Jordan, and endorse the contents of the memorandum submitted by the inhabitants of Jerusalem on 24 July 1967, in which they reject, together with all the people of this country, all measures taken by the Israeli authorities to detach the City of Jerusalem from Arab territory and to place it under Israeli control.[72]

A separate letter was sent to the military governor of the West Bank, registering similar support for the Higher Islamic Board.

The first action of the Higher Islamic Board was to denounce the Israeli government's annexation of East Jerusalem and to protest its practices regarding Islamic holy places.[73] The Higher Islamic Board also set about reactivating the religious life of the Muslim community on the West Bank. It arrogated to itself a number of important powers formerly located in Amman. The president of the Board was made acting *qadi al-quda'*, and a shari'a court of appeal was established in Jerusalem: these were given responsibility for the Awqaf Administration and the Committee for the Restoration of Al-Aqsa Mosque and the Dome of the Rock. It was through these channels that the Jordanian government was later able to reassert control over the religious establishment on the West Bank.[74]

The establishment of the Higher Islamic Board seemed to portend the formation of an embryonic Palestinian leadership. With significant funds and assets at its disposal, it had the potential for great influence in both the religious and political spheres. Indeed, the fact that Shaykh Abd al-Hamid al-Sa'ih, president of the Higher Islamic Board and therefore acting *qadi al-quda'*, was also made chairman of the semi-clandestine National Guidance Committee (precursor of the later Committee of the same name formed in 1978), indicated the potential for nationalist leadership and provided unity between Jordanian supporters and Palestinian nationalists.[75]

Although it is not the purpose of this book to trace the growth of a Palestinian national consciousness in the West Bank, it is important to place the Palestinian nature of the Higher Islamic Board in its political context. Here it is sufficient to state that the Palestinian nationalist organizations of the period were either undeveloped or strongly influenced by other Arab states. The Fateh guerrilla group had only recently been formed, and the Palestine Liberation Organization (PLO) was still controlled by the Arab League. Although there was without doubt a Palestinian identity of sorts in the West Bank, there was at that time no clear consensual alternative to the Jordanian government as representative and protector of Palestinian interests there.[76] By the mid-1970s, an independent PLO had become the recognized representative body for the vast majority of the Palestinian community, but it is important not to assign retroactively to it a role it did not have during the early years of the Israeli occupation of the West Bank. Thus, in the face of Israeli government attempts to encroach on the authority of the Higher Islamic Board and the Awqaf Administration, the Palestinian-Jordanian issue was of secondary importance. As the former director-general of the Awqaf Administration during this period, Hasan Tahbub, commented in a personal interview, the Awqaf Administration needed the Higher Islamic Board as a protective shield against the Israeli government. And at the time, the political composition of the board was not of immediate significance.[77]

The idea of an independent Palestinian state in the territories occupied in 1967 did not have great currency or appeal during the early years of the occupation. Jordan's actions to strengthen its links with the Awqaf Administration can perhaps be seen as an attempt to head off an independent Palestinian nationalist current, but this should not be given too much emphasis. Rather, Jordan was probably motivated more by the wish to reassert the *status quo ante* by reestablishing its authority over an important and prestigious religious institution; having been evicted from the Hijaz and thus losing its guardianship over Mecca and Medina, the Hashemite family was unwilling to lose its role as guardian over the holy Muslim sites in Jerusalem as well. In any case, the potential for the Higher Islamic Board to function as an independent institution mediating between the Israeli state and the Palestinian population was circumscribed by both the Israeli and Jordanian governments. Jordan's appointment of its own supporters to the Higher Islamic Board assured the body's depoliticization. Even if this had not been the case, however, the Israeli government would never have permitted the emergence of any kind of a political role for the board: from Israel's point of view, the entire point of preserving the existing administrative structures was to prevent autonomous action on the part of the Palestinian population and to secure for itself the levers of power.

The Israeli government was certainly more interested in undermining the board's legitimacy than building up its influence. This it tried to do in a number of ways. It refused to have any contact with the board or to recognize the shari'a court of appeal that the board had set up. Initially, it also refused to acknowledge the board's supervisory role over the Awqaf Administration. Israel also deported many leading members of the Higher Islamic Board, in contravention of the Fourth Geneva Convention.[78] On 20 September 1967, Shaykh Abd al-Hamid al-Sa'ih, president of the Higher Islamic Board and acting *qadi al-quda'*, was deported to Jordan.[79] In May 1969 another six board members were deported.[80]

The Jordanian government, on the other hand, did not undermine the Higher Islamic Board directly; rather, it sought to influence the board's decisions by altering its composition to include more of its own supporters. For example, in May 1969, the Jordanian government suggested the appointment of nine new members, appointments that diluted the preponderance of Jerusalemites on the board and increased the representation of the West Bank regions, shari'a courts, and waqf districts.[81] The new members were qadis and muftis who received salaries from the Jordanian government. In September 1969, another six persons regarded as Jordanian supporters were appointed to the Higher Islamic Board.[82] Thus, at the same time as it broadened the representation of the board, the Jordanian government also asserted greater control over its members.

It is difficult to determine whether there was tacit cooperation between the Jordanian and Israeli governments to tame the nationalist current in the Higher Islamic Board. What is clear, however, is that these appointments were part of the Jordanian government's attempts to reassert its control over the Awqaf Administration on the West Bank. This it was able to do, thanks to the expanding importance of the shari'a court of appeal, set up by the Higher Islamic Board and then made responsible for the religious affairs of the Awqaf Administration and other bodies. The central role of the shari'a court of appeal was consolidated when the board transferred to it its own executive powers.[83] The significance of this move lay in the fact that the Jordanian government paid the salaries of the shari'a court officials and appointed the qadis who sat on the court of appeal.[84]

Thus, the Awqaf Administration became part of the reconstructed Jordanian administrative machinery in the West Bank rather than part of a broader-based body partially representing Palestinian interests. Direct connections between the Ministry of Awqaf in Amman and the Awqaf Administration in Jerusalem were reestablished, and the position of Hasan Tahbub as director-general of the latter was confirmed by the ministry in Amman.[85] The Awqaf Administration's annual budget, which initially had been submitted to the Higher Islamic Board, was now submitted instead to the Ministry of Awqaf in Amman.[86] These developments led one member of the Higher Islamic Board to conclude:

> By 1973 the Higher Islamic Council [that is, Higher Islamic Board] abandoned its political role and lost its administrative control over the Islamic institutions, thus rendering itself helpless and useless.[87]

Clearly, the Israeli military government was not opposed to these developments. Dealing with weakened Jordanian institutions was far preferable to Israel than dealing with an incipient Palestinian nationalist institution. Thus, through its refusal to recognize the operations of the Higher Islamic Board and through the deportations of leading religious figures, the Israeli government was able to exploit the waqf system's links with Jordan and thwart the return of any kind of institution resembling the Supreme Muslim Council in the West Bank.

Depriving the Higher Islamic Board of a salient political role did not entail the complete subservience of the West Bank religious elite and the waqf system to the Israeli state. It simply meant that the political aspects of the system were exercised by the Jordanian government rather than by the religious leadership of the West Bank and the waqf system. The religious leadership was obliged to operate within these limits. The Muslim leadership was able to extend and improve the services of the waqf system. Mosques continued to be built, religious education programs were initiated, and so on. At the same time, however, the religious leadership deferred to the Jordanian government and the restrictions imposed on it by the Israeli government. The result was a further strengthening of the role of the waqf system and the religious leadership in the community while at the same time insulating them from contact with the Israeli state, thus limiting the political leverage they might have developed to enable them to exert an independent or mediating role. Still, although the Israeli state was successful in neutralizing the religious elite of the West Bank as a political force, its attempts at co-option were ultimately unsuccessful.

Integration of Administration: The Ibrahimi Mosque in Hebron

Despite early attempts by the Israeli government to take over the offices of the Awqaf Administration in Jerusalem and gain access to files, documentation, and shari'a court records (the *sijills*), the structure of the West Bank waqf system remained independent of the Israeli state. Nevertheless, the impact of the Israeli occupation on the management of the waqf system could be felt on two levels. First, the employees of the Awqaf Administration suffered the same effects of occupation as the other Palestinians living in the occupied territories, including detentions and the confiscation of land and property. The Israeli military occupation also impinged upon the actual functioning of the Awqaf Administration. This took many forms. Construction or repair permits often were denied; for example, work on the Ibn Walid mosque on the outskirts of Hebron was stopped by the Israeli military government for "security" reasons. Restrictions also were placed on external funds for social and charitable work.

The gradual transformation of the Awqaf Administration's role can be divided into three main phases. The initial period of disarray and confusion that followed the occupation and Israeli attempts at intervention was followed by low-level activity that extended to the late 1970s. This second phase can be characterized as both a consolidation of the Awqaf Administration on the West Bank and a test of the extent of its independence from Israel. A third period, up to the intifada in 1987, witnessed more vigorous activity, precipitated on the one hand by the increased Israeli settlement program, and on the other hand, by the oil price boom of the mid-1970s and the heightened pan-Islamic interest in the holy places of Palestine. These currents led to a greater availability of funds and to increased public interest in the activities of the Awqaf Administration.

Soon after the Israeli occupation and the separation of the Awqaf Administration from its Amman-based supervisory body, the newly-formed Higher Islamic Board established a West Bank-based supervisory body, known as the Council for Waqfs and Islamic Affairs (*majlis al-awqaf wa-shu'un al-islamiyya*). The director-general of the Jerusalem Awqaf Administration was made accountable to the council. Shaykh Abd al-Hamid al-Sa'ih, the acting *qadi al-quda'* and the chairman of the Higher Islamic Board, was made president of the council. Following his deportation, he was replaced by Shaykh Hilmi Muhtasib. The director-general, Hasan Tahbub, was also given a seat on the council.[88] In 1978, the Council was expanded from five to nine members to include a number of lay people. In 1982, Anwar Khatib, the former Jordanian governor of the Jerusalem district, and Anwar Nusaybeh, the former Jordanian defense minister, both members of the Higher Islamic Board, also joined the council.[89] By 1982 the Awqaf Administration had formed a large administrative structure covering a wide range of responsibilities and religious education activities in an increased number of waqf provinces (*mudiriyyat*). The new administration also placed greater emphasis on construction and repair work, establishing to this end a department for the restoration of historic buildings and monuments, the Department of Islamic Archaeology.[90]

Under the director-general was a general administrative director who presided over the heads of a number of departments; the two largest were the Finance Department and Preaching and Guidance Department. Other, smaller, departments dealt with personnel, waqf land, legal affairs, construction and maintenance, Islamic archaeology, statistics and documentation, and the operation of the Islamic Museum in the Haram al-Sharif.[91] A Department of Waqf Provinces was responsible for the local waqf administration, and it had offices in the Jerusalem, Hebron, Ramallah–al-Bireh, Bethlehem–Jericho, Nablus, Jenin, and Tulkarm districts. The Dar al-Aytam, the Awqaf Administration's orphanage, fell under this department.

The local waqf offices are responsible for general religious activities, including the management of mosques and waqf affairs. These responsibilities include the supervision of clerks and religious officials, the collection of rent, and the supervision of repairs. Rent levels can be fixed by the local waqf office after consultation with the department head in Jerusalem. According to one official in the Jerusalem department, the main criterion determining rent agreements was that the tenant should not sell.[92] The length of tenancies is fixed by Jordanian law and can be up to twenty-nine years. Rent revenues are sent to Jerusalem every fortnight. One type of tithe that is not collected by the Awqaf Administration is that collected from the waqf *tahsisat* villages, whose tithes used to be collected by the Ottoman and British governments, with a lump sum paid to the various waqf administrative structures. The Jordanian government abandoned this practice in the post-1948 period as a means of easing the burden of West Bank farmers, although it continues to pay the equivalent to the Ministry of Waqfs. The Awqaf Administration has not sought to revive this practice; the tithes have not been collected for a long time and, it was felt that under the conditions of the Israeli occupation it would not be appropriate to place a further burden on the farmers.[93] The exact extent of waqf property and land in each waqf province is difficult to determine; no complete records are publicly available.

Evidence suggests that the Israeli government initially sought to operate within the limits set down by international law.[94] The early measures the government took toward the holy places indicate an awareness of the sensitivity of the issue. On 27 June 1967, in accordance with Article 27 of the Geneva Convention, the Knesset enacted the Protection of Holy Places Law. A military order was issued extending this law to the West Bank and Gaza Strip.[95] Additional military orders refined the regulations issued for the care of and conduct in holy places on the West Bank.

In addition, other orders were issued extending the jurisdiction of the Israeli Department of Antiquities to sites on the West Bank in accordance with Proclamation No. 2, which gave the Israeli military administration all the powers of the Jordanian government in this respect.[96] Although these were primarily aimed at the preservation and upkeep of Jewish sites, they included many Islamic historical sites other than mosques (for example, the Caliph Hisham's palace near Jericho). The

Ministry of Religious Affairs had oversight of a number of key Jewish sites such as the Western (or Wailing) Wall in Jerusalem and the Tomb of the Patriarchs in the Ibrahimi Mosque in Hebron.[97]

This early respect for international law was eventually eroded, due to pressure from Israeli Jewish militants for increased access to Jewish sites, the perceived security needs of the military government in the regulation of Palestinian Muslims, and the desire to promote tourism among diaspora Jews. These considerations were expressed when the government clashed with the Awqaf Administration over this issue of access to and control of the Tomb of Abraham in the Ibrahimi mosque in Hebron. Although the intensity of the controversy in Hebron is anything but typical, it nevertheless illustrates the degree to which the Israeli government was prepared to act; it could also be said to exemplify the gradual encroachments on Muslim jurisdiction that have taken place in other locations in the West Bank and the Gaza Strip. Whereas the controversy was mainly over access to and control over a shared Jewish and Muslim holy place, a number of subthemes added to the intensity and passion of the situation. These include questions of whether the site (and indeed of the whole of Hebron) was Jewish or Islamic, the political strength of the local Israeli settler communities both in relation to the Israeli state and to the Palestinian residents, and, finally, the dual role of the military as protectors of the status quo and as guardians of the settlers. In examining the developments that took place during the first decade of the occupation, one can see how the mutually agreed-upon arrangements initially established concerning times of worship for Jews and Muslims were gradually undermined to give greater access to the settlers.

As early as October 1967, the minister of defense, Moshe Dayan, made arrangements with the Awqaf Administration for the use of the Ibrahimi mosque wherein the Tomb of the Patriarchs was located. Jewish visitors were admitted between 7:00 A.M. and 11:00 A.M. and between 1:30 P.M. and 5:00 P.M., and these hours were enforced by guards provided by the Israeli army chaplaincy. It was also agreed that a Yom Kippur service could be held in the evening. The rest of the time the building would remain a Muslim place of worship, and during Ramadan the building would be closed to Jewish worshippers during the afternoon.[98] In October 1968 a special Yom Kippur service was extended by Jewish worshippers in the mosque beyond the agreed hours. This led to tension in the town, culminating in a grenade attack on Jewish worshippers. In apparent retaliation, the military government demolished an eighth-century stairway leading to the mosque, an action that produced widespread objections against Israeli policies. Israeli officials claimed the demolition was unrelated to the grenade attack but carried out in accordance with a town landscaping program.[99] The following year, in an attempt to defuse the conflict, the army permitted no Yom Kippur service.

By 1972, the Israeli settlement of Kiryat Arba on the outskirts of Hebron had considerably expanded, and many more worshippers were attending the mosque, particularly on Sabbath eves and feast days. Consequently, the Israeli government unilaterally enlarged the praying area allocated to Jews and extended the permissible hours for prayers. This antagonized the Palestinians, and frequent clashes ensued. After several people were wounded in 1973, the Israeli government banned Jews from the mosque.[100] Nevertheless, in 1975, as a result of pressure from orthodox Jews and militant settlers, the government introduced new arrangements to allow Jews to pray inside the mosque, which again led to widespread protests by Palestinian Muslims and disturbances in Hebron. The increased tension culminated in fights inside the mosque and Tomb area during which religious paraphernalia, both Muslim and Jewish, were seriously damaged. Finally, settlers set fire to part of the mosque. The army arrested a number of prominent Israeli settlers and Palestinians and clamped a two-week curfew on the Old City of Hebron while allowing settlers to attend services.[101]

During this period the Israeli government did not wish to antagonize the Palestinians over the question of Jewish access to the Tomb of the Patriarchs, but it also was not prepared to allow the Awqaf Administration to exercise its role of overseeing Muslim holy sites. At most, the government denied the Israeli settlers unlimited access to the tomb. After the Likud party's victory in the 1977 elections, however, the settlers in Hebron began to receive much greater political, economic, and military assistance. By 1979 the government seemed to have decided that the interests of the settlers overrode any government fears about antagonizing the local community or any concerns about adhering to the conventions of international law. In January, hundreds of settlers marched into the mosque and drove out the Muslims at prayer, clashing with Israeli soldiers in the process. Rather than mete out punishment, the government yielded to the settlers' demands and gave Jews access to the mosque on Saturdays.[102]

Disputes over access to and control over other sites, such as the tomb of Samuel on the northern outskirts of Jerusalem and the tomb of Moses just off the road from Jerusalem to Jericho, resulted in the government's gradual usurpation of the Awqaf Administration's jurisdiction over these sites. It appears that although the Israeli military government in the West Bank was not able to fully integrate the administration of the waqf system, as it had done in Israel proper, it was able gradually to undermine important areas of its responsibilities, such as the management of holy places.

Control over Resources: Waqf Land and Property

The chief means by which the waqf system was brought under state control in Israel itself was the confiscation of waqf land and property. Without access to waqf sources of income, the administration and any putative Muslim leadership of the waqf system was powerless. By contrast, the system on the West Bank received a considerable portion of its income from the Jordanian government treasury in Amman, which meant that the Awqaf Administration was not totally dependent upon West Bank sources for its income. Thus, even given the Israeli military government's extensive acquisition of waqf land and property and the consequent loss of funds, the role of the Awqaf Administration could not be paralyzed in the West Bank in the same way it was by land losses in Israel proper. Indeed, the financial support it received from the Jordanian state enabled it to respond to the Israeli occupation by extending its responsibilities and activities.

Detailed figures for the budget of the Awqaf Administration are not public. The two reports (*bayans*) on its activities that are available contain general budget figures. The 1977–82 report, for example, simply provides two short tables, one for annual expenditure and one for annual income, without giving a breakdown of the sources of income.[103] Some information concerning these sources can be found in an earlier *bayan* for the years 1967–76, which also includes the subventions received by the Awqaf Administration from the Ministry of Waqfs in Amman.[104] These documents provide a sketchy picture of the Awqaf Administration budget.

Apart from funds for the restoration of the al-Aqsa mosque (a pan-Islamic effort), income to the Awqaf Administration comes from two main sources: income generated on the West Bank, and the Jordanian Treasury.[105] The proportion from either source is not indicated, but according to the Administration's former director-general, on average only 15 percent of the Awqaf Administration's income came from West Bank sources.[106] As will be shown, this estimate can apply only to the 1960s and 1970s, since by 1982 the percentage of income coming from the Jordanian Treasury was considerably greater.

Of the income originating in the West Bank, the 1967–76 *bayan* gives five sources. One of these is rental income from waqf property and land such as shops, workshops, warehouses, wholesale markets, agricultural land, residences, and offices.[107] Another source is income from *hikr* property and land.[108] A third source is income generated by the Awqaf Administration's management of *dhurri* waqf properties on behalf of families.[109] A fourth, surprisingly important, source of income is admission fees from tourists to the Haram al-Sharif and proceeds from the sale of guidebooks.[110] The last source of income derived from the West Bank is termed miscellaneous and includes donations and the proceeds from the Muslim Vocational Orphanage.[111] In theory, another source of income from the West Bank is the *'ushr* income derived from the tithes traditionally obtained from villages throughout Palestine.[112] In practice, however, the Jordanian government has not collected these tithes but instead has made subventions to the Awqaf Administration in equivalent amounts; this income should therefore be classified as income from the Jordanian government. The following table is based on both *bayans* and presents an estimate of the total income figures.

Table 1: Income of the Awqaf Administration from West Bank Sources, 1967–1982

Year	*JD*
1967	130,388
1970	207,195
1975	260,494
1980	495,949
1982	362,437
1987	650,000*

(Source: *bayan* I, p. 14; *bayan* II, p. 141.)

[* Author's estimate, derived from the following calculations: From the table we can calculate a rise in income from 1967 to 1982 of 277 percent. This figure is exceedingly low when one takes into account that inflation during this period was over 1000 percent. It is also a little misleading since the drop in income in 1982 can be largely attributed to the fall in revenue from admission fees to the Haram al-Sharif due to a sharp and temporary decline in tourism. From 1983 onward this figure almost certainly picked up. One can use this figure to estimate the income for 1987. If the 1980 figure is more representative of the rate of increase than the 1982 figure, the rate of increase is 380 percent on the 1967 figure. A conservative estimate for 1987 of a 500-percent increase on the 1967 figure provides an estimated income in 1987 of approximately JD 650,000.]

Figures for the expenditure of the Awqaf Administration during the same period are similarly sketchy. As with the figures for income, the first *bayan* of 1967–76 provides more of a breakdown than the second. It divides expenditure into four parts. The first comprises wages and salaries for the officials and auxiliary staff of the Awqaf Administration. This amounts to 62.2 percent of the total expenditure in the period 1967–76.[113] The second category specified in the first *bayan* is termed "operating expenses" (excluding wages). This category averages 26.3 percent of the total expenditure and includes travel expenses, transportation, postage, electricity, and general operating expenses.[114] The third category comprises a range of honoraria and grants. These include contributions for building mosques, purchasing carpets and amplification equipment, and grants to students attending the Dar al-Aytam, the al-Aqsa shari'a secondary school, and other Awqaf Administration-run shari'a schools, and for funding Quranic schools and shari'a instruction in independent schools.[115] The final category is labelled capital expenditure and includes the provision of furniture and equipment as well as construction and repair work. Apart from the day-to-day repair and maintenance of existing mosques and waqf buildings, the Awqaf Administration has also undertaken an extremely ambitious restoration and renovation program in the Old City of Jerusalem, a mosque building program covering all the main towns and most of the villages, and a construction program designed to maximize waqf income derived from waqf land and property.[116]

Also under this last category is the agricultural renewal project undertaken by a section of the Awqaf Administration.[117] This project was initiated largely in an effort to stave off land acquisitions that were being carried out by the Israeli military government and settler groups. Uncultivated or grazing lands being particularly vulnerable to expropriation, the Awqaf Administration provided grants and carried out land reclamation schemes and planting and fencing programs.[118] The program also provided the Awqaf Administration with an additional income. Between 1981–1987, 617 dunums of land were planted, mostly with olive trees.[119]

Although the exact extent of waqf land and property is difficult to determine,[120] an estimate can be attempted. One can state with certainty that there was considerably more waqf land and property on the West Bank prior to 1967 than is being managed by the Awqaf Administration today. In many cases, waqf land and property have been lost because of the lack of accurate records and difficulties in legal enforcement and administrative follow-up arising from the uncertain political situation. Tenancy agreements have lapsed or been forgotten without the tenants being removed or payments kept up. This is particularly the case with *hikr* land.

We estimated earlier that in the whole of Mandate Palestine, 15 percent of the approximate proportion of agricultural land was waqf. It is extremely improbable that waqf land in the West Bank amounted to much more than 15 percent of agricultural land, because a higher proportion of the agricultural and waqf land of Mandate Palestine was located in the coastal and low-lying areas that were incorporated into Israel.[121] A cautious estimate of the proportion of West Bank agricultural land that was waqf would lie in the region of 10 percent, or approximately 600,000 dunums. As we noted earlier, any estimates for urban waqf property would be pure speculation. In analyzing the extent of Israeli control over the resources of the waqf system, the following examination includes only the Israeli military government's acquisition of agricultural land.

Determining the extent of land acquired by the military government is daunting because no laws or military regulations pertain specifically to waqf land and property. In the West Bank, as in Israel, waqf land was treated no differently from any other land. Nevertheless, some deductions as to the extent of acquisitions of both types of waqf land (waqf *madbut* and waqf *mulhaq*, administered and supervised by the Awqaf Administration, as well as waqf *dhurri* managed independently by *mutawalli*s) can be made by examining the laws and military orders that have resulted in land confiscations.

The Israeli government has used three chief methods by which to confiscate land on a large scale. The first is the expropriation of land and property for military purposes. This method of expropriation is permitted by innumerable military orders and has been used on approximately 35,000 dunums on the West Bank. In addition, certain areas are closed off for military purposes, and in many cases they are later requisitioned for civilian settlement. Closed military zones apply to some 1.11 million dunums, or 53 percent of the land seized by the Israeli government.[122] The second method, detailed earlier, is to declare land and property abandoned or "absentee" (Military Order 58). Absentee property has in many cases been defined broadly to include land where the owner is still present but over which the Israeli Custodian of Absentee Property completed a transaction in "good faith" (see Chapter Two). It is estimated that the Israeli Custodian for Absentee Property has acquired some 430,000 dunums on the West Bank under Military Order 58, some of which it leased out for Jewish settlements for 49 years.[123] The third method, which has had the greatest impact upon waqf land and property, is to declare parcels of unregistered land to be state land.[124]

Under the Ottoman Land Code, *mulk* (private property) and *waqf sahih* (true waqf, that is, waqf endowed on privately-owned property) were registered and documented in title deeds. But three other categories of land—*miri*, *mewat*, and *mahlul*—were not usually registered since their ownership theoretically rested with the sultan by virtue of conquest. They were not owned by the sultan in the sense that he derived private gain from them, but merely in the sense that they belonged to him as the head of the state. An analogy can be drawn with Crown lands in the United Kingdom, which are separate from the private property of the Royal family and from government-owned land.[125] Occupiers of *miri* land were tenants, in the sense that they retained all the usual rights of ownership except the right to sell, while the ultimate ownership lay with the sultan.

Following the Elon Moreh case, when the Israeli High Court thwarted an attempt to confiscate land for a settlement on security grounds, the government resorted to Military Order 59 issued in July 1967 to take over Jordanian state property. To make the order applicable, the government extended it to the three categories of land noted earlier, despite the fact that the Israel Land Law of 1969 grants occupants of *miri* land inside Israel full ownership rights. While in 1967 only approximately 13 percent (or 730,214 dunums) of the land on the West Bank was registered in the name of the Jordanian state, under Order 59 "hundreds of thousands of dunums" have been declared state land and used for Jewish settlement on the West Bank.[126]

Waqf land that was endowed on privately-owned property, waqf *sahih*, technically should not be affected by this order, but many villages in the West Bank are *miri mawquf* lands—that is, land that was *miri* but whose income or use was endowed as waqf. These included both the waqf *tahsisat* lands managed by the Supreme Muslim Council, which traditionally had their tithes commuted, and many lands belonging to the Tamimi waqf around Hebron.[127] Although it is not known exactly how much of this *miri mawquf* land has been acquired by the Israeli government, senior Awqaf Administration officials on the West Bank believe that the Israeli government rationalizes its expropriation of significant percentages of waqf land on the grounds that it is *miri*.[128] Indeed, the threat of confiscation on these grounds hangs over all *miri mawquf* land in the occupied territories. A former legal advisor to the Awqaf Administration on the West Bank maintained that evidence of the waqf status of parcels of land acquired by the Israeli government or army is usually ignored in military courts, particularly if the waqf land is in the middle of the area to be confiscated. (If it is on the margins of the area, there is some possibility of its status being taken into account and the area slightly redrawn.)[129]

Figures for the extent of waqf land confiscated from the Awqaf Administration are not easily available. Nablus *mudiriyya* figures suggest that acquisitions there amounted to 54,968 dunums. Of this, 17,490 dunums were acquired in 1967—presumably, given the date, for military purposes. In 1982 another 12,978 dunums were acquired, and in 1988 24,500 dunums were acquired near the village of Kufr Haris. The last two expropriations were based mainly on the Israeli state's interpretation of *miri* land as state land.

With regard to the Tamimi waqf lands in the Hebron area, the Israeli government brought a case against the Tamimi waqf trustees, claiming that the Tamimi waqf land outside the municipal boundaries of Hebron was in fact *miri mawquf*—that is, not true waqf (*sahih*)—and could consequently be classed as state land under the new interpretation of *miri* land and be expropriated. The trustees were able to prove that their land was true waqf and the Israeli High Court ruled in its favor in August 1988.[130] Despite this legal victory, more than 500 dunums of this waqf were confiscated for settlement and military purposes under Military Order 59, according to Anwar Khatib, the *mutawalli* of the Tamimi waqf in Hebron and former Jordanian governor of the District of Jerusalem. He also maintained that much of the property occupied by Jewish settlers in Hebron was actually Tamimi *hikr* (waqf property under long leases) on the grounds that it had belonged to Jews who left the city after the 1929 troubles. As evidence for this assertion, he provided receipts of annual rents up to 1936, when the former Jewish residents stopped their payments, probably having decided that they would never return.[131] However, such receipts are not accepted as sufficient proof by the Objections Committee appointed by the Israeli military government, which looks into disputed cases of land acquisition.[132]

By 1987, the state had used Military Orders 58 and 59 to acquire approximately 52 percent of the total area of the West Bank, ostensibly for military purposes according to Meron Benvenisti.[133] Using this figure, one can estimate the percentage of waqf land acquired. Thus, if waqf land in the West Bank is estimated at 10 percent of the agricultural land, or 600,000 dunums, then it is possible to project, on the basis of Benvenisti's 52 percent figure, that approximately 312,000 dunums of waqf land has been acquired by the state. However, in some cases the waqf nature of the land would have a marginal deterring effect, and a lower figure of 270,000 (i.e., 45 percent) of West Bank waqf land may be more accurate. Although this does not compare to the wholesale confiscation that took place in Israel, 45 percent still represents a dramatic loss of landed wealth and income. It should be remembered that not all of this waqf land is managed by the Awqaf Administration, and it is not possible to determine whether the property of the Awqaf Administration was more or less likely to be confiscated.

In considering the question of state control over the resources of the waqf system, one may conclude that Israel has not directly assaulted the system's land and property. Even if it had done so, one can speculate that the proportion of income lost would not have been sufficient to paralyze the activities of the Awqaf Administration, although they would have been seriously hampered. From the state's perspective, then, it was not worth antagonizing and alienating the influential Muslim leadership and the whole Muslim community when such acquisitions would not eliminate the Awqaf Administration. Instead, by acquiring waqf land in the course of pursuing its general territorial aims, Israel was able simultaneously to undermine the independence of the Awqaf Administration at the expense of the Jordanian government and to acquire land for its own military and settlement policies.

The Awqaf Administration in the Gaza Strip

Israel's relationship with the waqf system in the Gaza Strip differs from its parallel relationships with the system inside Israel and in the West Bank. Two main reasons account for the difference. Unlike the Jordanian government on the West Bank, the Egyptian government ceased to act as financier and protector of the Gaza Strip waqf after the Israeli occupation of the Gaza Strip in 1967. Indeed, the system was left in an exceedingly weak and vulnerable position. Second, as described earlier, the Egyptian government had to some extent incorporated the administrative structure of the waqf system into the Egyptian military administration of the Gaza Strip. With the office of the *ma'mur al-awqaf* already accountable to the Egyptian military government, the way was open for the Israeli military government to take the same position. Nevertheless, since the Gaza Strip remained under military rule and was not annexed to Israel, there remained a separation between the state itself and the Gaza Strip waqf system.

Before examining the degree of co-optation of the religious elite, of integration of the administration, and of control over resources by the Israeli state—the three components of the analytical method adopted here—some qualifications need to be made. First, almost no official documents and records are available on this subject, and as a result, this section is based on extended personal interviews, which, given the political sensitivity of the subject, cannot always be attributed.[134] The lack of sufficient "hard" facts has prevented a comprehensive analysis of the relationship between Israel and the Gaza Strip waqf system.

Second, the system in the Gaza Strip is much smaller than in other areas of historical Palestine, both in terms of the personnel involved and the land and property under its management. As noted earlier, the Gaza Strip's waqf administrative structure was merely an over-extended district echelon of the Supreme Muslim Council—the local waqf office—but with relatively little land. This has meant that a clear separation of the three components of the analytical method used here is especially difficult to achieve. For example, while in the West Bank and Israel a working distinction can be made between the religious leadership and the waqf administrative structure, in the Gaza Strip the smaller numbers involved make this distinction more difficult to maintain.

Finally, factors other than the Israeli military occupation have undermined the position and influence of the religious leadership and the waqf system in the Gaza Strip. The rise of Islamic fundamentalism has led to the establishment of many Islamic associations with little connection to the established religious hierarchy and waqf system. Information on the activities and structure of these groups in relation to the Gaza waqf system is limited. Consequently, the following examination of the waqf system in the Gaza Strip is confined to the historical waqf system and developments, and excludes consideration of the administration and management of the property of the newly constituted Islamic associations and groups.

Co-optation of the Leadership

The defeat of the Egyptian army in 1967 resulted in the withdrawal of the Egyptian military administration from the Gaza Strip: the first proclamation of the military governor, appointed by Israel, for the Gaza Strip took over the powers held by the Egyptian governor-general.

One persistent characteristic of Gazan politics before and since 1967 has been the divisions between the long-established Gazan families (such as the Rayes, Abu Sha'ban, Tarazi, Surani, and Shawwa families) on the one hand, and the more nationalistic organizations in the refugee camps, on the other.[135] This division has prevented Palestinians in the Gaza Strip from presenting a united front, and consequently, in the wake of the occupation, no serious attempt was made to set up an umbrella body such as the Higher Islamic Board in the West Bank. The qadis of the shari'a courts could have assumed this role, but chose not to. The absence of such a body left the Gaza Strip system and the office of the *ma'mur al-awqaf* in a vulnerable and isolated position. Having lost most of its income-producing land in the 1948 war, the Gaza Strip waqf administration had been made dependent upon Egyptian grants to fulfil its traditional functions. Following the withdrawal of the Egyptian military administration, there was little income to pay the salaries of its staff or to make repairs and provide services. In these circumstances, the religious leadership was obliged to accept a delicate *modus vivendi* with the Israeli military government.

It is difficult to determine the degree of state co-optation of the waqf-supported religious leadership in the Gaza Strip. Relevant indications of co-optation include oaths of allegiance, participation in state ceremonies, and censorship, as well as the appointments procedure and the payment of salaries. In the Gaza Strip, these last two indicators are less easily discernable than elsewhere. The most senior official in the Gaza Strip waqf administration, the *ma'mur al-awqaf*, was appointed in 1945 and did not retire until 1986; his tenure thus spanned the entire Egyptian period and most of the Israeli period under review. The appointment of his successor—the single such appointment—can hardly be said to illustrate a pattern or to constitute a procedure. Similarly, the question of payment of salaries is obscure. No payments from the Israeli military government are publicly admitted. Ostensibly, senior officials in the Gaza Strip waqf administration have the freedom to act independently. Yet this researcher was informed by individuals who were sympathetic to the waqf administration of regular payments and grants by the Israeli military government. Without reliable evidence in the public domain, however, assessing the degree of co-optation on the basis of such unattributable information must remain tentative.

Reference to the relationship between the Gaza Strip qadis and the Israeli military government help by analogy to create a clearer picture of the relationship between the military government and Gaza's waqf administration. There are five shari'a courts in the Gaza Strip—in Gaza City, Khan Yunis, Rafah, Jabalya, and Dayr al-Balah. The last two were established after 1967.[136] Each of the courts has a qadi paid by the Israeli military government. The qadis maintain that their salaries actually come out of the fees collected by the courts, and that the Israeli military government is merely acting as an agent replacing the Supreme Muslim Council; in this way they assert their independence. But appointments of new qadis require the approval of the Israeli military government, a fact that the religious leadership downplays, stressing instead the consultation that takes place among themselves before each new appointment. Be that as it may, it is clear that the Israeli military government has the ability to play an interventionist role, and that whatever intervention does occur has not been seriously challenged by the Gaza Strip's established religious leadership. In the light of these precedents, we can get a better idea of the situation that probably exists with regard to the waqf administration itself.

One of the Israeli military government's first acts in the Gaza Strip in 1967 was to appoint an Israeli army officer to the post of *dhabat raqn al-adyan*, the person responsible for religious affairs. His chief responsibility was to act as a liaison between the Israeli military government on the one hand and the Muslim and Christian communities in the Gaza Strip on the other. With regard to the waqf system, the Israeli officer took over the functions exercised by the Egyptian governor-general and the Finance Department in the Egyptian General Administration. This placed him at the apex of the administrative pyramid that had been set up by the Egyptians. The functions of the officer, who assumed the role of representative of the Supreme Muslim Council, therefore included the appointment of the *ma'mur al-awqaf* and the appointment of the permanent employees of the Gaza Strip waqf administration.

Concerning the degree of the Israeli military government's actual intervention in the appointment process, the only important exchange we have, as already mentioned, is the 1986 appointment of the *ma'mur al-awqaf* after the retirement of the incumbent, Rif'at Abu Sha'ban. According to the version of the procedure offered in interviews by members of the religious elite, the qadis of the Gaza Strip shari'a courts, in the absence of a Muslim government, consulted with each other until a consensus was reached on a single individual. The main criterion was for a religious person with administrative ability; the candidate did not necessarily have to be a religious scholar. The agreed name was then presented to the Israeli officer, acting as *ra'is al-majlis* of the Supreme Muslim Council, who then approved it. According to the religious figures, then, the decision-making process remained with the Muslim community and was merely rubber-stamped by the Israeli military government. It is by no means clear that there was in fact much more state intervention than reported, especially since the Israelis may not have considered the appointment actually made to be controversial, the man finally selected being the nephew of the previous *ma'mur*. This kept the post in the Abu Sha'ban family and in the hands of the traditional religious elite. If a more outspoken and politically engaged individual had been chosen, the Israeli response may well have been different, especially given the state's loss of control over the independent Islamic associations discussed below. Nevertheless, some secular Palestinian leaders suggested to the author that the very appointment of another member of the Abu Sha'ban family raises questions about the degree of separation between the appointment system and the Israeli state.

In this context, it is interesting to note that the Christian communities in the Gaza Strip are managed by independently-appointed lay councils. Nine such communities are recognized in the Strip, two of which (the Greek Orthodox and the Roman Catholic) have ecclesiastical courts. As in the West Bank, these courts are paid for by the communities they serve.[137] As a result, they also enjoy far greater independence from the Israeli military government in terms of appointments and financial controls.[138]

One can conclude, therefore, that although the religious leadership of the waqf system remains outside the formal structure of the Israeli state, there is sufficient scope for state intervention in appointments and salaries to presume a measure of co-optation.

Control over Resources

Determining the extent of Israeli control over the resources of the Gaza Strip waqf system presents similar difficulties. No figures regarding either the extent of waqf land and property in the Gaza Strip or the income and expenditure of the administration are publicly available. Unlike the West Bank, the Gaza Strip lacks the *bayan*s from which deductions can be made. However, a bare sketch can be made on the basis of British Mandate figures and from interviews with members of the religious elite.

The main expenditures of the Gaza Strip waqf administration fall into two categories: the salaries of its administrative staff and mosque officials, and the maintenance and construction of mosques and other properties. In 1987 the office of the *ma'mur al-awqaf* employed a staff of approximately 250, including clerks, preachers, imams, muezzin, cleaners, and caretakers. No figures are available of the total actual salaries, but if one estimates $250 per month as the average wage in the Gaza Strip in 1987, the total expense comes to $62,000 per month and $747,000 per year.

No figures are available for the second expenditure category. The waqf administration is responsible for seventy-six mosques in the Gaza Strip, sixteen of which were built after 1967 in refugee camps. An Egyptian Military Order made the Gaza Strip waqf administration responsible for all mosques in the Gaza Strip, but limited resources prevent it from fulfilling this mandate. A large number of independently-run mosques occasionally receive grants from the waqf administration, but it has no organizational control over them; it has no say in the appointment of imams and it has no control over the content of the *khutba*, the Friday sermon. In 1987 the waqf administration estimated that there were a total of 170 mosques in the whole of the Gaza Strip, a figure that rose to 200 in 1989.[139] This means that more than half of the mosques in the Gaza Strip are outside the administrative control of the waqf system.

The responsibility of the waqf administration for the mosques under its management includes maintenance and the purchase of equipment and furnishings. The Gaza Strip waqf administration is also responsible for the upkeep of thirty-eight cemeteries, amounting to more than 6,000 dunums of land. Many of these cemeteries are in poor condition and require new walls and railings. Other urban properties also require extensive repair and renovation, which cannot be covered by the income of the waqf administration.

The Gaza Strip waqf administration has two main sources of income that are publicly admitted. The first is rents from urban property and rural land. Many shops, garages, residential and commercial buildings, markets, and offices are waqf-owned. Two Israeli journalists, Ze'ev Shiff and Ehud Ya'ari, suggest that up to 10 percent of "real estate" in the Gaza Strip is waqf.[140] It should be borne in mind that rents from urban properties are characteristically low. In most instances urban waqf property is old and dilapidated, requiring extensive maintenance. As the waqf administration has no surplus funds for capital investment, only the most crucial (minor) repairs are carried out, and these do not improve the property's general condition. In addition, the rents of much of the older properties were frozen at 1940 levels following a rent review that was never completed by the Mandate government.[141] After the cost of repairs is deducted from the (nominal) rents, these properties function at a loss. Israel has acquired little urban waqf property in the Gaza Strip, largely, it is presumed, because the Jewish presence there historically was slight. The largest single acquisition has been the occupation of the Abu Khadr waqf hospital complex, which has prevented the disbursement of endowed capital.

The most pressing concern faced by the Gaza Strip waqf administration is the need to invest in repairs and improvement in order to increase its income. A number of development projects have sought to use waqf land and property in a more profitable way.[142] The waqf administration has felt constrained by the nature of its work to avoid taking advantages of the political situation to increase its income. For example, it has adopted a two-tier policy concerning the lease of land and property: while leasing property at a commercial rate to maintain a good income for its work, it leases other land and property at low rates to charitable and humanitarian institutions.[143]

As noted previously, during the British Mandate period the waqf district of Gaza had much land that fell on the Israeli side of the armistice lines, with the result that the system lost a high proportion of its income from rural rents and tithes. Furthermore, a major dispute over the waqf status of the Mughaqa waqf, comprising some 7,000 dunums and involving many leading Gazan families, remains unresolved and has reduced the administration's income further.[144] Despite the lack of available figures, some deductions can be made.

Little income is generated by agricultural waqf property. The total land area of the Gaza Strip is approximately 360,500 dunums, of which, in 1967, possibly up to 190,000 dunums was cultivated.[145] If one takes the figure (cited in Chapter Two) of 15 percent of agricultural land of historic Palestine as being waqf, agricultural waqf land in the Gaza Strip, being situated on the more productive coastal plain, should amount to at least 15 percent. From this one can estimate waqf land in the Gaza Strip to be at least 28,500 dunums. American scholar Sara Roy estimates that by the mid-1980s one-third of the total land area had been acquired by Israel, but it is unclear what percentage of that land was agricultural. If we assume that it was a little less, say 25 percent, then we can conclude that approximately 25 percent of waqf land was also acquired, amounting to a loss of 7,125 dunums. Furthermore, the quantity of income-producing rural land has been drastically reduced by the restrictions the Israeli government has placed on water use and on marketing. Roy estimates that between 1968 and 1985 there was a reduction of 50 percent in cultivated land through a combination of the above factors.[146] From these figures, then, one can estimate that income-producing waqf land in the Gaza Strip is negligible (28,500 dunums less 50 percent, less 7,000 from the Mughaqa waqf, and less 7,000 seized by Israel).[147]

Another source of income for the Gaza Strip waqf administration is donations. Between 1979 and 1988, the administration received $56,000 from the Jordanian-

Palestinian Joint Committee, a fund set up especially to channel aid from the Arab and Islamic states to Palestinian institutions in the occupied territories. The sum of $38,000 was allocated to the salaries of preachers employed by the administration, and $18,000 for the restoration of mosques and waqf properties.[148] Another important item under "donations" is the interest accruing from waqf funds deposited in banks. Although this money cannot be used, it is regarded as a donation that can be used at some stage in the future. Probably the greatest proportion of this comes from the Abu Khadr waqf, which as noted earlier comprised money and land for a hospital in Gaza City. Construction of the 100-room hospital, situated on a 32-dunum site in the middle of Gaza City, was completed in 1956, but the hospital never functioned as such. In 1967 the Israeli military government took over the site and made it their headquarters, paying a nominal rent to the committee managing the waqf. The capital of the waqf cannot be used for any other purpose than for the hospital, and remains deposited in the bank.[149]

A further source of income for the Gaza waqf administration is not publicly acknowledged: income from the Israeli military government. It was not until the mid-1980s that the Israeli military government allegedly began to make regular contributions to the waqf administration, but it is quite likely that *ad hoc* grants were made available throughout the post-1967 period for specific repairs and projects; these are not acknowledged any more than the regular contributions, however. Because of the highly sensitive nature of the issue, which could seriously compromise the standing of the Gaza Strip waqf administration in the Muslim community, no figures are publicly available. Sources who spoke on condition of anonymity, and whose information could not be verified, claimed that in 1985 the waqf administration received a grant of 1 million New Israeli Shekels (NIS, approximately $300,000). This was followed by NIS 34,000 ($11,000) in 1986 and NIS 300,000 ($100,000) in 1988. The irregular amounts indicate that these grants were probably for capital projects as opposed to operating costs, and therefore need not signify a great reliance upon the Israeli military government. These figures do indicate the weakness of the waqf administration in relationship to the state and its growing propensity for incorporation into the state structures.

The Integration of Administration

The degree of integration of the Gaza Strip waqf administration into the Jewish state is equally difficult to ascertain. On one level the issue appears quite clear. While the Israeli military government has administrative offices in Gaza city itself, the offices of the Gaza Strip waqf administration are housed in a totally separate location, close to the Great Mosque in the center of the city. Furthermore, the management and direction of its staff are under the authority of the *ma'mur al-awqaf*. Administrative procedures follow those laid down by the Supreme Muslim Council and practiced during the Egyptian period. On another level, however, the issue is less clear and requires further exploration.

The main indication of some degree of integration of the waqf administration is that all checks issued by the office of the *ma'mur al-awqaf* are countersigned by the

Israeli liaison officer. This practice was introduced by the Egyptian governor-general in his assumed capacity as acting *ra'is al-majlis* of the Supreme Muslim Council. The Israeli military government has enforced the continuation of this practice; in this way it is able to scrutinize the operations and plans of the waqf administration. Any major expenditure that could be considered threatening to the security of Israel (including the borrowing of money or the raising of loans from Arab and Islamic sources) could thus be discouraged and ultimately vetoed. Similarly, the provision of activities and facilities for religious youth could be construed as a security threat. Whether the monitoring and restriction provided by the Israeli countersigning of checks amount to integration of the waqf administration is not entirely clear. Nevertheless, the fact that the accounts of the waqf administration are also audited by the Israeli military government serves to underline this relationship.

Whatever the degree of integration of the Gaza Strip waqf administration into Israel, the military government has not encouraged the waqf administration to build up and extend its services and activities. On the contrary: Until the late 1980s, the military government kept the religious establishment weak and politically marginal. Two examples give credence to this view. First, one of the most pressing problems in the management of the waqf administration's finances has been the delay in approving plans and granting permits to allow it to fully develop the property and land under its control. This has meant that the Gaza Strip waqf administration is constantly underfunded, despite the possibilities for developing its urban sites. If the Israeli military government had been interested in the waqf administration's securing an independent financial base, it seems clear that fewer impediments would have been placed in its path.

Second, although legally the Gaza Strip waqf administration has sole responsibility over all mosques in the Gaza Strip, as we have seen, more than one hundred mosques are not included in its administrative control. These independent mosques are financed and managed by Islamic associations affiliated with the Muslim Brotherhood or other pan-Islamic groups. The growth of these associations in the Gaza Strip during the late 1970s and mid-1980s was permitted by the Israeli military government as a means of counterbalancing the presence of the PLO in the Gaza Strip.[150] Functioning openly, they have constructed mosques and a network of centers that are independent of the existing religious establishment; some of their projects were funded in part by the Gaza Strip waqf administration. Without sufficient funds at its disposal, the Gaza Strip waqf administration has not been able to compete with these groups in responding to the rise of religious devotion during the 1980s. If the Israeli government had been interested in encouraging the work of the waqf administration, one would assume that it would have made available the necessary funds. When it became clear that the Islamic groups were not content merely to oppose the PLO secularists but were also turning against the Israeli state itself, the Gaza Strip waqf administration began receiving more funds from the Israeli military government. One can speculate that having lost control of the Islamic groups, the Israeli government sought new means to counter their influence.

Building up the traditional structures of the waqf administration may have been one of them.[151]

Given the weak financial position of the Gaza Strip waqf administration and the absence of a cohesive Muslim body to lend support and legitimacy to an independent religious institution, the activities of the waqf administration have been severely limited and have not carried the same political weight as those of its counterpart in the West Bank. In its weakened condition it served the interests of the state well. A minimum of services was provided, and no security or political challenge to the state was posed. With a weak financial base, and lacking a clearly demarcated independent leadership, the propensity for greater state incorporation already exists. If the provision of funds from the Israeli military government to the waqf administration continues at the rate assumed during the period from 1987 to 1989, then we can expect an increased monitoring of the waqf administration's activities and its subsequent graduated integration.

* * * * *

Israeli policies with regard to the waqf system in both the West Bank and Gaza Strip seem to have been implemented within the framework of the same overarching objectives: land acquisition and the curtailment of Palestinian political aspirations. Nonetheless, the actual policies in each of the two territories were determined by different factors and circumstances. In the West Bank, the existence of a strong waqf administration, a coherent united leadership, relatively independent resources, strong religious associations of the properties (Muslim holy places) under its management, and the active interventionism of Jordan all combined to introduce a more subtle and incremental Israeli policy. Direct intervention on the part of the Israeli government was liable to provoke extreme disorder and international opprobrium. Consequently, there was little co-optation of the leadership or integration of the administration. Control over the resources took place, but not to the extent of paralyzing the functions of the waqf administration, as income was still available from external sources, such as the Jordanian government. In the West Bank, the main efforts of the Israeli state focused on usurping the functions and undercutting the development of the waqf system to ensure that it was kept on the margins of political life.

In the Gaza Strip, the absence of a coherent Muslim body and a protective neighboring state that could resist the imposition of military rule allowed the Israeli state to take over powers already in place. Its objectives were assisted by the grave weakness of the Gaza Strip waqf administration, curtailed by the loss of lands in 1948 and overwhelmed by demands on its services by the huge influx of refugees. Even before the occupation by the Israeli state in 1948, the role of the waqf as an independent Palestinian institution representing the religious and political interests of the population was marginal. Israel was able easily to keep the waqf system in a marginal and weakened position while pursuing the main objectives of the occupation.

Thus the nonannexation of the occupied territories and the imposition of military rule preserved the existence of the waqf system in the Gaza Strip and West Bank, but under constraints that sought to depoliticize their roles. Moreover, comparing the state's waqf policies in the occupied territories to those inside Israel, one finds the same aim and the same basic means through which to achieve it: taking control of waqf resources, integrating the waqf administration into the Israeli state, and co-opting the waqf leadership. Thus, the thrust of the state's waqf policies in the West Bank, the Gaza Strip, and Israel proper fundamentally the same.

CHAPTER 5

The Muslim Waqf System in Jerusalem since 1967

On 7 June 1967, the Israeli armed forces captured the eastern part of the city of Jerusalem, which had been under Jordanian control since 1948 and inhabited by Palestinian Arabs for centuries. Three weeks later the Israeli Knesset passed two laws that extended Israeli legal jurisdiction and administration into Jordanian East Jerusalem and additional areas north and south of the city. These area were then incorporated into the West Jerusalem Municipality, which was given jurisdiction over the enlarged area. These laws in effect annexed East Jerusalem, including the Old City, to the State of Israel.[1] On 29 June the Palestinian mayor of East Jerusalem was ordered to dissolve the East Jerusalem Municipal Council and terminate its activities (see Map 4).

Despite the annexation of East Jerusalem, the waqf system was not incorporated into the Israeli state in the same way it had been inside the armistice lines of 1949. Indeed, it can be argued that state policy on the waqf system in East Jerusalem was less interventionist than in the occupied West Bank or even in the Gaza Strip. This situation raises the question of why Israel would permit such a political and legal anomaly to persist, especially at the heart of its "eternal capital," and what alternative action it took instead of absorbing the Jerusalem waqf. A second dimension of the question is the manner in which this anomaly has affected the development of the waqf system—that is, how the combination of occupation and annexation transformed the function and role of the waqf system for the Palestinian Muslim community in Jerusalem.

But although the Aqwaf Administration of Jerusalem was not absorbed by the Israeli state, neither did it assume the representative and mediating role that might have been expected under the circumstances. Indeed, a veritable political vacuum among the Palestinian population of Jerusalem followed the 1967 occupation. With the forced dissolution of the East Jerusalem Municipal Council (the municipal councils of other major urban centers on the West Bank, such as Nablus, Hebron,

Map 4. Jerusalem, Showing New Municipal Boundaries of 1967

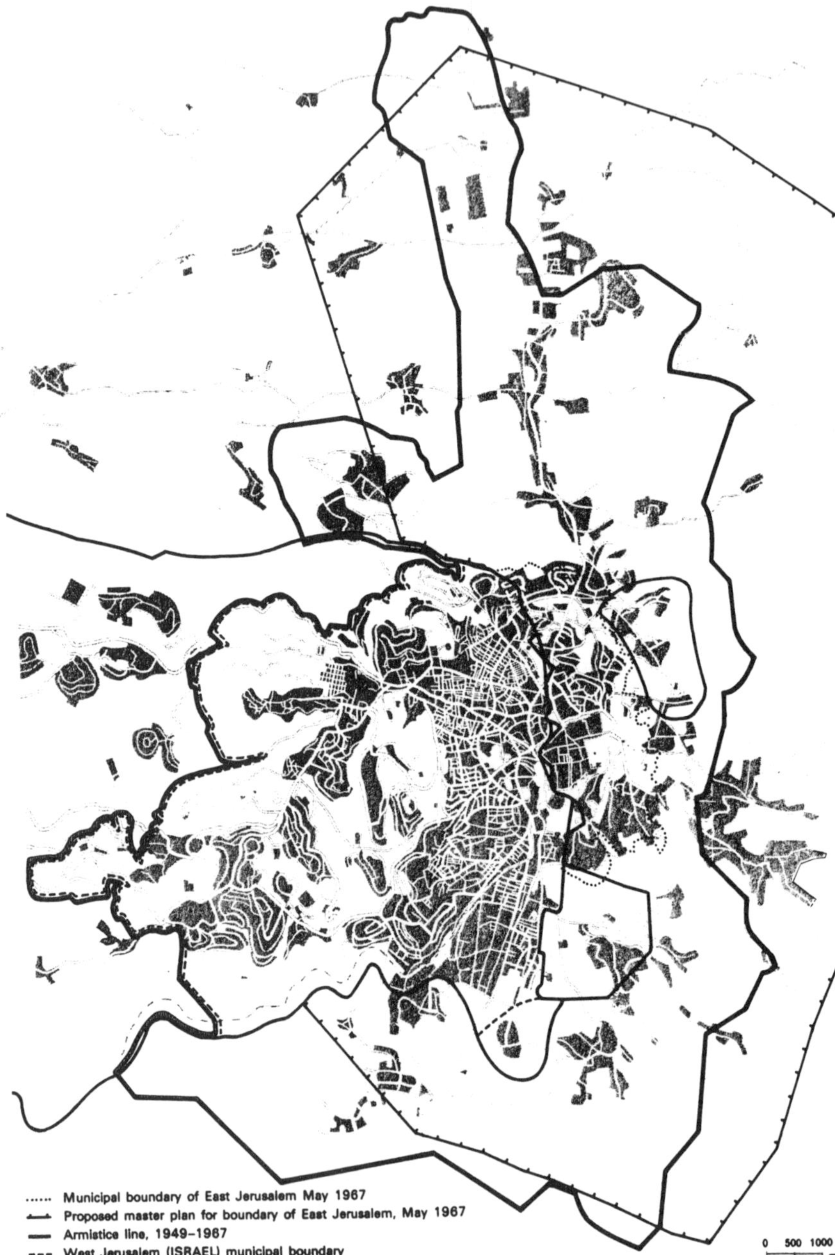

Source: D. Bahat, *Jerusalem* (Jerusalem: Carta, 1986), p. 81.

and Ramallah–al-Bireh, were allowed to continue their functions), the inhabitants of the city were without a national authority representing their interests. They refused to participate in the subsequent elections of the Israeli Jerusalem Municipal Council, arguing that this would confer recognition upon the annexation of East Jerusalem and the adjacent areas. In the absence of a politically acceptable representative forum for the Palestinian inhabitants of Jerusalem, the Awqaf Administration seemed particularly well placed to fill the gap. Given the large amounts of land and property it controlled, the staff it employed, the pan-Islamic interests it symbolized, and the breadth of its functions beyond the strictly religious, a more forthright leadership role might have seemed logical. Why it did not assume such a role is the second line of inquiry this chapter seeks to pursue in examining the activities of the Awqaf Administration in East Jerusalem. This chapter suggests that much of the reason lies in the determination of successive Israeli governments to prevent the waqf system from adopting such a mediating role.

Two key points need to be noted when considering Israeli policies towards Muslim waqf property and administration in Jerusalem. First, the Israeli state's underlying objective in East Jerusalem has been to establish supremacy over the city. Military dominance, certainly, had already been achieved.[2] But the objective also had cultural and political dimensions. Culturally, what was at stake was the character of the city, whether Jerusalem was to be an Arab city or an Israeli one, a Muslim and Christian city or a Jewish one. At a more fundamental and political level, the issue was to what extent East Jerusalem would be allowed to exist as a Palestinian Arab and Islamic enclave—whether its fate would be that of the other mixed cities in Israel, such as Acre and Jaffa, or whether it would develop into something entirely different and independent. And related to these issues was the other aspect of Israel's underlying objective: its determination to make certain that, in the event of a negotiated peace settlement between Israel and the PLO and the Arab states, there could never be any possibility either of a redivision of the city into two parts or an internationalization such as was proposed at the end of the British Mandate.[3]

These two considerations—assuming cultural dominance and securing permanent control over the city—coalesce and find expression in the Israeli government's long-term strategy of "Judaization"—or, more accurately, "Israelization"—of East Jerusalem and the Old City.[4] As was the case in the new Israeli state in the immediate aftermath of the 1948 war, the acquisition of land after 1967 is clearly of primary importance in this strategy. And the waqf system, because of the vast amounts of waqf property and land in East Jerusalem and its developed administrative structure that remained independent of the Israeli state, was at the very center of the struggle over the cultural character and political nature of Jerusalem. Its involvement went far beyond the military occupation's impingement on the use of mosques and other buildings under its control: By retaining land and property outside Israeli state control (holdings which by their very nature would have an Islamic or Arab character), the waqf system undermined the two key considerations in Israel's policy in Jerusalem. It is in Jerusalem, therefore, more than in any other city in

Palestine, that the political role played by the waqf system in the central feature of the Palestinian-Israeli conflict—the acquisition of land—is revealed.

An important counterpoint to the Israelization of Jerusalem is the revival of interest in the Islamic sites of the Old City of Jerusalem. In the early years of the occupation the sites tended to be neglected, partly because of lack of funds, but also in the belief that the neglect would stand as a testimony to the injustice of the Israeli occupation.[5] This view was superseded in the 1970s and 1980s by a determination to protect the sites as a means of consolidating the Arab and Islamic character of the city. In this the Awqaf Administration was assisted by a pan-Islamic and fundamentalist revival and by the greater availability of funds from the Arab oil-rich states. As a channel of funds, the administration was able both to preserve a role for itself independent of the Israeli state and to contribute to the vitality of the Palestinian and Muslim community in East Jerusalem.

Apart from a few minor adjustments, the methodology for this chapter can largely remain that of the previous chapters—that is, to examine the relationship between the state and the Muslim waqf system by assessing the degree of leadership co-optation, of integration of the administration, and of Israeli control over waqf resources. However, the observations made with regard to the co-optation of the waqf leadership in the West Bank (see Chapter Four) apply here as well, the West Bank and Jerusalem waqf being part of the same system and having the same leadership. Thus, in East Jerusalem, too, Israel was able to limit, with the acquiescence of the Jordanian government, the representative role of the Awqaf Administration. While not incorporated into the Israeli state, the Awqaf Administration and by extension the Muslim religious establishment were confined to the margins of political life. Only the question of the degree of administrative integration of the waqf system needs to be interpreted in a broader fashion, as the limitations faced by the Awqaf Administration within the civil jurisdictions of Israel itself were more far-reaching than those imposed by the Israeli military government on the West Bank.

The Historical Development of the Waqf System in Jerusalem during the Ottoman Period

Partly as a response to Christian interest and partly through the increase in Muslim pilgrimage, Jerusalem's status as a holy city in the Muslim world began to grow, increasing thereby its political significance. The Al-Aqsa mosque and the Dome of the Rock on the raised platform of the Haram al-Sharif, and the Mosque of Omar close by, had always been regarded as the holiest sites in Islam outside Arabia. They became a focus for pilgrimages, and many pilgrims came to Jerusalem following their *haj* to Mecca and Medina. A *ziyara* to Jerusalem and Hebron, where the grave of Abraham is located, was considered a lesser but still important act of piety.[6]

In order to support all this religious activity, waqfs were created, and the higher Jerusalem's status became, the more waqfs were endowed.[7] *Zawiya*s, *takiya*s, and other hostels established for pilgrims and travelers, *madrasa*s for scholars and teachers, tombs and mausolea for wealthy people, soup kitchens, orphanages, homes for the needy, public fountains, baths, prayer-rooms, mosques—all were supported by endowments drawing income from rented accommodation, *suq*s, markets, and *khan*s and from tithes from endowed villages and agricultural land around Jerusalem and other parts of Palestine.[8] Indeed, the religious prestige of Jerusalem was such that waqfs in the city were also supported by tithes and rents from endowed villages and property outside Palestine.[9]

The proliferation of waqfs in Jerusalem really began in the latter part of the thirteenth century with a construction program initiated by Mamluk amirs (princes). Exiled and removed from powerful positions but in many cases still retaining their wealth, the Mamluk amirs became patrons of architects and craftsmen, and conferred on the city many monumental buildings. To protect their own wealth and that of their children, these buildings were supported by extensive endowments.[10]

Fewer impressive constructions were built in Jerusalem during the Ottoman period, but the establishment of waqfs continued under both official patronage and that of wealthy families.[11] The walls surrounding the Old City had been built by Sultan Sulayman between 1537 and 1541, and a new aqueduct to supply water to Jerusalem from pools in the Bethlehem area was started.[12] The sultan's wife, Roxelana, established a famous waqf that was known throughout the Islamic world, well known not only for the soup kitchen, which continued to function until the end of the Mandate, but also because of the large amount of land that was taken from state domains to give financial backing to the charitable services the Ottoman state was interested in providing.[13]

During this period the well-known Jerusalem families, such as the Husaynis, the Khalidis, the Jarallahs, and the al-'Alamis began making endowments for their families and for public purposes. While many genuine endowments were made, sometimes leading Jerusalem families extended their influence over the management of *khayri* waqfs, which, over the years, came to be regarded as their *dhurri* waqfs, or even as private property.[14] Reiter has calculated that during the Ottoman period between four and five waqfs on average were created each year. Per capita, Jerusalem had far more waqfs than any other major Ottoman city, such as Istanbul, Cairo, Aleppo, and Bursa.[15]

New waqfs were still being created in Jerusalem in the twentieth century. In 1904 Raghib al-Khalidi endowed income from properties in Jerusalem for the establishment and upkeep of a library in Tariq Bab al-Silsila.[16] During the Mandate, another member of the Khalidi family, Amina al-Khalidi, endowed land and property for the construction of a hospital. In 1932 the al-'Alami family established a waqf for the poor of Jerusalem.[17] During the period of Jordanian rule, between 1949 and 1967, sixteen new waqfs were established in Jerusalem, all of them waqf *dhurri*.[18]

In trying to ascertain the extent of waqf properties in Jerusalem, the researcher is confronted with two difficulties. First, sources define "Jerusalem" in many different ways and a consistent framework is difficult to achieve. The confines of the Old City may be appropriate up to the late Ottoman period, but they would not take into account the rapid development of Jerusalem outside the walls that started during the latter part of the nineteenth century. For our purposes here, Jerusalem is defined as part of the city that was under Jordanian rule until 1967, first and foremost the Old City; it does not include the areas attached to Jerusalem by the Israeli government after 1967. West Jerusalem is defined as that part of the city captured by the Zionist forces in 1948, and which became the municipality of Jerusalem.

The second difficulty is that no concise records on the extent of waqf property are publicly available. Individual waqfs are recorded in the *sijill*s of the shari'a court in Jerusalem, but research has not yet produced sufficient comprehensive data. The Awqaf Administration has relevant records in its finance department, the *mudiriyyat al-amlak al-awqaf*, but these are not accessible to the public. Some research on individual *dhurri* waqfs has been carried out, but it is of a preliminary nature. No Mandate records are extant and Kupferschmidt, generally a meticulous historian of this period, is content with declaring that "most of Muslim buildings in Jerusalem are waqf."[19]

Some estimates concerning the extent of waqf properties in the Old City were obtained from a number of former officials in the Jordanian government and from employees of the Awqaf Administration.[20] Taking these figures together, the total of waqf property in the Old City (excluding the Haram area) can be estimated at between 45 and 50 percent. If the Haram area, which amounts to 17 percent of the Old City, is included, the total of waqf property in the Old City comes to approximately 67 percent, or slightly more than two-thirds.

Estimates for East Jerusalem and West Jerusalem as a whole are even more difficult to compute. One source is a survey of registered business properties in East Jerusalem conducted by the Israeli Ministry of Finance, which may or may not include the Old City. The survey concludes that 11.7 percent of registered business properties in East Jerusalem were waqf *khayri* and 17.6 percent were waqf *dhurri*, a total of 29.3 percent.[21] Interviews with *mutawalli*s of *dhurri* waqf also reveal that possibly up to 50 percent of the land in the al-Tur, Shaykh Jaraah, and Wadi Joz districts to the north and east of the Old City are also endowed.

Since 1948, waqf property in West Jerusalem has been administered by the Muslim and Druze division of the Israeli Ministry of Religious Affairs. Waqf land and property in West Jerusalem that was taken over by the Custodian of Absentee Property was not returned to the administrators and families living in East Jerusalem following the "reunification" of the city in 1967. The Amina Khalidi waqf, for example, which had land in West Jerusalem and in the "no-man's land" area near Shaykh Jarrah, was retained by the Custodian and the Israel Lands Administration. The administrators of the waqf still have not been able to build the hospital for poor Muslims for which it had been endowed.[22] Concerning the extent of waqf property still existing in West Jerusalem, no figures have been obtained but it is thought to be quite small, much of it having been sold or expropriated.[23]

The history of waqf administration in Jerusalem reflected most of the same general trends exhibited in other parts of Palestine. The late Ottoman period brought increasing state intervention and control over the waqf system. During the Mandate period, the local notable families assumed increasing influence over the waqf system through the offices of the Supreme Muslim Council and the waqf system evolved into a more cohesive and centrally organized body. The waqf system's relevance as a mediating role can first be seen during the Mandate period. After 1948, the Jordanian government, in trying to integrate the two banks of its kingdom, sought to subordinate the position of Jerusalem to Amman; the Jordanian administration of Jerusalem waqfs also followed this objective. Because of its unique religious status, however, the system in Jerusalem was both wealthier and its administration more developed than in other areas.

The status of Jerusalem as a holy city in Islam and the rise of Palestinian nationalism brought it growing political significance, which led to the establishment of administrative structures partially and sometimes wholly differentiated from other state administrations. During the Ottoman and Jordanian periods, these developments gave the waqf system in Jerusalem a special status, which diluted the centralizing tendencies of the state. During the Mandate period up to 1937, the uniqueness of Jerusalem and the expansion of the organizational base of the waqf system were further enhanced by the independent role of the Supreme Muslim Council.

The importance of these developments for this book lies in the dilemma they posed for Israel in 1967. The uniqueness of Jerusalem in Islam, underlined by the waqf system, meant that Israel could incorporate the waqf system only at the risk of provoking intense pan-Islamic and international opprobrium. At the same time, to leave it entirely outside the state structures would result in a state-within-state arrangement that would seriously undermine Israel's hold on and claim to a single and undivided Jerusalem. Indeed, the status of the Jerusalem qadis was such that they could undermine the judgment of Israeli-appointed qadis in Israel. The next section analyzes how the Israeli state dealt with this dilemma.

Integration of the Jerusalem Waqf System

During the early months of the Israeli occupation of Jerusalem, Israeli policies towards the waqf system there were inconsistent and confused. The government appeared unsure about the extent to which it should accept the existence of the East Jerusalem Muslim religious establishment and the Awqaf Administration. There was also the complex problem of integrating those parts of the waqf administration that applied to Jerusalem while not tampering with those parts that dealt with the West Bank: enforcing a separation of functions without direct intervention would be difficult. The government's lack of clarity could also be seen in its uncertainty about how strictly Israeli laws should be applied to waqf property, and to what extent the Israeli Ministry of Religious Affairs should supervise and appoint waqf administrators. The government was also undecided about which state body should be responsible for relations with the Muslim community in Jerusalem.

In the first weeks of the occupation, it is not surprising that the Ministry of Defense should have taken responsibility for all affairs in the city. In the meantime, the Knesset prepared the necessary legislation to integrate Jerusalem into the State of Israel, a move that would amount to annexation.[24] Following the passing of this legislation, the government transferred responsibility for the shari'a courts and waqf affairs from the Ministry of Defense to the Ministry of Religious Affairs.[25] Legally this was a logical step, and the Israeli Ministry of Religious Affairs sought to apply Israeli law to East Jerusalem, including the Old City and the West Bank areas Israel incorporated into the city. In practice, the application of the relevant Israeli laws meant the qadis of East Jerusalem would not be permitted to adjudicate on shari'a matters unless they renounced their Jordanian citizenship and swore allegiance to the president of Israel. Moreover, if they accepted these conditions they would also have to adjudicate according to the amendments in shari'a law enacted by the Israeli state and adopted by the Israeli qadis.[26] The ministry also insisted on its right to censor the Friday *khutba* delivered in the al-Aqsa mosque. As a first step towards this end, the Ministry of Religious Affairs tried to establish a Board of Guardians, composed of qadis from Israel as well as from East Jerusalem.[27]

More importantly, the ministry attempted to assert its authority over the administration of waqf properties in the city. Its representatives paid daily visits to the Awqaf Administration's offices in the Madrassa Manjakiyya and tried to persuade the director-general, Hasan Tahbub, to release files and documents relating to the waqf affairs in the city.[28] The Awqaf Administration, under the *qadi al-quda'*, Shaykh Abd al-Hamid al-Sa'ih, flatly refused all these demands and proceeded to convene the Higher Islamic Board. Instrumental in the establishment of the Board was the director-general's insistence that he needed the political support of other religious leaders as well as prominent persons in other fields in order to resist the Israeli demands for access to waqf files.[29]

The stage seemed set for a confrontation between the ministry and the Awqaf Administration. When Nissim Dana, the Jewish head of the Division of Muslim and Druze Affairs, attempted to see the text of the Friday sermon on 14 July 1967, the religious establishment boycotted the service and tensions escalated.[30] The prospect of an outright confrontation with the Jerusalem religious leadership, which was made more likely by the formation of the Higher Islamic Board, caused the Israeli government to retreat on this issue. On 31 July 1967, the Awqaf Administration was informed that the responsibility for Muslim affairs was being transferred back to the Ministry of Defense.[31] This was a significant concession gained by the Awqaf Administration, as the decision meant both that it retained exclusive control over waqf properties in East Jerusalem and that it remained institutionally connected to the West Bank, the situation that had obtained before the occupation. This greatly strengthened the role of the Awqaf Administration and gave substance to its efforts to act as a mediating institution. In effect, Israel had accepted a mini-Jordanian-Palestinian autonomous adminis-tration within the annexed parts of Jerusalem.

It is important to assess the implications of this retreat by the Israeli government, particularly as it relates to the waqf system in Jerusalem. Under Israeli law, extended to Arab Jerusalem, the position of waqf property and the independence of the Awqaf Administration implicit in the government's concession were anomalous and illegal on two accounts. First, the Israeli government considered itself the legal heir to the Mandate government, which had taken control of the Supreme Muslim Council in

1937. This being the case, it is the Israeli Ministry of Religious Affairs, not the Awqaf Administration, that should be running the waqf system and the shari'a courts. Second, since the Israeli government had never recognized Jordan's annexation of the West Bank, the Supreme Muslim Council was the last recognized legal body responsible for waqf property in Jerusalem. Since the Council was deemed "absentee" under Israel's 1950 Absentee Property Law,[32] waqf land and property should by Israeli law be placed under the jurisdiction of the Custodian of Absentee Property and thus be administered by the Ministry of Religious Affairs as its agent, as was the case inside Israel.[33] The return of responsibility for Muslim affairs in Jerusalem from the Ministry of Religious Affairs to the Ministry of Defense was a signal that these steps would not be implemented, and that the Jerusalem waqf system would not be integrated into the Israeli state.

Nonetheless, it would be incorrect to assume that Israel's reversal enabled the waqf system to operate irrespective of the interests of the Israeli state. The prospect of a Jordanian-Palestinian enclave in Jerusalem could not be countenanced in the long-term, and measures were taken to undermine both the legitimacy and the authority of the Awqaf Administration and its religious leadership. In the absence of a national or municipal authority representing the interests of the Palestinians living in the city, the Israeli government also saw to it that the Awqaf Administration should not be permitted to expand its social and political role.

Within a few years of the occupation, the situation had settled down to the extent that a new status quo had emerged. The Israeli government was obliged in 1970 to recognize the anomalies in its relationship with the Awqaf Administration with a new law whose primary purpose was to remove the legal obstacles to the Awqaf Administration's continuing de facto control even while not recognizing the Awqaf administration itself.[34] Article 2 of the 1970 law exempted "Holy Places" from the application of the Absentee Property Law and thus in effect accepted the Awqaf Administration's jurisdiction over the Haram al-Sharif and other mosques, cemeteries, and tombs in East Jerusalem. Concerning other forms of waqf property, the provision in Article 3(a) that the residents of East Jerusalem shall not "be regarded as an absentee within the meaning of the Absentee's Property Law, 5710-1950, in respect of property situated in that area" put many *dhurri* waqfs back under the control of their *mutawalli*s. As *dhurri* waqfs are indirectly supervised by the Awqaf Administration, this provision further enhanced its role. The passing of the 1970 law should be seen in the context of the Israeli government's general attempt to make the annexation of East Jerusalem more acceptable to Palestinian Muslims while not conferring a mediating role on the Awqaf Administration by recognizing its existence legally. The Palestinian researcher Sabri Jiryis has termed this legislation as a "law of absorption" designed "to ensure the basic political objective: the annexation of Jerusalem by Israel."[35]

One of the most important features in the relationship between the Israeli state and the waqf system has been the government's refusal to recognize the authority of the Awqaf Administration and the shari'a courts in East Jerusalem. While de facto management of waqf property was conceded by the government over time, this was not the case for the jurisdiction of the shari'a courts.

But even though the government refused to recognize East Jerusalem's shari'a courts, at the same time it was reluctant to enforce its control over them, a situation that has resulted in further anomalies. Under shari'a law waqf is regarded as a matter of "personal status" and consequently falls under the jurisdiction of the shari'a courts. After 1948, shari'a courts in Israel were run by the government, which also appointed its qadis. But the Jerusalem qadis refused to allow their courts to be absorbed in this way and continued to operate irrespective of Israeli pressure. In retaliation, the Israeli government refused to recognize marriage and divorce certificates and wills issued by the Jerusalem shari'a courts, insisting that only the Jaffa shari'a court had jurisdiction in these matters. Muslims in Jerusalem were obliged, therefore, to seek approval for these affairs from the Jaffa court as well. What developed, then, was another protracted procedure whereby the shari'a courts in Jerusalem continued to issue the required certificates, which were then stamped by the Jaffa court as a sign of official Israeli recognition.[36]

Reiter has carried out some useful research into the relationship between the shari'a courts of East Jerusalem and Jaffa. He discovered that although Palestinians from East Jerusalem used the Jaffa court half as much as they used their own, the Jaffa court provided an element of additional insurance to its East Jerusalem counterpart. The Jaffa shari'a court was also the one to which East Jerusalemites resorted when they did not agree with the judgment of the East Jerusalem shari'a court. Reiter cites an example where the two courts appointed a different *mutawalli* for the same waqf at the request of different branches of a family.[37] The opportunity for chaos is immense, but in general the greater prestige of the East Jerusalem court has ensured a measure of deference by the Jaffa court.

The Israeli government's lack of recognition of the shari'a courts or the Awqaf Administration has several implications for waqf property in the Old City and East Jerusalem. First, waqf cases decided upon in the shari'a courts, such as questions of rent levels or tenancy issues, could not be implemented since they required enforcement by civil courts, which are Israeli and therefore not recognized by the East Jerusalem shari'a court. As a result, *mutawalli*s of *dhurri* waqf and the Awqaf Administration have to rely on moral and community pressure to enforce decisions regarding their property. In practice, this pressure is not always sufficient. The combination of growing secularization and the Israeli occupation exacerbated the loss of authority and legitimacy of the Awqaf Administration and shari'a court system. Nevertheless, decisions can often be enforced if the defendants have family or business interests in Jordan. In addition, because the Awqaf Administration does not accept Israel's annexation of East Jerusalem, it refuses to take up litigation in the Israeli civil courts against its tenants, against the Israeli municipality, or against Israeli citizens. For that reason it has refused to contest expropriations, construction on its land, and restrictions on its activities. It is only as the defendant that the Awqaf Administration has appeared in Israeli civil courts.[38]

The Israeli occupation of East Jerusalem and the attempts to absorb it into the Israeli state have had two contradictory effects. On the one hand, commercial and cultural activities have flourished as Palestinians take advantage of the greater liberality of Israeli civil law compared with the military administration of the West Bank. On the other hand, investment in property and urban development were neglected as a result of the uncertainty and ambiguity with regard to the waqf system's jurisdictions and responsibilities. This neglect has led to a kind of property blight, particularly in the Old City. Poor conditions, overcrowding, insufficient health, social, and educational facilities, and the decline of traditional economic activities all meant that the Awqaf Administration presided over a disintegrating and discontented social and political environment. If the Administration was to maintain its authority and relevance in East Jerusalem, these problems had to be addressed.

The changes brought about by annexation have been responsible for a number of problems threatening the very survival of waqf property in the Old City, both waqf directly managed by the Awqaf Administration and waqf *dhurri*. Rent freezes, key-money arrangements, subletting without permission, and protected tenancies have all combined to make the administration of property and land in Jerusalem exceedingly arduous and complex.[39] The cumulative effect is neglect and maladministration that have led to dilapidation and in extreme cases abandonment. Some resourceful *mutawalli*s have sought to overcome these problems by putting pressure on their tenants or by being constantly vigilant for changes of use and subtenants. Nonetheless, in the absence of a local or national authority concerned about the survival of waqf *dhurri* in Jerusalem and the preservation of waqf buildings, the task will be an uphill struggle. To put it simply, for *mutawalli*s of waqf *dhurri* in particular, there is too much aggravation for insufficient financial return. In this context the Awqaf Administration's initiatives to renovate and subsidize repairs are of great significance for the future not only of waqf property but also of Palestinian and Islamic culture in Jerusalem.

The general history of the Awqaf Administration has been described in Chapter Four. The confusion and disorganization into which it was thrown by the occupation initially rendered it incapable of resisting the outright expropriations and demolitions of its property that occurred in parts of East Jerusalem just after the war. Following this initial period, and up to the mid-1970s, the Awqaf Administration faced a range of encroachments upon its authority and property by Israel. Tunnelling, archaeological excavation, demolitions, and redevelopment work by various Israeli institutions and ministries all affected waqf property. The Awqaf Administration sought to prevent these incursions by sending memoranda to the Israeli Ministry of Defense and cables to the United Nations. Through the intermediary of Jordan, it also sponsored resolutions in the UN General Assembly, the Security Council, and UNESCO condemning Israeli violations of international law regarding the holy places and waqf.[40] These protests had little effect and were not followed up by activities "on the ground" to regain confiscated waqf property, or to protect that which was threatened. Such inactivity reflected in part the general belief that an Israeli withdrawal was imminent, and that waqf matters would be properly addressed as a result of a negotiated settlement.

By the mid-1970s, however, it was clear that the Israeli occupation was to be a prolonged affair, and the Awqaf Administration began to take more ambitious initiatives to consolidate its position and protect its property. In this task it was greatly assisted by an increase in the availability of funds that resulted both from the growth in pan-Islamic interest in Jerusalem and the rise in oil revenues (see Table 2, p. 134). Part of these funds were spent on the renovation program, but some of the revenue went to consolidating the Arab and Islamic character of the Old City through educational programs.

The Awqaf Administration recognized that a vigorous religious education program could play an important role in maintaining its influence in the Palestinian Muslim community. Educating a new generation of Palestinians about the importance and centrality of Jerusalem to Islam and to the Arabs would show the importance of waqf property and ensure increased respect for its own role.[41] The "jewel in the crown" of the Awqaf Administration's educational program is the Dar al-Aytam, or Muslim Orphanage and Vocational School. Since its establishment in 1922, it has undergone considerable expansion, particularly in the last twenty years. Originally it provided residential accommodation and vocational courses for orphan boys in the Old City's Dar Sitt Tunshuq, the site of the old soup kitchen of the Khaski Sultan waqf. Following the Israeli occupation, the orphanage-school expanded and maintains premises in al-Ram and al-'Ayzariyya on the outskirts of the city.[42] By 1985, these premises together provided a mixture of academic and vocational courses for approximately 550 boys between the ages of six and twenty. The vocational training courses include printing, carpentry, metal-work, and tailory.[43]

It is important to recognize that waqfs have continued to proliferate in Jerusalem since 1967. Between 1967 and 1990, there were ninety new waqfs established—approximately four a year, compared to less than one a year during the Jordanian period and compared to virtually none inside Israel itself. One-third of these new endowments were public waqfs.[44] One of the reasons for this somewhat surprising increase may be the doubling of the Palestinian population of East Jerusalem from approximately 70,000 in 1967 to 130,000 in 1990. Other have also attributed the increase to the lack of social cohesion in the Palestinian Muslim community, leading wealthy benefactors to endow property rather than to allow their descendants to squander family wealth.[45] It is also important to recognize the political circumstances that are behind this increase. The survival of the Awqaf Administration and the shari'a court in Jerusalem, despite the Israeli occupation, has encouraged the perception that an endowment may offer property a greater degree of protection than privately-held property—echoing the age-old reasons for endowing property described in Chapter One. In addition, donations by Arab states and bodies have often been contingent upon the donation being converted into waqf. This was partly to provide the element of protection just mentioned, but also to ensure an element of accountability and supervision over the administrators in that they have to submit accounts to the shari'a courts. It is interesting to note that many of the well-known and leading charitable societies of East Jerusalem, such as the Dar al-Tifl

Association, the Arab Women's Association, the Muqassed Hospital, and the Hope Association, have endowed their assets by registering them as waqf.[46] In this context, one can understand the Israeli government's interest in attempting to undermine the role of the Awqaf Administration in East Jerusalem.

Meanwhile, the Awqaf Administration had embarked upon a renovation and restoration program designed to encourage the continued residence of Palestinian Muslims in the Old City.[47] The work began in the early 1970s, and during the 1980s the program was placed under the direction of a specially created department, the Department of Islamic Archaeology.[48] In interviews, officials and employees of the department emphasized the difficulties created by Israeli institutions and the ways in which they hamper its work. The most frequently cited areas of concern have to do with tunnelling and the installation of services. The Israeli Ministry of Religious Affairs has carried out excavations underneath the Muslim quarters along the length of the Haram wall. As a result, a number of historic waqf properties have collapsed or suffered structural damage.[49] Similarly, the installation of modern services such as sewage disposal, drainage, water supplies, and electricity, while welcomed in themselves, have caused serious damage to waqf properties in the Aqabat Saraya and beside the Tariq Bab al-Hadid.[50] The fact that most of the damaged properties are residences, gives credence to the argument that such activities reflect Israeli plans to reduce the Palestinian population of the Old City.[51]

The question of the legality of work by the Department of Islamic Archaeology has practical implications for the Awqaf Administration's restoration program. That the Israeli government, like the British Mandate government, declared the Old City an antiquities site meant that all restoration work had to be approved by the Israeli chief archaeologist for Jerusalem.[52] The chief archaeologist for most of the post-1967 period was Dan Bahat, who stated in an interview that his office was willing to approve projects of the Department of Islamic Archaeology since they generally were of a high standard.[53] However, the Department of Islamic Archaeology refused to ask for such permission; it considers the Israeli presence in the Old City illegal, and to seek permission would be to recognize its jurisdiction. Thus the legal status of the department's work is ambiguous, and to a significant extent undermines its authority. Projects continue irrespective of the chief archaeologist's consent, but planning and consultation are rendered partially clandestine and illicit.

A controversy over the Bab al-Huta quarter in the Old City provides another example of the difficulties encountered by the Department of Islamic Archaeology.[54] The Bab al-Huta quarter is one of the most densely-populated, impoverished, and dilapidated areas of the Old City. It is made up largely of waqf property managed by the Awqaf Administration. The Jerusalem Municipality expressed interest in undertaking restoration work there itself: the former mayor, Teddy Kollek, was quoted as supporting the "gentrification" of the Muslim quarters.[55] The Department of Islamic Archaeology, on the other hand, does not wish any action taken that could legitimize or assist the Israeli occupation of the city. This situation has resulted in an impasse over the question of major redevelopment and restoration work in the Bab al-Huta area. The Palestinian department, fearing that the aim of gentrification is the thinning out of the Palestinian population (in keeping with Israel's long-term plans to reduce the Palestinian population of the Old City), limits itself to making financial grants to tenants on an ad hoc basis to improve their situation. The municipality refuses to proceed with more comprehensive restoration without the cooperation of the Awqaf Administration, which, in turn, refuses to cede responsibility over its properties. This impasse may only be resolved after the conclusion of a peace settlement, or when the Israeli government decides it is in a strong enough position to override the interests of the Awqaf Administration.[56]

A more overt attempt to encroach upon the Awqaf Administration's authority and management of waqf property was the Jerusalem Municipality's "Roof-top Promenade" project. This was a proposed development of the roofs of the central market area in the Old City and was strongly opposed by the Awqaf Administration. The municipality argued that the Old City was in desperate need of "open spaces" and that the market roofs provided an ideal undeveloped site where playing areas, shrub beds and benches could be laid out. As owner of the area, the Awqaf Administration was more concerned that any municipality intervention in its use might lead to further acquisitions of property. It also argued that the project was not in character with the Arab and Islamic nature of the city. As a preemptive move, the Awqaf Administration repaired and repaved the market roofs, and the municipality refrained from proceeding with the proposal.[57]

Notwithstanding Israel's tunnelling and excavations, and its expropriations and demolitions (described in the next section), the state has refrained from direct intervention to integrate the Awqaf Administration into its own bureaucracy. An important result of this policy is that it enabled the Awqaf Administration to attempt to fill the vacuum created by the absence of a national authority representing Palestinian Muslims in the Old City by extending its role. Thus, the Administration's education and construction works aimed at maintaining the vitality of the Muslim community in East Jerusalem and its position in it, while its restoration program, under the Department of Islamic Archaeology, attempted to address the problem of neglect, dilapidation, and blight brought about by the uncertainties of the occupation.

At the same time, however, Israel's refusal to recognize the Awqaf Administration, coupled with its determination to secure Jewish demographic dominance in East Jerusalem, has undermined the Administration's authority and ability to respond to the challenges that the Israeli occupation posed. The authority problem becomes very clear when we look to the expropriations in the Old City and the semi-official activities of Israeli settler groups in the Muslim quarters.

Control over Resources

Despite the annexation of Jerusalem, the Awqaf Administration retained its structural unity and continued to manage the waqf system in both the West Bank and East Jerusalem as a single operation. As has been described, jurisdiction over the affairs of the Muslim community in East Jerusalem was not given to the Ministry of Religious Affairs, but kept with the Ministry of Defense, as on the West Bank.

Similarly, Israeli legislation that would have affected waqf property, such as the Absentee Property Law and its amendments, were not applied to East Jerusalem.[58] Israeli state control over the resources of the Jerusalem waqf system, therefore, took the form of the direct acquisition of waqf property, thereby undercutting the independent financial base of the Awqaf Administration in East Jerusalem.

No figures for the income or expenditure of the Jerusalem *mudiriyya* since 1967 are publicly available, which makes precise calculations of income from waqf property in Jerusalem alone impossible. An approximate estimate of income from waqf property in the Jerusalem *mudiriyya* would be in the region of JD 150,000, or 40 percent of the total income of the Awqaf Administration from West Bank sources.[59] This income is supplemented by subventions from the Jordanian Ministry of Waqfs and other pan-Islamic and pan-Arab bodies. Without these subventions the Awqaf Administration could not possibly support the restoration projects undertaken by the Committee for the Restoration of al-Aqsa Mosque and the Dome of the Rock and the Department of Islamic Archaeology. The following table indicates the Awqaf Administration's dependence on external subventions for its work in Jerusalem. On average these subventions amount to half a million dollars per year. Fluctuations in the transfer of funds, however, have underlined the importance to the Awqaf Administration of an independent financial base. Israeli acquisitions of waqf property in East Jerusalem are, therefore, a serious challenge to the functioning of the Awqaf Administration, not only reducing its income but also restricting its areas of jurisdiction and responsibility.

Table 2: Financial Participation in the Preservation and Restoration of the Holy Places and Historical Sites in Jerusalem, 1967–1987

source	*$*
Jordanian government	7,500,000
Arab League (Center for the Documentation and Preservation of Historical Sites in Jerusalem)	750,000
Islamic Conference (Joint Jordan-Palestine Committee)	100,000
UNESCO	100,000
Organization of Islamic Capitals and Cities	100,000
Organization of Arab Cities	260,000
Governorate of ʿAmman	100,000
ALESCO	25,000
Total	9,297,000

(Source: Nijm, "ʿard tarikhi," p. 37.)

In order to illustrate the consistency of Israel's acquisitions policy, three examples involving property acquisition have been chosen from three different periods: the demolition of the Magharib quarter in the immediate aftermath of the occupation; the expansion of the Jewish quarter in the 1970s; and the semi-official activities of the Israeli settler groups in the Muslim quarters of the Old City in the 1980s. Each example illustrates the assertion of Israeli state control over the Old City and the undercutting of the Awqaf Administration's resource base.

The Magharib Quarter

One of the first acts of the Israeli military towards the Palestinian population after the occupation of the Old City in June 1967 was the almost complete demolition of the Magharib quarter, also known as the Moroccan quarter, and the eviction of its inhabitants. This was carried out in order to create a large plaza for Jewish worshippers in front of the Western Wall of the Haram al-Sharif, also known as the Wailing Wall or Wall of Lamentations, which incorporates the last remaining part of the Second Temple. The demolition of the Magharib quarter is significant for our purposes here since it extinguished the ancient and important Abu Madyan waqf that included mosques, two *zawiya*s, and a great number of endowed residences. It also reflected the complete impotence of the Awqaf Administration and the Muslim religious establishment in the face of military force and its disarray in the immediate aftermath of the war.

The demolition was consistent with other actions taken later to assert Israeli sovereignty over the city. These included the acquisition of land and property for the construction of the ring of new Jewish settlements around the city, archaeological excavations and tunnelling along the Haram's southern and western wall, the redevelopment of an expanded Jewish quarter, and the government's encouragement of Israeli settlers to move into other Palestinian areas in the Old City. The demolition also removed both income and territory from the jurisdiction of the Awqaf Administration.

The shock caused by this action was considerable, but the Awqaf Administration and the Abu Madyan trustees were still reeling from the military occupation and were in no position to resist it. It was not until 24 July, when the *haya't al-islamiyya al-'ulya* (the Higher Islamic Board) was formed that these actions were finally condemned. In the memorandum it sent to the military governor of the West Bank, the new body cited, among other examples of Israeli government interference in the conduct of the Muslim community's religious affairs: "c) the demolition by the Israeli authorities of two mosques in the Moroccan quarter of Jerusalem. Furthermore the whole of this quarter is waqf property."[60] None of the Israeli government ministries was prepared to accept responsibility for the destruction of the quarter, and no attempt was made to offer the evicted residents any alternative accommodation.[61] At a later date, when the entire area was expropriated for the redevelopment of the Jewish quarter, the residents of the quarter were offered compensation by the Israeli government, but the offer was essentially an empty one: The properties of the quarter were well known to be waqf and not the private property of the residents.

As administrators of the endowment, the Awqaf Administration and the Abu Madyan trustees were bound by shari'a law not to accept any change in the status of the area, which acceptance of compensation would require.[62]

While to some extent the destruction of the Magharib quarter reflects the drama and impetuosity associated with war, it also indicates that on crucial matters of state interest the Israeli government would brook no resistance. Securing access to the Western Wall was a national imperative that overrode any concern for the sensibilities of the Palestinian Muslim community and religious establishment. Nevertheless, the government realized that such actions would consolidate the religious and political opposition to its occupation and could not be repeated without serious consequences for its claims to the whole of Jerusalem. Later actions were tempered by legislative and administrative processes that gave the acquisition of property a veneer of legality. With or without such veneer, the end was the same: enabling the Israeli state to gain control over the waqf resources of East Jerusalem.

The Expansion of the Jewish Quarter

The disarray that had paralyzed the Muslim religious establishment in the immediate aftermath of the occupation, preventing it from resisting the destruction of the Magharib quarter, did not last. By the time the government sought to expropriate more waqf land in the 1970s for its plans to extend and redevelop the traditional Jewish quarter, the Higher Islamic Board had been formed and had received recognition both locally and from abroad. The Awqaf Administration was starting to function, and the shari'a court system was falling into place. Even in this situation, however, the religious establishment could do little in the face of Israeli expropriations and further demolitions. Its impotence with regard to the expropriations in the Jewish quarter indicated the strength of the government's position and its determination to overcome resistance when the question of sovereignty over land was at stake.

Following the 1948 war and the evacuation of the Jewish quarter by the Jewish inhabitants, many Palestinian Arab refugees from residential quarters in West Jerusalem, to which they were not permitted to return, took up residence in empty Jewish and Arab properties in the quarter. At first their residence was administered by the International Red Cross, but later, and until their eviction in the 1960s and 1970s, it was placed under the jurisdiction of the United Nations Relief and Works Agency (UNRWA).[63] Property that had been actually owned by Jews was placed under the control of the Jordanian Custodian of Enemy Property, who rented it out to both individuals and to UNRWA.

On 18 April 1968, the Israeli minister of finance, Pinchas Sapir, issued an order expropriating twenty-nine acres (116 dunums) of the southern part of the Old City for "public purposes," as defined by the British Ordinance of 1943.[64] The purpose of this order was to develop the area to house Israeli Jewish families and reestablish a Jewish presence in the Old City. The boundaries of the expropriation zone stretched from the Western Wall in the east to the edges of the Armenian convent in the west, and from the Tariq Bab al-Silsilah in the north to the walls of the city

Map 5. The Old City of Jerusalem before the Israeli Occupation

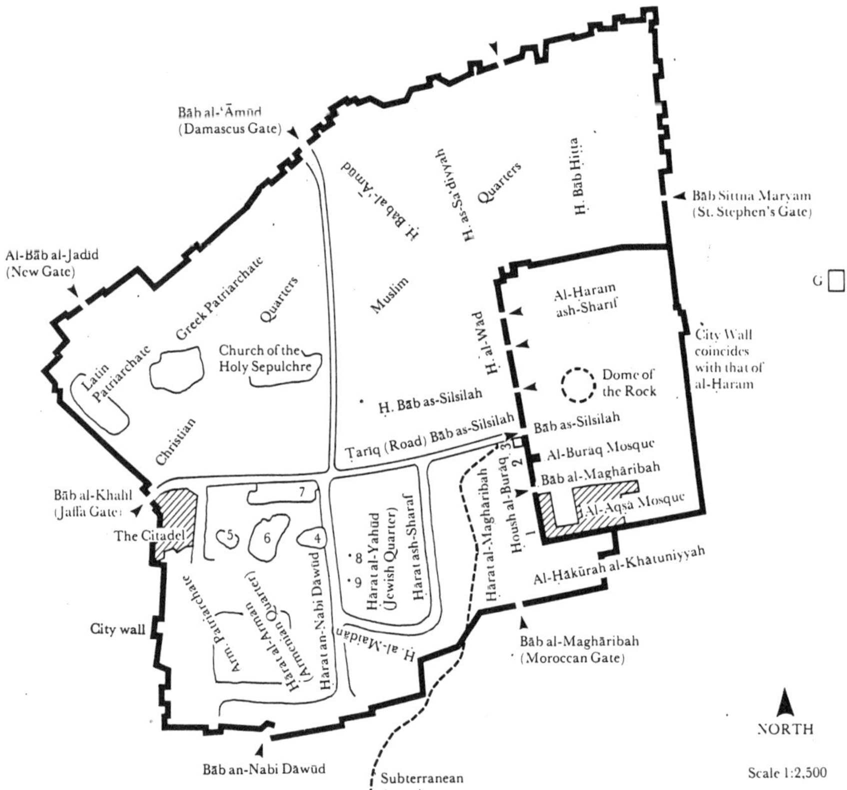

Source: Tibawi, *Islamic Pious Foundation in Jerusalem* (London: Islamic Cultural Centre, 1985).

in the south. Included in the expropriation were 700 stone buildings, only 105 of which had been owned by Jews before 1948. Of the Palestinian Arab properties expropriated, there were 1,048 flats or apartments housing 6,000 Palestinians, and 437 workshops or commercial stores providing employment to approximately 700 workers.[65]

Of the expropriated properties, twelve belonged to the Awqaf Administration (three to the Muhareb Mosque waqf) and ninety-nine to the Abu Madyan al-Ghauth waqf.[66] Figures for waqf *dhurri* are harder to ascertain, but my own fieldwork shows that at least fifty-five properties of this kind were expropriated, including sixteen from the Khalidi family, thirteen from the al-'Asali family, and eight from the Ja'ouni family.[67] These figures cannot be considered complete: There are certainly more waqf *dhurri* properties than I have been able to count. Nevertheless, the figures give a general indication of the effect of the expropriation order on the waqf system in the Old City. At the very least, 27 percent (and probably as much as 33 percent) of the non-Jewish-owned properties were endowed in some way, amounting to approximately 24 percent of the total property expropriated. The former mayor of Jerusalem declared in protest:

> By these new expropriations Arabs in the City will lose properties which have belonged to them for hundreds of years, and more than 6,000 Arabs will be evacuated from the City and dispersed...while more than 700 employers and workers will be deprived of their means of livelihood, and forced to swell the ranks of the homeless....while the landlords and beneficiaries of Waqfs, who used to enjoy and live on the rent of their properties and Waqfs, will be deprived of their sources of livelihood and forced to join the ranks of the needy, if not of the refugees.[68]

The eviction of waqf tenants was not carried out in one day, as it had been in the Magharib quarter. An Israeli company, "The Company for the Reconstruction and Development of the Jewish Quarter" (CRDJQ), was created to renovate and rebuild the expropriated area as the new Jewish quarter; it was directly accountable to the Israeli prime minister and the interministerial Committee for Jerusalem Affairs. The CRDJQ notified tenants of the expropriation and offered compensation to leave and help with mortgages for alternative housing. Some tenants were happy to accept the terms, but many refused. In such cases litigation was begun and a long process of harassment and coercion followed, which has been well-documented in the international press.[69]

The process of eviction lasted ten years, partly because the Awqaf Administration, the *mutawalli*s of waqf *dhurri*, and most private landlords refused to accept compensation or to recognize the change of ownership that the CRDJQ wished to have clearly settled. For both nationalist and religious reasons, the religious leadership affirmed that waqf property was not for sale and compensation could not be accepted. Although in shari'a law *istibdal*, or the exchange of waqf property for one equal or better, is permitted, no such arrangement was offered by the Israeli government, and in any case it would not have been accepted. In order to circumvent the owners' refusal, the government was forced to resort to changing the law, and in 1973 the Knesset passed an amendment to the Absentee Property Law that allowed it to bypass the ownership issue and gave the expropriation a veneer of legitimacy.[70] The law declared that if a tenant accepted compensation, then all property rights were liquidated and the government would recognize the transaction as a valid change of ownership.[71] This would apply even if it was clear that the tenant was not the owner of the property concerned. In the face of such measures all the Awqaf Administration was able to do was to protest and refuse to recognize the legality of the expropriations.

On the grounds of principle, the Higher Islamic Board and the Awqaf Administration refused to contest the expropriations in the expanded Jewish quarter in Israeli courts, which greatly weakened their own positions. Their reasons for doing so, however, were not without validity: They argued that to resort to Israeli courts would confer legitimacy on the occupation and annexation of East Jerusalem and would constitute a form of recognition. There was also a fear that to appear in court as representative of the Ministry of Waqfs in Jordan would, under Israeli law, be tantamount to accepting its Israeli-defined "absentee" status and pave the way for the Israeli Ministry of Religious Affairs to take over its functions.[72] A fallacy in this last argument is that the Israeli government failed in its early attempts to incorporate the East Jerusalem functions of the Awqaf Administration into the Israeli state system, and it is not clear why they would have succeeded this time. In any event, the Awqaf Administration dropped its refusal to contest expropriations twenty years later when it decided to contest a case in May 1987.[73]

Whatever reservations one might have of the Awqaf Administration's stance at the time of the expropriations in the late 1960s and 1970s, the refusal to contest may have reflected an accurate assessment of the chances of success that such cases would have. Landlords of private properties in the expropriation zone were all unsuccessful in their court cases. Indeed, the failure rate led one judge to comment that to the best of his knowledge all attempts to get the expropriation order rescinded had failed.[74]

Israeli Settlers in the Muslim Quarter

The activities of Israeli settlers in the Muslim quarters of the Old City are not exclusively directed against Muslim waqf properties. Nevertheless, their actions have important implications for the moral and political authority of the Awqaf Administration in the Old City, and thus for the long-term survival of the waqf system in Jerusalem. While the settlers' long-term plans include the takeover of the Haram al-Sharif area and the construction of a Jewish Temple on the site, which would undercut much of the *raison d'etre* of the Awqaf Administration in Jerusalem, their short-term plans involve the acquisition of waqf *khayri* and waqf *dhurri* property, of mosques, tombs, and prayer-rooms; this would not only undercut the Awqaf Administration's resource base in the Old City but would lead to the emigration of the Palestinian population. The settlers' activities also show how the nationalist groups, initially working independently of government policy, have been able through their determination not only to override municipality concerns about offending Muslim sensibilities in East Jerusalem, but also to establish, through skillful politicking and lobbying, considerable covert government support.

During the early part of the twentieth century the expansion of the modern city in the west and north of the Old City eased the flow of Jews wishing to settle in the Muslim quarters.[75] In 1929, intercommunal rioting led to the start of a gradual emigration of Jews from the Muslim quarters to the new city. The tensions and rioting of the 1930s accelerated this movement until finally in 1936 the last Jewish family left the quarters.[76] Properties that had been bought by Jewish institutions were either sold or leased to Palestinian Arabs or abandoned. The yeshiva Torat Hayyim, for example, in the Harat al-Wad had been abandoned by 1932.[77] As already noted, Palestinian refugees from West Jerusalem and other parts of Palestine that had fallen to Israel "squatted" in the Muslim quarter's empty former Jewish properties, which in 1950 were placed under the management of the Jordanian government's Guardian of Enemy Property. It was his responsibility to continue to collect the rents and maintain the properties until a peace settlement was reached with Israel. After the Israeli occupation of the Old City in 1967, the functions of the Guardian were transferred to the Israeli Custodian of Absentee Property. The properties were not returned to their original owners, and the Palestinian Arab inhabitants were recognized as protected tenants or given new leases to sign in accordance with the municipality's "mosaic" policy.

In the years following the Israeli occupation of Jerusalem, Israeli private and governmental agencies were focused on the reconstruction of the enlarged Jewish quarter. In the early 1970s, however, a number of individuals became interested in the former Jewish properties in the Muslim quarters and sought to reactivate a Jewish presence there.[78] A yeshiva was established in the late 1970s on the second floor of the former Torat Hayyim premises in Harat al-Wad, and a group of Sephardi Jews began trying to occupy the Bet Ma'aravim complex, a former hostel for North African Jews on the Aqabat Khalidi.

These activities were sporadic and uncoordinated and attracted little attention compared to the activities of Israeli settlers in Hebron and other parts of the occupied territories. The 1980s, however, were marked by the surfacing of a number of ultranationalistic and religious groups, inspired by and composed of Gush Emunim members, the militantly nationalistic settler group. These groups were committed to the large-scale Jewish settlement of the Muslim quarters, in line with their Messianic vision of replacing the Dome of the Rock and the al-Aqsa Mosque with a Jewish Temple.[79] The activity of these groups marked the end of the municipality's attempts to pursue its "mosaic" policy while simultaneously ensuring Israeli demographic dominance in East Jerusalem. The support the settler groups began to find from Israeli national political figures and governmental departments also meant that the Awqaf Administration faced a much more hostile and provocative Israeli state policy.

This was particularly the case following the growing involvement of "hawkish" political leaders such as David Levy and Ariel Sharon of the Likud party, Professor

Yuval Ne'eman of Tehiya, and Zevulun Hammer of the National Religious Party, all of whom openly proclaimed their support for the settlers.[80] In December 1987, Sharon rented the Moshe Wittenberg house in the Harat Bab al-'Amud from one of the groups, Ataret Cohanim, as an act of support for their goal.[81] These leaders also used their control over various government ministries to secure practical support for the settlers. As minister of religious affairs, Hammer allocated at least one grant worth $250,000 to a settler project in the Muslim quarters and set up a commission to pursue the possibility of restoring synagogues there.[82] As minister of housing, Levy allocated a grant of $40,000 to another settler group for its restoration work, although these funds were not approved in the annual budget of the ministry.[83] In May 1987, Sharon, as minister for trade and industry, called on the government to increase the resources available for settlement in the Muslim quarters.[84] Meanwhile Ne'eman, a former minister for science and technology, called for the renewal of the charter of the Company for the Reconstruction and Development of the Jewish Quarter and for the extension of its work throughout the entire Old City. This would probably entail more expropriation orders.[85]

Such explicit government support led the settler groups to drop the relatively low-profile approach that characterized their early activities. Conscious of ministerial protection, they became more public in their fund-raising activities. In 1986, for example, the settler groups held celebrations for the twenty years of "unification" of Jerusalem in the Muslim quarters. Their properties were festooned with Israeli flags, and visiting days were held in the yeshivas with exhibitions, video shows, lectures, and guided tours of Jewish properties in the Muslim quarters, including various sections of the Haram wall.[86] They also solicited support from Christian and Jewish groups abroad. An "American Friends of Ataret Cohanim" was set up in the United States; it produces glossy brochures on the work and plans of Ataret Cohanim. (One brochure carried endorsements from virtually all senior right-wing Israeli politicians.)

The settlers have a strategic aim in the choice of the properties they target for acquisition. Former Jewish properties along the Aqabat Khalidi that are in the hands of the Custodian of Absentee Property have been selected. From this initial base, properties adjacent or within close reach were identified for further acquisition. Inducements, threats, court cases, and physical violence encourage the Palestinian residents to leave.[87] In this way the settlers intend to create a chain of properties, extending from the Jewish quarter, across the rooftops to the Kolel Galicia, down the Aqabat Khalidi to the old Hungarian synagogues on the Tariq al-Wad, and linking up to the army post at the entrance to the underground passage to the Western Wall plaza. Establishing such a chain is consistent with the traditional pattern of Zionist settlement prior to 1948 and in the occupied territories after 1967.

The presence of the settler groups in the Muslim quarters has been perceived as the chief threat facing the Awqaf Administration and the waqf system in Jerusalem.[88] Settler activities have led to great anxiety and fear among the Palestinian inhabitants, many of whom are waqf tenants. For example, during the demonstrations and torch-lit march through the Old City by nationalist right-wing Israelis following a stabbing in December 1986 of a member of the Shuvu Banim yeshiva off the Aqabat Khalidi, shop-fronts were smashed, fire-bombs were thrown, and Palestinian residents were harassed.[89] According to one senior Awqaf Administration official, the immediate effect of this violence was to create panic among the Palestinian residents, many of whom started to make preparations to leave the Old City. The Awqaf Administration's concern was that this panic would spread and result in the depopulation of the Muslim quarters.[90]

By occupying former Jewish properties in the Muslim quarters, by buying (often through dubious means) other Palestinian-owned properties, evicting tenants, and precipitating the departure of their Palestinian neighbors through harassment and intimidation, the settler groups contribute to the long-term Israeli plans to reduce the Palestinian population in the Old City and undermine the independence of the Awqaf Administration. Dependent upon external funds for much of its work, and with the prospect of its internal resource base further diminishing, the Awqaf Administration faces the most serious challenge to its existence in East Jerusalem.

* * * * *

Despite the Israeli military takeover and the political annexation of the Old City and East Jerusalem, the waqf system in East Jerusalem, as represented by the Awqaf Administration, has operated since 1967 with a certain measure of autonomy. Indeed, as a consequence of the Israeli occupation it has acquired additional social and political functions. It was able to create and maintain this anomalous position largely as a result of Jerusalem's unique status as Islam's third holiest city and because the historical basis for the management of waqf land and property provided a strong institutional framework. A further factor in creating this situation was that the traditional religious and institutional leadership in East Jerusalem remained there and was supported by the Jordanian government. In that situation, it was possible to continue managing the waqf system without serious and lasting interruption and to consolidate its positions.

Under these circumstances Israel was obliged to act more circumspectly than it had done inside Israel proper. The status of Jerusalem and the difficulties involved in dividing waqf administration from the West Bank was such that it was forced to accept the relative autonomy of the Awqaf Administration. Its conundrum lay in allowing this while taking care not to allow the Awqaf Administration to develop a mediating role in relation to the East Jerusalem Palestinian Muslim population. This last would have unravelled the state's attempts to curtail Palestinian political aspirations in the West Bank and Gaza Strip, and would have fanned the dissatisfaction of Palestinian Muslims in Israel proper who would have either clamored for the creation of a similar institution for themselves or begun to look to the Awqaf Administration as their representative in religious affairs.

The Israeli state sought to resolve this conundrum both by undermining the authority of the Awqaf Administration and by undercutting its resource base. It undermined the institution's authority partly by refusing to recognize the jurisdiction of the shari'a court and partly by restricting the development of the Awqaf Administration's potential social and political roles. It undercut the resource base by acquiring land either directly or through state-supported organizations. These acquisitions had a direct impact in the form of removing property from the Awqaf Administration and an indirect impact by creating socially and politically hazardous conditions in which only the very poorest Palestinians would live. Thus, despite the Awqaf Administration's apparent freedom of activity, the policy of the Israeli state towards the waqf system in East Jerusalem was entirely consistent with its policies towards the waqf system in other territories under its control.

CHAPTER 6

A Perspective on the Muslim Waqf System's Past and Future

Students of Islamic history and politics have long recognized the importance of the waqf system in Muslim society. Similarly, those following the ebb and flow of the Palestinian-Israeli conflict have long been aware of the central role played by land and property in the dispute. This study has drawn together the two issues to reveal a hitherto much-neglected aspect of the Palestinian-Israeli conflict: the Palestinian Muslim waqf system. Given the prominence of religious movements and associations in the conflict, the hope is that the perspective offered here will add to our understanding of Palestinian and Israeli behavior. The study has focused on the role of the waqf system as a mediating institution in order to draw out the interplay between Islam, land, and the Palestinian-Israeli conflict.

During the late Ottoman period both the structures of the state and the waqf system were undergoing a process of centralization and rationalization. It was not until the mid-nineteenth century that government procedures were codified and began, as a result, to impinge upon the administration and autonomous development of the waqf system. During most of this period the waqf system remained the preserve of the regional elite, the notable families who themselves acted as mediators between the state and the population. It was not until the period of the *tanzimat* reforms and the centralizing policies of the Young Turks that the structures of what can be regarded as a modern state can be discerned.

These changes had two contradictory effects on the waqf system: it became at one and the same time the vehicle through which the state extended its influence in education and welfare provision and a bastion of regional and conservative opposition to the state. It is this "double-facing" aspect of the waqf system during this period that reveals its potential as a mediating institution. Thus, while the state sought to take advantage of its pervasiveness in Muslim society, the waqf system supported the independent action of a local elite and provided services to the population at large. In this way, state penetration was pitted against regional opposition, and the waqf system was essential to this dynamic.

The potential of the waqf system as a mediating institution became all the greater when the state ceased to be Muslim. The "oppositional" characteristics of the waqf system both cohered and responded in varying ways to the degrees of control over the system exercised by the state. During the British Mandate period the separation of the waqf system from the state heightened these characteristics. As the waqf system's functions, responsibilities, and resources increased, so did the influence and power of the local religious elite. While the state continued to retain the ultimate coercive power within which the waqf system operated, the system was nevertheless able to play a mediating role, protecting and promoting the interests of the Muslim population in particular and, to a large extent, the Palestinian people in general. That mediating role was terminated when the state determined that the waqf system's oppositional role had taken precedence over its mediating role.

A similar mediating role for the Muslim waqf system was also possible under the succeeding non-Muslim state authority in Palestine, the state of Israel. We have sought to explain here why this did not occur, and have concluded that two interconnected reasons account for it. The waqf system was not permitted to play a mediating role because (1) the state needed to acquire land to strengthen its territorial integrity, and (2) in order to preserve its territory, the state needed to deny the Palestinian people the opportunity to reclaim it or establish an independent state. By refusing to confer a mediating role on the waqf system, the state was simultaneously able to acquire the resources of the waqf system in the form of land and property, and to constrain Palestinian political aspirations by restricting Muslim leadership and organization. We have examined these policies here by way of the three key linkages—co-optation of leadership, integration of administration, and control over resources—and our study has revealed a decisive policy of control and land acquisition. Given the continued presence of a substantial Palestinian minority in Israel, these policies of control and acquisition have produced an ultimately destabilizing reaction. One conclusion here is that Palestinian Muslim resistance was inherent in a policy that refused to allow the Muslim waqf system to play a mediating role.

When the Israeli state adopted new legislation in 1965, it was partly to address this consequence of its policy. The new legislation, often characterized as reforms consistent with those carried out in other parts of the Middle East, was in fact encumbered by the same state policies that had earlier failed to stabilize the situation. By examining the activities of three boards of trustees established by the 1965 amendment, we were able to demonstrate how the co-optation of the waqf system's leadership, the integration of the administration, and the transfer of resources were all pursued to the same extent as before. The need to acquire land and to constrain Palestinian political aspirations overrode the need to address Muslim demands that the waqf system be given some form of representative and mediating role. The state's establishment of boards of trustees, therefore, was a gesture in the direction of allowing the remnant of the waqf system to play a mediating role, but one which lacked real substance.

The political configurations in the West Bank and the Gaza Strip after the Israeli occupation in 1967 provide useful contrasts to the situation inside Israel itself. While Israeli policies remained essentially the same, the state was compelled to take into account a number of additional political factors. On the West Bank, the potential for the waqf system to act as a mediating institution was far greater than inside Israel. The leadership had remained in place, the administration was not structurally absorbed by the state, and the resources did not suffer from wholesale confiscations, as in Israel. Nevertheless, this potential mediating relationship was never realized. The Jordanian government's involvement in the administration of the West Bank and its control over the waqf system obscured the relationship between the waqf system and the Israeli state. The waqf system was accountable to and directed from Amman, which minimized its links to the Israeli state. Moreover, Israel sought to undermine its potential mediating role by "de-Palestinianizing" its leadership, usurping and restricting its responsibilities, and undercutting its resource base. In the period under review, the Israeli state has to a large extent succeeded in neutralizing the waqf system's political role without, however, completely marginalizing it. By contrast, the waqf system in the Gaza Strip was almost completely marginalized. The small size of the waqf system there, its financial weakness, and its lack of external support all meant that it was unable to respond to the challenges of the Israeli occupation. As a result it could not play a significant political role. The leadership of the waqf system in Gaza has been co-opted, though to an undetermined extent, and its administration penetrated and made dependent upon covert Israeli financial support. Without more funds and independent financing, it had no potential for playing a mediating role.

The situation in annexed East Jerusalem, where civilian rule and military occupation converge, is of especial interest to this study. As a result of the annexation of East Jerusalem and the adjoining parts of the West Bank, this part of the waqf system technically came under Israeli law. One might therefore have anticipated that its leadership would have been co-opted into the Israeli system, its administration integrated into the Muslim and Druze Division of the Israeli Ministry for Religious Affairs, and its resources transferred to the Custodian of Absentee Property or to the Muslim and Druze Division acting as agent for the Custodian. None of these possibilities materialized. In fact, the waqf system of East Jerusalem, like the rest of the West Bank, remained under the jurisdiction of the Israeli Ministry of Defense and under the administrative control of the Jordanian Awqaf Administration. Several reasons account for this anomaly: the continued presence in Jerusalem of the religious leadership after 1967 (in contrast to the situation in Israel after 1948), continued and expanded Jordanian and Islamic financial support, the unique religious status of Jerusalem in Islam, which conferred upon its waqf system an aura of holiness and prestige, and the strong institutional foundations built up over the past century. These factors compelled the state to treat the East Jerusalem waqf system more circumspectly than it had inside Israel itself. Nevertheless, Israel denied the waqf system a mediating role, not only because the state wanted to acquire symbolically important property in East Jerusalem and the Old City and because it wanted to forestall any possibility of the leadership adopting a representative role, but also because it was determined to avoid a precedent being set in the (enlarged) capital. Indeed, a mediating role for the Jerusalem Awqaf Administration would fuel Muslim demands and pressures for a more independent waqf system inside Israel and therefore unravel the state's control over the waqf system there.

It is now time to return to the principle research questions posed at the beginning of this study. Why does the Palestinian Muslim waqf system still constitute a threat to the Israeli state and, given that threat, why does the Israeli state permit it to continue to exist? Does the continued existence of the waqf system indicate that the interests of the Israeli state are in some way being served, or that there are limits on the coercive power and the sovereignty of the state? The answer to the first question should by now be clear: The waqf system presents a fundamental challenge to the Israeli state and its territorial and ideological hegemony. To cede to the demands of those supporting the waqf system would lead to the unravelling of the state's control over its land and to a loosening of constraints on Palestinian political aspirations.

Concerning the question of why Israel has allowed the waqf system to continue to exist, the answer is also relatively clear. As we have seen, a leadership under Israeli control, co-opted to varying degrees in the different areas, provides a conduit for the transfer of waqf resources from the Muslim community to the Jewish community. It also assures a domesticated elite, exacerbating the political and religious vacuum in Palestinian society. At the same time, however, limitations upon Israeli coercive power and sovereignty can be observed, particularly in East Jerusalem. Israeli policy has been a balancing act between accepting the waqf system's existence and constraining its ability to operate effectively and to develop its resources.

It is hoped that this study has succeeded highlighting the extreme durability of the waqf system as a Muslim institution in the modern world. As for the future of the Palestinian Muslim waqf system in Israel and the occupied Palestinian territories, it would be reasonable to assume that without a peace settlement that gives the Palestinians a national authority of their own, the trends examined in this study will persist: continued acquisition of land, continued usurpation of administrative functions and responsibilities, continued attempts to co-opt and control leadership.

With the establishment of a Palestinian state, one can envisage two scenarios: If relations between Israel and Palestine remain hostile, the waqf system inside Israel will be subjected to even greater state control than before since an unrestricted waqf system would form the potential base from which any Palestinian irredentism could be launched. Palestinian attempts to reclaim the waqf system from the Israeli state will lead to greater confrontation between Palestinians and Israelis inside Israel. Alternatively, if the peace settlement is an authentic one based upon mutual security and compensation, it is possible that the grievances held by Palestinian Muslims will be seriously addressed. Under this scenario, we cannot rule out the return of limited amounts of waqf land and property, particularly waqf *dhurri*, and an enlarged but state-controlled waqf administration. However, the Israeli body politic is unlikely to contemplate an autonomous, nationwide, and centralized administrative structure staffed by Palestinians. To a greater of lesser degree, any future waqf system inside Israel will be state-controlled.

In the West Bank and the Gaza Strip, we have found little evidence of Palestinian scholars or politicians showing interest in modernizing the waqf system or considering more democratic means of administering it.[1] Under a Palestinian state, it will most probably be absorbed into a Ministry for Religious Affairs or Social Welfare and administered in much the same way as is the case in Jordan. Some *mutawallis* of waqf *dhurri* may face increased pressure for greater accountability and entrepreneurialism. The future of the waqf system in East Jerusalem is more difficult to predict. The range of options for the final status of East Jerusalem in a peace settlement is much broader than for that of the West Bank and Gaza Strip. In the face of Israeli determination to retain full sovereignty over both halves of the city, it is hard to envisage the waqf system surviving in its present form. Judging by present policies, an agreement that concedes some autonomy to the Awqaf Administration in, say, the Old City, would not be free of difficulties. The most likely outcome of this scenario would be a periodic and consistent erosion of the Awqaf Administration's resources, its independent administration, and its leadership. A final point must highlight the irony that it is the waqf system, this most conservative of Palestinian national institutions, which is in fact the chief vehicle and standard bearer for Palestinian and Muslim claims in Jerusalem and the most likely means through which limitations on Israeli sovereignty can be placed.

NOTES

Notes to Preface

1. G.C. Kozlowski, *Muslim Endowments and Society in British India* (London: Cambridge University Press, 1985), p. 1.

2. J.N.D. Anderson, "Recent Developments in Shari`a Law. IX: The Waqf System," *The Muslim World* 42, No. 4 (October 1952): 257–76.

3. For a more detailed discussion on the theoretical aspects of these linkages see M.R.T. Dumper, "Muslim Institutions and the Israeli State: Muslim Religious Endowments (waqfs) in Israel and the occupied territories, 1948–1967," Ph.D Diss., University of Exeter, 1991, pp. 5–15.

4. The main theoretical formulation of the control model can be found in I. Lustick, "Stability in Deeply Divided Societies: Consociationalism versus Control," *World Politics* 13, No. 3 (April 1979): 325–44. His case is forcefully argued in a later book, *Arabs in the Jewish State: Israel's Control of a National Minority* (London: University of Texas Press, 1980).

5. Conversation with senior Israeli official concerned with the waqf system in Israel, 1988.

Notes to Chapter 1

1. See his interesting analysis of the interplay of political influences over the control of the Khaski Sultan waqf in O. Peri, "The waqf as an instrument to increase and consolidate political power: The case of Khaski Sultan waqf in late eighteenth-century Ottoman Jerusalem," in *Studies in Islamic Society*, ed. by G. Gilbar and J. Warburgy (Haifa: Haifa University Press, 1984), pp. 47–62.

2. See for example "You will not attain piety until you expend of what you love," "The Family of Imran," Sura 3, v. 86, translation from A.J. Arberry, *The Koran Interpreted* (Oxford: Oxford University Press, 1964), p. 57; "True piety is this...to give of one's substance, however cherished, to kinsmen, and orphans, the needy, the traveller, the beggars, and to ransom the slave." From "The law," Sura 2, v. 173, *ibid*., pp. 22–23; or "Be kind to parents and the near kinsmen and to orphans and to the needy, and to the neighbor who is of kin, and to the neighbor who is a stranger, and to the companion at your side, and to the traveller...." "Women," Sura 4, v. 41, *ibid*., p. 78. Discussions as to the origins of the waqf institution have been extensive. See for example, discussions outlined in A.A. Abdullahi, "A New Definition of Waqf: A Basis on which the legal personality of Waqf is established," *Journal of Comparative Islamic Law* 7 (1978): 57–72; J.N.D. Anderson, "The Religious Element in Waqf Endowments," *Royal Central Asian Society Journal* 38, pt. 4 (October 1951): 292–99; M. Pacha Aly, "Le Waqf, est-il une institution religieuse?" *L'Egypte Contemporaine* 18 (1927): 385–402, and "Le Probleme de Waqf" *L'Egypte Contemporaine* 18 (1927): 501–24; M. Bekhit "De l'institution du waqf," translated by J. Cassis, *L'Egypte Contemporaine* 18 (1927): 403–31.

3. S. Vesey-Fitzgerald, *Muhammedan Law, an Abridgement* (London: Oxford University Press, 1931), p. 208; D. Pearl, *A Textbook of Muslim Law* (London: Croom Helm, 1979) p. 162. See also H. Khayat, "Waqfs in Palestine and Israel—From the Ottoman Reforms to the Present," Ph.D. thesis, American University, Washington D.C., 1962, p. 14.

4. J.B. Barron, *Mohammedan Wakfs in Palestine* (Jerusalem: Greek Convent Press, 1922), p. 14.

5. H.A.R. Gibb and H. Bowen, *Islamic Society and the West*, vols. I and II (London: Oxford University Press, 1957), p. 165; and Khayat, "Waqfs," pp. 21, 24.

6. See for example G. Furlonge, *Palestine is My Country: The Story of Musa Alami* (London: John Murray, 1969), pp. 24-25.

7. Pearl, *Muslim Law*, p. 163. See also Khayat, "Waqfs," pp. 49–50; and F.M. Goadby and M.J. Doukhan, *The Land Law of Palestine* (Tel Aviv: Shoshany's Co. Ltd., 1935), p. 71. Over the centuries a number of exceptions were made such as "exchange," *istibdal*, or varieties of long leases, such as *ijaratayn* and *hikr*. Baer has also conducted some research on *khulu*, which is an indemnity for carrying out repairs on a waqf property that may be passed on. See G. Baer, "The Dismemberment of Awqaf in Early 19th Century Jerusalem," *Asian and African Studies* 13, No. 3 (1979): 220–41.

8. Pearl, *Muslim Law*, p. 163.

9. Gibb and Bowen, *Islamic Society*, II, p. 175. A. Granott, *The Land System of Palestine: History and Structure* (London: Eyre and Spottiswoode, 1952), p. 129; Barron, *Mohammedan Wakfs*, p. 28. Some medieval jurists, notably those of the Hanafi school, permitted the revocation of a waqf, but once a qadi had delivered his *fatwa*. See Pearl, *Muslim Law*, p. 164. See also Abdullahi's views on these matters, "New Definition," p. 58.

10. See Baer's comments in G. Baer, "Jerusalem's Families of Notables and the Wakf in the Early 19th Century," in *Palestine in the Late Ottoman Period*, ed. by D. Kushner (Jerusalem: Yad Izhak Ben-Zvi Press, 1986), p. 113.

11. Khayat, "Waqfs," pp. 9–10; Goadby and Doukhan, *Land Law*, pp. 69–70; Barron, *Mohammedan Wakfs*, pp. 9, 17; Granott, *Land System*, p. 129; Gibb and Bowen, *Islamic Society*, pp. 174–75. These procedures also applied to the non-Muslim communities. See *ibid.*, p. 174.

12. Gibb and Bowen, *Islamic Society*, II, p. 171.

13. *Ibid.*, p. 173; Barron, *Mohammedan Wakfs*, p. 25. See also Pearl, *Muslim Law*, p. 165; and Vesey-Fitzgerald, *Muhammedan Law*, p. 221.

14. Gibb and Bowen, *Islamic Society*, II, pp. 167–68; Granott, *Land System*, p. 129.

15. Granott, *Land System*, p. 136; Khayat, "Waqfs," p. 70. See also Massignon, L., "Documents sur certains waqfs des lieux saints d'Islam," *Revue des Etudes Islamiques* (1951): pp. 73–120, who refers to a resolution passed at the International Muslim Congress held in 1929 in Jerusalem, affirming the waqf character of the Hijaz railway.

16. Pearl, *Muslim Law*, p. 162; Khayat, "Waqfs," p. 14; Baer, *Land Ownership*, p. 135.

17. Technically it was only the usufruct, or *tassaruf*, which *miri* tenants owned and thus converted into waqf; the land itself belonged to the Sultan. See Goadby and Doukhan, *Land Law*, pp. 75–77; and also Granott, *Land System*, p. 138. In special circumstances *miri* land could be converted into *mulk* but the Sultan's permission was required. The Ottoman Land Code of 1858, Article 121, encapsulated this provision. See A. Layish, "The Muslim Waqf in Israel," *Asian and African Studies* (Journal of the Israel Oriental Society) 2 (1966): 46 n.18; and Khayat "Waqfs," p. 78.

18. Barron, *Mohammedan Wakfs*, p. 22; Granott, *Land System*, p. 145; and Khayat, "Waqfs," pp. 24–25.

19. Barron, *Mohammedan Wakfs*, p. 22.

20. In Turkey, *dhurri* waqf was known as *zorri*. See Granott, *Land System*, p. 152; G. Baer, *Population and Society in the Arab East* (London: Routledge and Kegan Paul, 1964), pp. 141–42. See also Khayat, "Waqfs," p. 23; and Pearl, *Muslim Law*, p. 167.

21. Granott, *Land System*, p. 154.

22. See, for example Khoury, *Urban Notables*, p. 30.

23. Granott, *Land System*, p. 130.

24. Baer, *Population and Society*, pp. 141–42; Khayat, "Waqfs," p. 23. The Palestinian term for the *khayri* waqf is *ummy* but it is not used sufficiently widely to warrant its substitution for *khayri* which is more widely known.

25. Anderson, "Religious Element," p. 296; Granott, *Land System*, p. 153; see also Baer, *Land Ownership*, p. 155 on the problems reformers encountered when they tried to differentiate between the two. C. Cahen, "Reflexions sur le Waqf Ancien," *Studia Islamica* 14 (1961): 47–48. Cahen argues that waqf *khayri* was subsumed under waqf *dhurri*. As we have already mentioned the origins of the waqf system are disputed and some scholars even suggest a non-Islamic beginning. For examples see Gibb and Bowen, *Islamic Society*, II, pp. 165–66; and Khayat, "Waqfs," pp. 15–17. For later division into categories see Anderson, "Religious Element," p. 296; and Baer, *Land Ownership*, p. 155. For examples of *hadith* relating to waqf, see Bekhit, "De l'Institution," pp. 424–45.

26. Heyd, *Ottoman Documents*, pp. 146–50.

27. Data for this waqf was obtained from a series of translations of waqf documents held in the private library of Bernhard Dichter, a member of the Rotary Club of Acre. This information was then supplemented by interviews with various local inhabitants, including members of the Boards of Trustees for waqf property in Acre, the qadi of Acre, local municipal councilors and Palestinian Arab academics active in local affairs; see also M. Dumper, "The Palestinian Muslim Waqf: a Study in the Transformation of a Religious Symbol," M.Phil. dissertation, Lancaster University, 1983, pp. 29–31.

28. Interview with Shaykh Muhammad Hubayshi, qadi of Acre, 3 March 1981, cited in Dumper, "Transformation of a Religious Symbol," p. 30.

29. For the extent and income of waqf properties in Acre see Vaschitz, *The Arabs*, p. 296; and Barron, *Mohammedan Wakfs*, p. 63. See also Reiter's comments in Chapter Four.

30. See N. Makhoul, *Guide to Acre* (Jerusalem: Government of Palestine, Department of Antiquities, 1941), p. 51 and pp. 92–93.

31. Interview with qadi Hubayshi, 3 March 1981, cited in Dumper, "Transformation of a Religious Symbol," p. 30. Also in the north of Palestine was the waqf endowed for the benefit of the Shadhilyya Sufi order, which had a *takiya* north of Acre. Granott, *Land System*, pp. 144–145. The Shadaliyya are also known as the Yashruti and the *takiya* is mentioned in F. de Jong, "The Sufi Orders in Nineteenth and Twentieth Century Palestine," *Studia Islamica* 58 (1983): 160.

32. Barron refers to a list of waqf properties in Jerusalem which was lost, *Mohammedan Waqfs*, p. 56.

33. See comments made by A. Manna', "The Sijill as a Source for the Study of Palestine During the Ottoman Period, with Special Reference to the French Invasion," in *Palestine in the Late Ottoman Period*, ed. by D. Kushner (Jerusalem: Yad Izhak Ben-Zvi Press, 1986), p. 354.

34. S.B. Himadeh, *Economic Organization of Palestine* (Beirut: American Press, 1938), p. 90.

35. Baer, *Land Ownership*, pp. 148–52.

36. J. Hope-Simpson, *Palestine: Report on Immigration, Land Settlement and Development.* Command Paper 3686. H.M.S.O. London, 1930, p. 30.

37. *Ibid.*, p. 159.

38. Barron, *Mohammedan Wakfs*, p. 63, Appendix 1.

39. Y. Shimoni, *The Arabs of Palestine* [in Hebrew] (Tel Aviv, 1947), p. 86, cited in Kupferschmidt, *Supreme Muslim Council*, p. 109.

40. Y. Vashitz, *The Arabs in Palestine*, (Meravya, 1947), p. 296; cited in Kupferschmidt, *Supreme Muslim Council*, p. 111.

41. Granott, *Land System*, p. 142.

42. Figure obtained from Hope-Simpson, *Land Settlement*, p. 30; see also Granott, *Land System*, p. 142.

43. Granott, *Land System*, p. 142.

44. Shimoni, *The Arabs of Palestine*, p. 90, cited in Kupferschmidt, *Supreme Muslim Council*, p. 109; and Granott, *Land System*, p. 142.

45. Abrahamovitch, "Palestine Waqfs," p. 289.

46. Barron, *Mohammedan Wakfs*, p. 59; see also H. Luke and E. Keith-Roach, E., *The Handbook of Palestine and Transjordan* (London: Macmillan, 1934), p. 44.

47. Kupferschmidt, *Supreme Muslim Council*, p. 109.

48. For the total agricultural area of Palestine, see Hope-Simpson, *Land Settlement*, p. 159.

49. Granott, *Land System*, p. 142.

50. Granott, *Land System*, p. 154., that is, 40,000 dunums of agricultural land and much urban property, under Hope-Simpson's reckoning.

51. For further details see Dumper, "Muslim Institutions," pp. 63–67.

52. Barron, *Mohammedan Wakfs*, p. 46n; H. Gerber, *Ottoman Rule in Jerusalem, 1890–1914* (Berlin: Klaus Schwarz Verlag, 1985), pp. 183–94.

53. Gerber, *Ottoman Rule*, p. 193.

54. Barron, *Mohammedan Wakfs*, p. 57; Granott, *Land System*, p. 140; Kupferschmidt, *Supreme Muslim Council*, p. 116. The Supreme Muslim Council later claimed that sixty-eight waqfs had been expropriated by the Ottomans largely on this basis. See *Committee for Muslim Religious Affairs*, p. 21.

55. Barron, *Mohammedan Wakfs*, p. 56.

56. Khayat, "Waqfs," pp. 84–85.

57. Barron, *Mohammedan Wakfs*, p. 56; Granott, *Land System*, p. 140.

58. Barron, *Mohammedan Wakfs*, pp. 58–59; *Committee for Moslem Religious Affairs*, pp. 21–22.

59. Barron, *Mohammedan Wakfs*, pp. 43–45.

60. F.M. Goadby, "Religious Communities and Courts in Palestine," *Tulane Law Review* 8, No. 2 (1934): 225; R.H. Eisenman, *Islamic Law in Palestine and Israel: A History of the*

*Survival of the Tanzimat and the Shari`a in the British Mandate and the Jewish State* (Leiden: E.J. Brill, 1978), pp. 17–18; Khayat, "Waqfs," pp. 91–92. For a history of the incorporation of Islamic law into Mandate and Israeli legislation, and for the changes in shari`a law itself, see Eisenman, *Islamic Law*; and A. Layish, "Muslim Religious Jurisdiction in Israel," *Asian and African Studies* (Journal of the Israel Oriental Society) I (1965). For the political aspects of these changes see Y. Porath, *The Emergence of the Palestinian Arab National Movement, 1918–1929.* (London: Frank Cass, 1977), pp. 187–88 and 194–95. The authority to appoint muftis was also transferred to the Supreme Muslim Council; see *Committee for Moslem Religious Affairs*, p. 7.

61. See Barron, *Mohammedan Wakfs*, pp. 49–50 for details of the formation of the electoral college.

62. *Committee for Moslem Religious Affairs*, and Government of Palestine, *Order-in-Council*, 20 December 1921, cited in Barron, *Mohammedan Wakfs*, Appendix 2.

63. *Order-in-Council*, 20 December 1921, Article 8.1(a).

64. See for example *Order-in-Council*, Articles 7, 81(a), (b), 8.4.

65. The opposition was known as the *mu'aridun*, comprising mainly members and allies of the Nashashibi family; see D. Gilmour, *The Dispossessed* (London: Sidgwick and Jackson, 1980), p. 50; and Kupferschmidt, *Supreme Muslim Council*, pp. 66–72.

66. Kupferschmidt, *Supreme Muslim Council*, pp. 26–27.

67. *Ibid.*, p. 174.

68. *Order-in-Council*, Article 16.2.

69. See *Committee for Moslem Religious Affairs*, Appendix II; Kupferschmidt describes the Supreme Muslim Council's efforts in this direction in great detail in *Supreme Muslim Council*, pp. 117–28.

70. Granott, *Land System*, p. 147; Kupferschmidt, *Supreme Muslim Council*, p. 138. See also *Report by His Britannic Majesty's Government to the Council of the League of Nations on the administration of Palestine and Transjordan for the Year 1926*, Colonial Paper No. 26, p. 36; and *Report of 1928*, Colonial Paper No. 40, p. 57, cited in Khayat "Waqfs," p. 108.

71. Anyone who sold land to Jewish immigrants was to be regarded as "a traitor to his nation and country, and an enemy of God his Prophet and believers," cited in Y. Porath, *The Palestinian Arab National Movement, 1929–1939: From Riots to Rebellion* (London: Frank Cass, 1977), p. 95.

72. The traditional view of the hinterland of Jerusalem being *al-ard al-muadassah* helped in this respect. See Porath, *Emergence*, p. 5.

73. At one such meeting the Mufti was reported as having said: "The lands that were sold in this country contain the corpses of your fathers and forefathers, the martyrs and friends of the prophet and the early warriors. The daring of the criminals who sell it and act as brokers in the sale of it is a great crime which God and country do not pardon," *jami'a al-arabiyya*, 30 December 1934, cited in Porath, *National Movement*, p. 97. The Mufti also went on to say that if the land sales continued there would be no land left to bury the Muslim dead. There is a picture of one of the meetings organized in this campaign in B. Erskine, *Palestine of the Arabs* (London: Macmillan, 1937), p. 166. A report of the meeting is in *ibid.*, p. 163. As Porath notes, the term for broker, *simsar*, acquired derogatory connotations in Arabic; see Porath, *National Move-*

ment, p. 92. Violence was also directed against brokers, one of whom was killed in Jaffa. J. Reudy, "The Dynamics of Land Alienation," in *The Transformation of Palestine*, ed. by I. Abu-Lughod (Evanston: Northwestern University Press, 1971), p. 133.

74. See Baer, *Population*, pp. 148–49; and Porath, *National Movement*, pp. 95–96.

75. Eisenman, *Islamic Law*, p. 95; Porath, *National Movement*, pp. 97–98.

76. Cited in Porath, *Emergence*, p. 198.

77. Minutes prepared by Shuckburgh, 11 March 1926. Colonial Office 733/113. Cited in Porath, *Emergence*, p. 201.

78. See A.L. Tibawi, "Religious and Educational Administration in Palestine of the British Mandate," *World of Islam* 3, No. 1 (1953): 5. A former employee in the Department of Education of the Government of Palestine, Tibawi writes:

> The sort of nationalism that was stressed in Muslim schools in Palestine was simply an aspect of religion. Nationalism and religion were in fact forces working in close alliance and unison. Texts from the Qur'an or Hadith of the Prophet were expounded in such a way that the outcome might be presumed to come from a modern political treatise. Conversely, political events and current local affairs were so subtly represented in a religious garb, with an irresistible appeal to the minds of the young, that they gave the impression that the outcome was in accord with the wishes of the early caliphs or indeed of Muhammad himself.

79. Details of this incident can be found in Porath, *Emergence*, pp. 259–73; P. Mattar, *The Mufti of Jerusalem: al-Hajj Amim al-Husayni and the Palestinian National Movement* (New York: Columbia University Press, 1988), pp. 33–49. Mattar argues that the Mufti only became involved after the incident had already flared up and during the course of the whole affair was reluctant to antagonize the Government. See also A. Lesch, *Arab Politics in Palestine, 1917–1939: the Frustration of a Nationalist Movement* (London: Cornell University Press, 1979), pp. 208–12; M.E. Lundsten, "Wall Politics: Zionist and Palestinian Strategies in Jerusalem, 1928," *Journal of Palestine Studies* 8, No. 1 (Autumn 1978): 3–27.

80. Mattar, *The Mufti*, p. 48; Porath, *Emergence*, p. 271.

81. See Mattar, *The Mufti*, p. 77; and Porath, *National Movement*, p. 172 for a different interpretation of the Mufti's commitment to the strike.

82. These regulations referred specifically to the waqf system.

83. Lesch, *Arab Politics*, pp. 121–23; Porath, *National Movement*, p. 172.

84. Khayat, "Waqfs," p. 116.

Notes to Chapter 2

1. UN Resolution No. 181 (II), 29 November 1947, *UN Resolutions on Palestine, 1947–72* (Beirut: Institute of Palestine Studies, 1974).

2. See H. Cattan, *The Palestine Question* (London: Croom Helm, 1988), p. 39 for figures concerning land areas; see Appendix I to Report of Sub-Committee 2 to the Ad Hoc Commission on the Palestine Question, Official Records of the 2nd Session of the General Assembly, Doc. A/AC 14/32, p. 304, cited in Cattan, *Question*, p. 39 for population figures.

3. J. Abu-Lughod, "The Democratic Transformation of Palestine," in *Transformation*, ed. by Y. Abu-Lughod, pp. 153–61. Abu-Lughod demonstrates convincingly how she arrives at

these figures. See also Zureik, *The Palestinians in Israel: A Study in Internal Colonialism* (London: Routledge and Kegan Paul, 1979), pp. 108–109.

4. Statistical Abstracts of Israel, cited in S. Jiryis, *The Arabs in Israel*, Appendix, Table I, p. 289.

5. Zureik, *The Palestinians*, p. 109.

6. See L. Mayer and Pinkerfield, *Some Principal Muslim Religious Buildings in Israel* (Jerusalem: Government Printer, 1950), pp. 15–17.

7. *Ibid.*, pp. 14, 16.

8. For example the Great Mosque in Lydda, *ibid.*, pp. 30–31. In the Raslan mosque in Jaffa a group of Sephardi Jewish refugees had taken up residence (p. 34). Palestinian and Arab prisoners of war were also quartered in a mosque in Umm Khalid, near Netanya; see A. Magil, *Israel in Crisis* (New York: International Publishers, 1950), p. 61, cited in Khayat, "Waqfs," p. 132.

9. O. Stendel, *The Minorities in Israel* (Jerusalem: Israel Economist, 1973), p. 20; Layish, "Muslim Waqf," p. 42, n3.

10. The Shadhiliyya, or Yashruti, near Acre, and the Rahmaniyya in the village of Baqa' al-Gharbiyya in an area close to Tulkarm known as the Triangle. Khayat, "Waqfs," p. 136. For further details see also F. de Jong, "The Sufi Orders in 19th and 20th Century Palestine," *Studia Islamica* 58 (1983): 179, who writes that only the *zawiya* in Acre and Tarshiha remained to the Shadhiliyya order.

11. Mayer and Pinkerfield, *Religious Buildings*, p. 17.

12. Eisenman, *Islamic Law*, p. 224.

13. Layish, "Muslim Waqf," p. 42; Khayat, "Waqfs," pp. 130–33; Eisenman, *Islamic Law*, p. 224.

14. Eisenman, *Islamic Law*, pp. 159–60.

15. For a thorough study of the policies of the military government, see Jiryis, *The Arabs*, pp. 9–56.

16. Khayat, "Waqfs," pp. 134–36.

17. Affidavit made by S.Z. Kahana, Director-General of the Ministry of Religious Affairs, *Judgements of the Supreme Court*, HCJ 282/61. Mahmud al-Suruji et al. v. Minister of Religious Affairs and the Muslim Council, Acre.

18. Khayat, "Waqfs," pp. 155–57; Jiryis, *The Arabs*, p. 118.

19. UN Resolution No. 181 (II), 29 November 1947. Part 2, Article 4.

20. H.Z. Hirschberg, "be'ayot ha-shari`a bi-medinat yisra'el" [Islamic legal problems in the state of Israel] *Hamizrah Hehadash*, No. 2 (January 1950), pp. 97–108, cited in Jiryis, *The Arabs*, p. 198, n117. Kupferschmidt's interpretation of Hirschberg's arguments implies the opposite. See *Supreme Muslim Council*, p. 258.

21. *Knesset Debates*, 16 May 1949, p. 502, cited in Jiryis, *The Arabs*, p. 118.

22. Reudy, "Land Alienation," p. 135. Jews owned approximately 12 percent in Mandatory Palestine; 75 percent of that figure would come to 9 percent for Jewish ownership, but since most of the holdings were in the area that became Israel, 10 percent would be more accurate.

23. D. Peretz, *Israel and the Palestine Arabs* (Washington D.C.: Middle East Institute, 1958), p. 143.

24. Article 1. Absentee Property Law, 5710-1950, *Laws of the State of Israel* (Official English translation), vol. 4 (1949/50), p. 68; cited in Jiryis, *The Arabs*, p. 83, n34.

25. Peretz, *Palestine Arabs*, p. 152.

26. Absentee Property Law, Article 1.

27. Eisenman, *Islamic Law*, p. 225.

28. In contrast, as noted later in this chapter, the Custodian released ecclesiastical holdings to the Greek Orthodox Patriarchate and the Melkite Archdiocese. See Layish, "Muslim Waqfs," p. 60; Lustick, *Jewish State*, p. 134.

29. Development Authority (Transfer of Property) Law, 5710-1950, *Laws of the State of Israel*, vol. 4, cited in Jiryis, *The Arabs*, p. 78, n10.

30. The Development Authority was also given the authority to sell property to an organization responsible for Palestinian refugees inside Israel. Whether this organization was ever established is uncertain. See Jiryis, *The Arabs*, p. 78. See also W. Lehn and U. Davis, *The Jewish National Fund* (London: Kegan Paul International, 1988), p. 131.

31. Reudy, "Land Alienation," p. 138. See also S. Hadawi and W. Lehn, "Zionism and the Lands of Palestine," *The International Organization for the Elimination of All Forms of Racial Discrimination*, Paper no. 17, p. 13.

32. A. Granott, *Agrarian Reform and the Record of Israel* (London: Eyre and Spottiswoode, 1956), pp. 100–101.

33. Peretz, *Palestine Arabs*, pp. 178–81; Reudy, "Land Alienation," pp. 137–38; Jiryis, *The Arabs*, p. 78; Lustick, *Jewish State*, p. 99.

34. Peretz, *Palestine Arabs*, p. 181. Lehn and Davis made some more recent calculations that confirm this estimate, see *National Fund*, pp. 133–34.

35. See A. Granott (Granovsky), *Land Problems of Palestine* (New York: Bloch, 1940), pp. 2–3, for an exposition of this principle by the former Chairman of the Jewish National Fund; and Lehn and Davis, *National Fund*, pp. 58–59. See also *Report to the Israel Lands Administration, 1961–62* [in Hebrew] cited in Lehn and Davis, *National Fund*, pp. 113–14; see also Lustick, *Jewish State*, pp. 98–100.

36. See Lehn and Davis, *National Fund*, pp. 109–11.

37. *Laws of the State of Israel*, vol. 7 (1952/53), p. 43, cited in Jiryis, *The Arabs*, p. 96, n84.

38. Layish, "Muslim Waqfs," p. 58.

39. Jiryis, *The Arabs*, pp. 119–20. See also S. Hadawi, "Israel and the Arab Minority," *International Organization for the Elimination of All Forms of Racial Discrimination*, n.d., p. 35. From private conversations with a senior official concerned with Muslim religious affairs, it appears that the sales were in fact little more than a legal formality and that no real transfer of money took place.

40. Written question submitted to Dr. Nissim Dana, director of the Muslim and Druze division of the Ministry of Religious Affairs. Answer delivered verbally and in note form by his Secretary, Dalia Yenom, on 3 May 1989. (Hereafter referred to as Interview with Nissam Dana, 3 May 1985.)

41. Interview with Nissim Dana, 3 May 1989.

42. Lustick, *Jewish State*, p. 189.

43. Reudy, "Land Alienation," p. 135.

44. *Ha'Aretz*, 13 December 1965, cited in Jiryis, *The Arabs*, p. 119, n38.

45. Eisenman, *Islamic Law*, p. 229; Khayat, "Waqfs," p. 144; Layish "Muslim Waqf," p. 57.

46. "Israel's Kadis meet in Jerusalem," *Jerusalem Post*, 5 October 1954.

47. A summary of the report submitted to the Ministry in February 1949 is provided in Mayer and Pinkerfield, *Religious Buildings*, p. 14. See also Gideon Weigert, "Wakf Funds Will Aid Israel's Moslems," *Jerusalem Post*, 2 February 1951.

48. *Jerusalem Post*, 17 September 1949. The questioner was Seif al-Din el-Zu'bi of the Nazareth Democrats list. He was also one of the organizers of a conference on waqf issues held in Acre in November 1952.

49. See *State Controller's Report 1966/67*, 18 (1968), cited in Jiryis, *The Arabs*, pp. 118, 119, n37, n43. As noted earlier, Jiryis claims that in fact no money was paid over to the Custodian for these sales, and up to 1967 no record of payment had been made.

50. Interview with Nissim Dana, 3 May 1989.

51. Layish, "Muslim Waqf," p. 57.

52. One estimate for the annual income from waqf property for the first five years of the state of Israel is IL 45,000. See Gideon Weigert, "New Authority for Waqf Holdings," *Jerusalem Post*, 9 March 1954. However, an earlier article reports that the annual income is estimated at IL 180,000; see "Administration of Waqfs," *Jerusalem Post*, 17 December 1951.

53. Layish, "Muslim Waqfs," p. 58.

54. Weigert, "New Authority," *Jerusalem Post*, 9 March 1954; also articles in *Jerusalem Post* on 10 and 14 September 1954. See also Layish, "Muslim Waqf," pp. 42–43; Khayat, "Waqfs," p. 148; Eisenman, *Islamic Law*, p. 224. Interview with Shaykh Muhammed Hubayshi, qadi of Acre, 3 March 1981, who spoke of the lack of a seminary.

55. Layish, "Muslim Waqf," p. 58.

56. Eisenman, *Islamic Law*, pp. 169–70.

57. Mayer and Pinkerfield, *Religious Buildings*, p. 17. Khayat, "Waqfs," pp. 145–46; Eisenman, *Islamic Law*, p. 224, refers to 120 mosques.

58. *Laws of the State of Israel*, vol. 8 (1953/54), p. 4. See also Jiryis, *The Arabs*, p. 198.

59. Jiryis, *The Arabs*, p. 198; Layish, "Qadis and the Shari`a Law in Israel," *Asian and African Studies* (Journal of the Israel Oriental Society) 7 (1977): 238; N. Hawari, "The Moslem Community," *New Outlook* 5, No. 3 (March-April 1962): 77; Eisenman, *Islamic Law*, p. 169.

60. In reality they have taken it upon themselves to conduct exegesis. See Layish, "Qadis," pp. 238–40 and 269–70. Further examples can be found in A. Layish, *Women and Islamic Law in a Non-Muslim State* (Jerusalem: Israel Universities Press, 1975).

61. Eisenman, *Islamic Law*, p. 224.

62. Jiryis, *The Arabs*, p. 119; Eisenman, *Islamic Law*, p. 229; Khayat, "Waqfs," p. 146; Layish "Muslim Waqfs," p. 58.

63. Khayat, "Waqfs," p. 146.

64. See "Administration of Waqfs," *Jerusalem Post*, 17 December 1951, and untitled piece, *Jerusalem Post*, 25 February 1952.

65. *Knesset Debates*, 27 May 1957, p. 1981, speech by Zirach Werhaftig, Minister for Religious Affairs, cited in Jiryis, *The Arabs*, p. 119, n41.

66. Some concerted action was undertaken by the committees, such as preparing detailed proposals for the reform of the Israeli waqf administration that would enhance their powers. See Layish, "Muslim Waqfs," p. 59, n65.

67. Until 1972, the Arab Evangelical Episcopal Church (Anglican) was not registered as a religious community and had no officially recognized governing body in Israel. Its property was registered in the name of different communal organizations (Ottoman societies), clergymen, and individuals. The Custodian took over Anglican church property, since it was regarded as absentee. The chair of the Evangelical Episcopal Council managed the property as the agent of the Custodian. See Layish, "Muslim Waqf," pp. 60–61, n70; see also Khayat, "Waqfs," p. 138, n22, where it is incorrectly stated that the church had no waqfs at all; most of the waqfs are in the Galilee, West Bank and Jerusalem. Sixty percent of the church's waqf property continues to be in the hands of the Custodian, and the church derives no income from it. After official recognition was given in 1972, the Custodian still refused to release waqf property until a Board of Trustees was set up whose members it approved. Negotiations over the composition of the Board continued until 1987. Interview with Rev. Abu al-Assal, Vicar of Christchurch, Nazareth, 2 April 1980; Interview with Nabil Zu'mot, Property Department, Jerusalem Diocese, Episcopal Church in Jerusalem and the Middle East, 1 October 1988.

68. Layish, "Muslim Waqf," pp. 59–60.

69. Khayat, "Waqfs," p. 131.

70. Layish, "Muslim Waqf," p. 60.

71. Layish, "Muslim Waqfs," p. 60; Khayat, "Waqfs," p. 131. Some pressure was required before the release was completed. See "Bishop Hakim Asks Return of Property," *Jerusalem Post*, 2 August 1956.

72. In 1962 Israel contained three Greek Orthodox courts; two Greek Catholic; one Latin Catholic; one Maronite and one Armenian Orthodox courts. Khayat, "Waqfs," p. 153.

73. The Druze community was not legally recognized until 1957. Lustick, *Jewish State*, pp. 133–35 and 209–10. Jiryis, *The Arabs*, pp. 199–202; Layish, "Qadis," p. 238. For a detailed study on the Druze community in Israel, see G. Ben Dor, *The Druze in Israel* (Jerusalem: Magnes Press, 1979).

74. See *Ha'Aretz*, 21 April 1952, and *al-Mirsad*, 7 January 1960, cited in Eisenman, *Islamic Law*, p. 226. Tahir Fahum, a politically active lawyer from Nazareth, also wrote an article in which he defined the waqf system in the new situation as *mulk musha'*, private property of the Muslim community, asserting that it should be administered by Muslims. See article in *Da'wat al-Jabha*, 15 February 1960, cited in Layish, "Muslim Waqfs," p. 59, n64.

75. *Jerusalem Post*, 14 November 1954.

76. See reports on Knesset debates in *Jerusalem Post*, 19 December 1951 and 4 December 1952.

77. For example, as part of the campaign to secure the release of waqf property, a Christian lawyer, Elias Kusa, asserted in a letter to the *Jerusalem Post* that if the Israeli government was

to free these properties, Palestinians would be less dependent upon state support. *Jerusalem Post*, 12 March 1952, cited in Lustick, *Jewish State*, p. 16.

78. Khayat, "Waqfs," p. 155; Bentwich, *Israel, Resurgent* (London: Routledge and Kegan Paul, 1960), p. 180.

79. Jiryis, *The Arabs*, p. 120.

80. The first case, in 1952, was brought against the Custodian. The Supreme Court ruled that the shari'a court could not remove the Custodian from the management of a waqf and appoint a new *mutawalli.* The second case was brought in 1955 against the Minister of Development; by then, waqf property had been transferred by the Custodian to the Development Authority. The Supreme Court affirmed the right of the shari'a courts to appoint a *mutawalli* and voided the management rights of the Custodian. This particular property was retrieved. See "Law Report," *Jerusalem Post*, 22 May 1956; Layish, "Muslim Waqf," p. 55; Jiryis, *The Arabs*, p. 118.

81. See Layish, "Muslim Waqfs," p. 44, n9. Justice Landau declared, "I hesitate from ruling definitively on this question, which was not exhaustively argued in these hearings, but I incline to the view, that the 1937 Regulations exist independently, without being linked to the 1921 Order, although the commission replaced the body instituted by the 1921 Order." *Judgments of the Supreme Court*, HCJ No. 282/61.

82. Layish, *Women*, pp. 296–98, and "Muslim Waqfs," p. 48.

83. Layish, "Muslim Waqfs," p. 70, n101. It is also possible to endow *mulk* as waqf to prevent property being declared absentee if the heir to the property is an absentee. Layish, "Religious Jurisdiction," p. 75; Baer, *Population*, pp. 39–40.

Notes to Chapter 3

1. See A. Haidar, "The Different Levels of Palestinian Ethnicity" in *Ethnicity, Pluralism, and the State in the Middle East*, ed. by M. Esman and I. Rabinowich (London: Cornell University Press, 1988), p. 88, for negative impressions of Palestinians from the occupied territories by Palestinians inside Israel.

2. The Koenig Report, English translation in *Journal of Palestine Studies* 6, No. 1 (Autumn 1976): 191–92. Considerable research has now been carried out on this theme. See for example K. Nakleh, "Cultural Determinants of Palestinian Collective Identity: The Case of the Arabs in Israel," *New Outlook*, (October-November 1975): 31–40; Y. Peres and N. Yuval-Davis, "Some Observations on the National Identity of the Israeli Arab," *Human Relations* 22, No. 3 (1969).

3. In 2000 they are projected to make up 23 percent. *The West Bank and Gaza: Israeli's Options for Peace* (Tel Aviv: Jaffee Center for Strategic Studies, 1989), p. 207. Following the recent large-scale immigration of Soviet Jews, this estimate will have to be revised downwards.

4. Amendment No. 3 to the Absentee Property Law. Release and Use of Endowment Property Law 5725-1965, *Laws of the State of Israel*, vol. 19 (1964/1965), p. 55.

5. See Layish, "Muslim Waqf," pp. 61–63 for outline terms; see also Eisenman, *Islamic Law*, p. 230; and Jiryis, *The Arabs*, p. 120.

6. Absentee Property Law, Amendment to Section 4(ca) (1A) (1), 1(b).

7. Absentee Property Law, Section 29A (b).

8. Land Acquisition Law (Validation of Acts and Compensation), 5713-1953, *Laws of the State of Israel*, vol. 7 (1952/53), p. 43.

9. Moshe Sharett, a former foreign minister of the Israeli government, referred to this law as a "scandalous robbery," cited in Jiryis, *The Arabs*, pp. 120–21. It is also possible that the low take-up rate was because there were numerous beneficiaries, making the share of each so small that it would not have been worth their while to take it up. A similar result occurred in post-reform Gaza and Egypt. See Chapter Five.

10. Absentee Property Law (Third Amendment), Section 29G.

11. Jiryis, *The Arabs*, pp. 120–21; see also Lustick, *Jewish State*, p. 190.

12. Absentee Property Law (Third Amendment), Section 29E (1).

13. *Ibid.*, Section 29E (2).

14. Eisenman, *Islamic Law*, p. 333. By "later days," it is assumed that he is referring to the period after 1937, when the waqf was directly controlled by the High Commissioner.

15. *Ibid.*, p. 232.

16. Layish, "Muslim Waqf," pp. 67–68.

17. *Ibid.*

18. Absentee Property Law (Third Amendment), Sections 29A (b), 29E (2).

19. See Layish, "Religious Jurisdiction," pp. 58–79.

20. Khayat, "Waqfs," p. 178; for general accounts of waqf reform in the Arab world in the immediate post-1948 period, see J.N.D. Anderson, "Recent Developments in Shari`a Law, IX: The Waqf System," *The Muslim World* 42, pt. 4, (1952): 257–76; for a more comprehensive account of the same period, see G. Bussons de Janssens, "Les Wakfs dans l'Islam contemporain," *Revue des Etudes Islamiques* (1951): 1–72.

21. For a discussion of Jordanian reforms see Chapter Five.

22. G. Baer, "Waqf Reform in Egypt," *St. Antony's Papers* 4 (1958): 15. The abolition also applied with amendments to *mushtarak*. See also Khayat, "Waqfs" p. 175.

23. Baer, "Waqf Reform," p. 73.

24. *Ibid.*, p. 73.

25. *Ibid.*, p. 71.

26. *Ibid.*, p. 75. In return, *nazirs* received "Land Reform Bonds" and in this way capital held in land was transformed into productive investment.

27. Waqf *dhurri* remains under the jurisdiction of the shari'a courts in Israel; see also Eisenman, *Islamic Law*, pp. 232–33.

28. Jiryis, *The Arabs*, p. 121.

29. R. Kislev, "Where Are the Waqf Treasures?" *Ha'Aretz*, 13 January 1984.

30. *Ibid.*

31. Article by R. Kislev in *Ha'Aretz*, 11 January 1984; and Kislev, "Waqf Treasures," *Ha'Aretz*, 13 January 1984. See also Lustick, *Jewish State*, p. 190.

32. The secretary of the Acre Board of Trustees in 1980, for example, was employed in the finance office of the Acre Municipality. See Dumper, "Transformation of Religious Symbols," p. 168. See also M. Dumper, "Suppressing a National Identity," *Middle East International*, 21 January 1983.

33. Conversation with senior Israeli civil servant concerned with Palestinian issues in Israel, 1988.

34. See "al-Judhur" [Roots], the regular column by Fathi Furani, secretary of the Islamic Initiative Committee, in *al-Ittihad*. In the mid-1980s, the government tried to persuade more respected Muslim community leaders to sit on the boards, but because of their reputation these efforts had little success, particularly in those areas where the corruption was most blatant–Jaffa, Haifa, and Acre. (Personal communication by a senior Israeli civil servant dealing with Muslim affairs in Israel, 1988.) It would be interesting to discover what, if any, guarantees of independence and autonomy were offered.

35. Section 29D of the 1965 amendment states that the board[s] "shall prepare an annual budget of income and expenditure in connection with the property under its control. The budget shall require the approval of the Government and upon such approval being given shall bind the Boards of Trustees."

36. Kislev, "Waqf Treasures," *Ha'Aretz*, 13 January 1984. A similar situation existed with the Acre Board of Trustees; see Dumper, "Suppressing a National Identity," *Middle East international*, 21 January 1983. Interview with Walid Daoud, secretary to the Board of Trustees in Acre, 3 March 1981.

37. Before 1948 there were approximately 15,000 Palestinians in Acre; after the war only 3,500 remained. By 1971 the number had increased to nearly 10,000, as compared with 35,000 Israeli Jews. See E. Cohen, *Integration and Separation in the Planning of a Mixed Jewish-Arab City in Israel* (Jerusalem: Hebrew University, 1973), pp. 6–16 for an account of the political and social conditions of the Palestinians in the Old City of Acre; see also Lustick, *Jewish State*, p. 131.

38. Cohen, *Integration*, p. 8; see also A. Abdel-Fattah, "Acre's Never-Heard Facts," *al-Fajr* English weekly, 20–26 September 1981.

39. Interviews with Shaykh M. Hubayshi, qadi of Acre, 3 March 1981; Walid Daoud, secretary of the Board of Trustees in Acre, 3 March 1981; Muhammad Abu Shunub, councillor on the Acre Municipal Council, 31 January 1981; Ramsey Khoury, lawyer and former councillor on the Acre Municipal Council, 31 January 1981. These interviews are recounted in Dumper, "Transformation of Religious Symbols," pp. 167–71. See also Barron, *Mohammedan Wakfs*, p. 63, for information about the receipts from waqf rents and the amount of waqf property in the Acre district was that urban. Reiter, on the other hand, disputes the commonly held view of the extent of waqf property in the Old City by arguing that much of it was *hikr*, which had lapsed into *mulk* by the beginning of the Mandate period. See note 41.

40. Interview with Muhammad Abu Shunub, 31 January 1981; see also A. Abdel Fattah, "Acre," *al-Fajr* English weekly, 20–26 September 1981.

41. Y. Reiter, "Muslim Endowments in Acre," [in Hebrew] Master's thesis, Hebrew University, Jerusalem, 1986, p. 63 refers to one-third of Acre as being al-Jazzar *hikr*, which suggests that the total of waqf properties comprised more than one-third of Acre.

42. Y. Reiter, "An Assessment of the Reform in the Muslim Waqf Institution in Israel: Acre

as Case Study," draft of English summary of article in *Hamizrah Hehadash* (Quarterly of the Israel Oriental Society) 32 (1988).

43. N. Makhouly and C.N. Johns, *A Guide To Acre* (Jerusalem: Greek Convent Press, 1946).

44. A. Kesten, *Survey of Old Acre* (Tel Aviv: Government Printers, 1962).

45. Cohen, *Integration and Separation*, pp. 9–10. See also Lustick, *Jewish State*, p. 132; regarding plans in the Old City of Jerusalem, see Chapter Six. In the context of these two cities, it is interesting to read Gilsenan's comments on "museum-cities" as an imposition of the dominant class's conception of what is "traditional." See his *Recognising Islam*, p. 210.

46. Cohen, *Integration and Separation*, p. 8.

47. Interview with Mahmud Abu Shunub, 31 January 1981; Interview with Ahmad 'Ammar, resident of the Old City and organizer of Slum committee, 4 February 1981; see also *al-Fajr* English weekly, 20–26 September 1981.

48. *Al-Fajr* English weekly, 20–26 September 1981; "Makr Village is First Arab Development Project," *Jerusalem Post*, 26 November 1980.

49. According to informal conversation held with a senior Israeli civil servant concerned with these issues, the board took eighteen months to agree to the release of waqf property on these grounds and then did so reluctantly.

50. *Al-Fajr* English weekly, 20–26 September 1981.

51. Conversation with senior Israeli civil servant concerned with waqf affairs, 1988.

52. See F.M. Abel, "Jaffa au Moyen-Age," *Journal of the Palestine Oriental Society* 20: 6–28; and C. Comte de Volney, *Voyage en Syrie et en Egypte pendant les annees 1783, 1784, et 1785* (Paris: Jean Gaulmier, 1958), pp. 336–37, cited in Peters, *Jerusalem*, pp. 553–54 for a history of Jaffa and the role of pilgrimages during Middle Ages.

53. Barron, *Mohammedan Wakfs*, p. 63.

54. See discussion over different estimates in R. Kislev, "Slums from another world," *Ha'Aretz*, 30 December 1983.

55. Kislev, "Slums," *Ha'Aretz*, 30 December 1983.

56. Some of these premises sell alcohol, which has caused offense to many Muslims in Jaffa. For attempts to halt such sales, see I. Shehori, "Nationalist organizing—Arabs in Jaffa," *Ha'Aretz*, 28 May 1981.

57. Islamic Initiative Committee, *Islamic Waqfs in Israeli Mixed Cities*, 31 August 1988. See also A. Abdel Fattah, "Muslim Outcry Changes Tel Aviv's Mind," *al-Fajr* English weekly, 30 October–5 November 1981, which reports that al-Siksik mosque was also once a plastics factory.

58. Shehori, "Nationalist Organizing," *Ha'Aretz*, 28 May 1981.

59. Kislev, "Waqf Treasures," *Ha'Aretz*, 13 January 1984.

60. *Jerusalem Post*, 15 April 1973.

61. Kislev, "Waqf Treasures," *Ha'Aretz*, 13 January 1984.

62. The implications for the local politics of Jaffa are discussed in M. Shokeid, "Strategy and Change in the Arab Vote: Observations in a Mixed Town," in *The Elections in Israel—1973*, ed. by A. Asher (Jerusalem: Jerusalem Academic Press, 1975), pp. 145–66.

63. Kislev, "Waqf Treasures," *Ha'Aretz*, 13 January 1984.

64. *Ibid.* Similar difficulties were experienced by the Acre Board of Trustees.

65. The issue had actually first been raised in 1972 but it received little publicity. One member of the board, Zuhadi Siksik, tried to prevent the mosque being leased by obtaining a court injunction. (*Jerusalem Post*, 1 September 1972.) As is made clear below, the board was apparently able to overturn the injunction at a later stage and proceed with the lease.

66. Kislev, "Waqf Treasures," *Ha'Aretz*, 13 January 1984.

67. *Jerusalem Post*, 23 and 30 October 1981, 6 November 1981, and *al-Fajr* English weekly 30 October–5 November 1981.

68. Kislev, "Waqf Treasures," *Ha'Aretz*, 13 January 1984.

69. *Jerusalem Post*, 23 and 26 October 1981, 6 November 1981. A donation amounting to IS 45,000 was also made by the Mufti of Jerusalem. *Jerusalem Post*, 1 November 1981.

70. *Jerusalem Post*, 11 November 1981.

71. *Ibid.*

72. *Ibid.*

73. *Jerusalem Post*, 24 April 1987. The Awqaf Administration in Jerusalem also contributed JD 70,000, see R. Nijm, "`ard tarikhi masuri 'an 'am al-muqaddisa fi filastin w-al-'ajra'at alati tamat li-siyanat al-turath," *Fifth Conference on the Holy Places, Tradition and Culture in Palestine*, p. 35.

74. A. Abdel-Fattah, "Muslim Outcry," *al-Fajr* English weekly, 30 October–5 November 1981.

75. "Double Probe Set into Cemetery Sale," *Jerusalem Post*, 24 April 1987; and "Plan to Sell Cemetery in Jaffa Foiled," *Jerusalem Post*, 27 November 1987.

76. "Jaffa Murder Linked to Huge Land-sale Scandal," *Jerusalem Post*, 17 November 1988.

77. The exact figure for the Haifa administrative district, which is larger than the municipal boundaries, on 11 August 1948 was 8.4 percent; cited in Jiryis, *The Arabs*, p. 290.

78. Department of Occupied Territories Affairs (PLO), *al-awqaf al-islamiyya taht al-ihtilal: 1948–1985* [Muslim waqfs under the Occupation, 1948–1965] (Amman: Dar ibn Rashid, 1987), p. 31.

79. "Muslim Trust Files Claim to 46 Sites in Haifa," *Jerusalem Post*, 19 February 1979; see also Islamic Initiative Committee, *Israeli Mixed Cities*, p. 1.

80. See *Jerusalem Post*, 1 November 1943 and 10 February 1943.

81. *Jerusalem Post*, 14 October 1959; see also Islamic Initiative Committee, *Israeli Mixed Towns*.

82. The Shukris are a prominent Haifa family. Suhil Shukri was the son of a former mayor of Haifa during the Ottoman and Mandate periods. His brother, Zawja Samir Rifa'i, became a high-ranking minister in Jordan during the reign of King Abdullah. See F. Furani, *Difa' al-judhur* [Defense of Roots] (Nazareth: matba'at al-sha'biyyat, 1984), p. 25; see also *Jerusalem Post*, 19 February 1979.

83. *Jerusalem Post*, 19 February 1979.

84. *Jerusalem Post*, 15 October 1969.

85. *Jerusalem Post*, 10 March 1972.

86. "Fighting to Maintain Palestinian Presence," interview with Fathi Furani, secretary of the Islamic Initiative Committee, *al-Fajr* English weekly, 20–26 November 1981.

87. Islamic Initiative Committee, *Israeli Mixed Towns*; *al-Fajr* English weekly, 21-27 June 1981.

88. Interview with Fathi Furani, Secretary of Islamic Initiative Committee, 26 March 1981. See also *al-Fajr* English weekly, 21–27 June 1981; Islamic Initiative Committee, *Israeli Mixed Towns*, pp. 1–2.

89. *Al-Fajr* Arabic daily, 11 January 1984, cited in Furani, *Difa'*, p. 87.

90. Interview with Fathi Furani, 26 March 1981.

91. *Jerusalem Post*, 12 June 1981; *al-Fajr* English weekly, 14–20 June 1981.

92. Furani, *Difa'*, p. 28.

93. *Al-Fajr* English weekly, 14–20 June 1981. For details of the activities of the Islamic Initiative Committee during this period see Furani, *Difa'*, pp. 25ff.

94. *Jerusalem Post*, 12 June 1981.

95. A number of Palestinians were arrested when they tried to prevent the work of the bulldozers, and a sizeable police presence was required. *Jerusalem Post*, 12 June 1981; *al-Fajr* English weekly, 14–20 June 1981.

96. See *Kol Haifa* Hebrew weekly, 21 December 1984, cited in Islamic Initiative Committee, *Israeli Mixed Towns*; see also Furani, *Difa'*, pp. 78–80.

97. Unlike an earlier conference (which failed to elect a national committee), the 1961 Conference established a steering committee to press for Muslim demands. However, of the twenty-three members on the committee twenty belonged to the MAQI (Israeli communist) party, which at the time had little influence in the Muslim community in Israel. See J. Landau, *The Arabs in Israel: A Political Study* (London: Oxford University Press, 1969), p. 83. The steering committee soon dissolved. One result of the 1985 Conference was the establishment of a secretariat that was to commission reports on the state of waqf property in Israel; see S. al-Aboudi, "Conferees Seek Ways to Regain Islamic Land," *al-Fajr* English weekly, 13 September 1985. As yet there has been no sign of these reports.

98. *Jerusalem Post*, 17 April 1983.

99. *Al-Fajr* English weekly, 6–12 November 1981. Also interview with Rev. Shehadi, 30 November 1980.

100. Interview with Ramzi Khoury, 31 January 1981, lawyer, Communist councillor on the Acre municipal council. See also S. al-Aboudi, "Conferees Seek Ways," *al-Fajr* English weekly, 13 September 1985; and Furani, *Difa'*, p. 60, where he describes the part played by Tawfiq Tubi, Rakah member of Knesset, in the campaign to defend the Istiqlal cemetery.

101. *Information Bulletin of the Communist Party of Israel*, December 1980, p. 21.

102. *Al-Fajr* English weekly, 15 June 1984.

103. The author witnessed two such workcamps in Lydda and Kabul village in 1980.

104. See Ben Kaspit, "Khoumeinism, Ten Minutes from Tel Aviv," *Ma'ariv*, 14 Septem-

ber 1990, for examples of recent such calls.

105. See A. Abdel Fattah, "Muslim Outcry," *al-Fajr* English weekly, 30 October–5 November 1981 for comments by Shaykh Bassam, imam of the Mahmudiyya mosque in Jaffa.

106. Y. Reiter, "An Assessment of the Reform in the Muslim Waqf Institution in Israel: Acre as a Case Study," *Hamizrah Hehadash* 32 (1988).

107. Kislev, "Waqf Treasures," *Ha'Aretz*, 13 January 1984.

108. Government sensitivity to the waqf issue has been reflected in its evasiveness. According to one Israeli newspaper report, a survey of waqf property inside Israel commissioned in 1984 by the prime minister's Advisor for Arab Affairs, Arieh Gur, had disappeared from his office when Palestinian Knesset members made requests to see it. *Hadashot*, 1 June 1984, cited in *al-Fajr* English weekly, 15 June 1984.

Notes to Chapter 4

1. The shari'a courts played a similar role. Interview with Ibrahim Daqqaq, director of the East Jerusalem Arab Thought Forum, former chief engineer in the al-Aqsa restoration program, 9 October 1988.

2. E. Mogannam, "Developments in the Legal System of Jordan," *Middle East Journal* 6 (1952): 196–97.

3. Some 350,000 Palestinians were cut off from their homes in Israel. For further details of demographic impact of refugees on the West Bank, see D. Peretz, *The West Bank: History, Politics, Society and Economy* (Boulder: Westview Press, 1986), pp. 31–33.

4. Busson de Jansens, "Les Wakfs," p. 38.

5. Article 61, cited in *ibid.*, p. 38.

6. Law No. 25, 1946, Law of Muslim Waqfs, Art. 3, cited in Busson de Janssens, "Les Wakfs," p. 64.

7. Article 8, cited in *ibid.*, p. 65.

8. Busson de Janssens, "Les Wakfs," p. 40.

9. *Ibid.*, p. 39.

10. *Ibid.*, p. 40.

11. This view is shared by Kupferschmidt, *Supreme Muslim Council*, p. 258.

12. Kupferschmidt, *Supreme Muslim Council*, p. 257.

13. J.P. Richardson, *The West Bank: A Portrait* (Washington, D.C.: Middle East Institute, 1984), p. 45; and Peretz, *West Bank*, p. 37; see also A. Cohen, *Political Parties in the West Bank under the Jordanian Regime, 1949–1967* (London: Cornell University Press, 1982), p. 148.

14. A. Layish, "Mahkama," *Encyclopaedia Islamica* (forthcoming), p. 31.

15. Kupferschmidt, *Supreme Muslim Council*, p. 258.

16. Interview with Hasan Tahbub, former director-general of the Awqaf Administration (1960–1983), 4 October 1988.

17. D. Farhi, "ha-mo'atza ha-muslemit be-mizrah yerushalayim u-vi-yehuda ve-shomron

me'az milhemet sheshet ha-yamin" [The Muslim Council in East Jerusalem and in Judea and Samaria since the Six Day War, unofficial translation] *Hamizrah Hehadash* [The New East] 28 (1979): 4.

18. Kupferschmidt, *Supreme Muslim Council*, p. 258.

19. Layish, "Mahkama," p. 31; Kupferschmidt, *Supreme Muslim Council*, p. 258.

20. This was partly at the request of local employees so that their positions, salaries and pensions would fall in line with other governmental employees. Interview with Hasan Tahbub, 2 May 1989.

21. Interview with Hasan Tahbub, 4 October 1988.

22. See Eisenman, *Islamic Law*, p. 95; see also Porath, *National Movement*, pp. 97–98; *Official Gazette* 3, Law No. 41 (Amman 1953).

23. Interview with Hasan Tahbub, 14 November 1985.

24. Interview with Hasan Tahbub, 11 October 1988; Interview with 'Ala al-Din al-Bakri, lawyer with shari`a court cases, 10 September 1988.

25. Interview with Hasan Tahbub, 4 October 1988.

26. *Ibid.*

27. *Official Gazette*, Law No 26, (Amman 1966).

28. *Ibid.*, Regulation No. 142.

29. *Ibid.*, Article 8, iii–v.

30. See for example, *Ibid.*, Article 9, iii, iv, and vi.

31. *Ibid.*, Article 47.

32. M. Ma'oz, *Palestinian Leadership on the West Bank* (London: Frank Cass, 1984), pp. 9–11; See also Cohen, *Political Parties*, for a thorough description and analysis of political opposition to the Hashemite monarchy.

33. There were some exceptions. Dr. Husayn Fakhri al-Khalidi, "supervisor of the holy sites," resigned in 1952 in opposition to the centralizing policies accelerated by King Hussein following his father's assassination in 1951. *Filastin*, 14 August 1952, cited in N. Sofer, "The Political Status of Jerusalem in the Hashemite Kingdom of Jordan, 1948–1967," in *Palestine and Israel in the 19th and 20th Centuries*, ed. by E. Kedourie and S.G. Haim (London: Frank Cass, 1982), p. 270. Opposition from *hizb al-tahrir* and the Muslim Brotherhood was limited to criticism of specific policies; it did not extend to calls for the overthrow of the regime. See Ma'oz, *Palestinian Leadership*, p. 9; Cohen, *Political Parties*, pp. 147–48, regarding the Muslim Brotherhood.

34. The only study on waqf in the Gaza Strip that I was able to find is M. Kafrawi, "al-waqfiyya dar`a'sha wa makram abu khadr" [The Waqfiyya of 'A'sha and Makram Abu Khadr Family], *Hoda al-Islam* (September 1985): 26–31.

35. Similar difficulties are reported in S. Roy, "The Gaza Strip: Critical Effects of the Occupation," *Arab Studies Quarterly* 10, No. 1 (Winter 1988): 61–63; see also S. Graham-Brown, "The Economic Consequences of the Occupation" in *Occupation: Israel over Palestine*, ed. by N. Aruri (London: Zed Press, 1984), p. 168; and B. Van Arkadie, *Benefits and Burdens: A Report on the West Bank and Gaza Strip Economics since 1967* (New York: Carnegie Endowment for International Peace, 1977).

36. Interview with Farraj Sarraf, lawyer to the Gaza Strip office of the *ma'mur al-awqaf*, 27 September 1988.

37. Order-in-Council, *op. cit.* Arts. 10 - 14. See also Barron, *Mohammedan Wakfs*, p. 51.

38. See details of waqfiyya in Kafrawi, "abu khadr." See also *Jerusalem Post*, 29 January 1943, which specifies 3,000 dunums.

39. Kupferschmidt, *Supreme Muslim Council*, p. 127.

40. For shops reference see Massignon, "Documents," p. 117; for al-Huda waqf, see Barron, *Mohammedan Wakfs*, p. 62.

41. Kupferschmidt, *Supreme Muslim Council*, p. 112 mentions that the Tamimi waqf has property in Gaza, but the sources he gives do not actually mention it. See Massignon, "Documents," pp. 79–81; and Barron, *Mohammedan Wakfs*, p. 62.

42. *Civil Appeal*, No 108/41.

43. Interview with Farraj Sarraf, 27 September 1988.

44. Barron, *Mohammedan Wakfs*, p. 63.

45. Interviews. See also Kupferschmidt, *Supreme Muslim Council*, pp. 142, 144.

46. Interviews.

47. See Roy, "Gaza Strip," pp. 64–65 for details of early days of Egyptian administration.

48. Shlaim makes no mention of the waqf system in his recent article. See A. Shlaim, "The All-Palestine Government," *Journal of Palestine Studies* 20, No. 1 (Autumn 1991); see also Ma'oz, *Palestinian Leadership*, p. 8. J. Migdal, *Palestinian Society and Politics* (Princeton, N.J.: Princeton University Press, 1980) mentions on p. 36 that the All-Palestine Government existed only on paper.

49. Interview with Farraj Sarraf, 27 September 1988.

50. Figures from Roy, "Gaza Strip," p. 63.

51. Interviews.

52. Military Order No. 297, published in Gaza 3 March 1954, cited in *Majmu'at al-Qawanin al-Filastiniyya*, p. 711. See also Article 2. For Egyptian reforms see G. Baer, "Waqf Reform," pp. 71–73. See also discussion in Chapter Four.

53. *Ibid.*, Articles 3–4.

54. Interview with Farraj Sarraf, 27 September 1988. Similar problems in Egypt are outlined in Baer, "Waqf Reform," p. 72.

55. For details of this period see Roy, "Gaza Strip," pp. 64–65; A. Lesch, "The Gaza Strip: Heading Toward a Dead End," *UFSI Reports*, part 1, No. 10 (1984): 3–5.

56. Military Order 564, *Majmu'at al-Qawanin al-Filastiniyya*, pp. 716–17.

57. Interviews.

58. Interviews. Specifically, interview with Farraj Sarraf, 27 September 1988.

59. Examples of this perspective can be found in Peretz, *West Bank*, pp. 51–52; Richardson, *Portrait*, pp. 111–17; Ma'oz, *Palestinian Leadership*, pp. 188–98; and G. Aronson, *Creating Facts: Israel, Palestinians and the West Bank* (Washington, D.C.: Institute for Palestine Studies, 1987), pp. 59–61.

60. See Roy, "Gaza Strip," pp. 66–67; Lesch, "Dead End," p. 6.

61. No attempt was made to annex the West Bank, other than those parts incorporated into an enlarged Jerusalem, but some exploratory steps were taken in the Gaza Strip, hence the strong resistance encountered by the Israeli army. See Roy, "Gaza Strip," p. 66, and Lesch, "Dead End," pp. 5–6.

62. R. Shehadi, *The West Bank and the Rule of Law* (New York: International Commission of Jurists and Law in the Service of Man, 1980), p. 10; A. Gerson, *Israel, the West Bank and International Law* (London: Frank Cass, 1978), pp. 78–82. See also a clear exposition of the juridical issues in Cohen, *Human Rights*, pp. 37–56.

63. See for example the section in Shehadi, *Rule of Law*.

64. The Civil Administration, Judea and Samaria, *Annual Report, 1985*, p. 38.

65. A. Layish, "Mahkama," p. 32.

66. Interview with Hasan Tahbub, 14 November 1985. However they did agree to accept IL 25,000 (US $8,000) for salaries for their employees in June 1967. *Jerusalem Post*, 6 July 1967 and 29 August 1967, cited in Lesch, p. 43. According to Tahbub, banks were closed and this was a temporary loan. It was returned with a receipt for repayment within twenty days. Interview, 3 May 1989.

67. M. Benvenisti, *Jerusalem: The Torn City* (Minneapolis: Israeltypset Ltd. and University of Minneapolis, 1976), p. 287.

68. Another effect of this transfer of responsibility was goodwill; the Muslim community appreciated that gestures were being made to reassure it of Israel's good intentions. After some disagreement over the acceptance of censorship, permission was given to broadcast live the customary Friday sermon from al-Aqsa mosque on Israel radio in an uncensored form. See A. Lesch, *Israel's Occupation of the West Bank: The First Two Years* (Santa Monica, CA: RAND Advanced Research Project Agency, 1970), pp. 42–43. See also Benvenisti, *Torn City*, p. 278. To mark Ramadan the Israeli government also released 193 prisoners and distributed IL 4,000 (US $1,150) to poor families at the 'Id al-Fitr. In February 1968 two busloads of pilgrims from Hebron were permitted to leave on a 2-month permit for Mecca. Lesch, *First Two Years*, p. 43.

69. See article by Shaykh Abd al-Hamid al-Sa'ih, "al-hay'at al-islamiyya l-'ulya fi al-quds" [The Higher Islamic Board in Jerusalem], *al-Quds al-Sharif*, No. 1 (April 1985): 9–14, reference.

70. I. Daqqaq, "Back to Square One: A Study in the Re-emergence of the Palestinian identity in the West Bank, 1967-1980," in *Palestinians over the Green Line*, ed. by A. Sch_lch (London: Ithaca Press, 1983), p. 70.

71. Daqqaq, "Square One," p.70. Tahbub says there were 25 members of the board, but 2 could not attend (Interview, 14 November 1985); Benvenisti, *Torn City*, p. 284, says 22 attended. See also A.H. al-Sa`ih, "al-hay`at," p. 11. They included Anwar Khatib, Jordanian governor of Jerusalem; Anwar Nusaybeh, former Jordanian minister of defence; Ruhi al-Khatib, mayor of Arab Jerusalem; two members of the Upper House and six from the Lower House of the Jordanian parliament, six lawyers, two members of the Arab Higher Committee for Palestine; the chairman of the Jerusalem Arab Chamber of Commerce; and three members of the Arab Municipal Council.

72. *Resistance of the Western Bank of Jordan to Israeli Occupation* (Beirut: Institute for Palestine Studies, 1967), p. 22.

73. Interview with Hasan Tahbub, 14 November 1985. Daqqaq notes that this first letter was sent on Hashemite Kingdom of Jordan notepaper. Daqqaq, "Square One," p. 70. The full text of this letter can be found in *Resistance*, pp. 11–14. Part of it can be found in Benvenisti, *Torn City*, pp. 284–85.

74. Daqqaq, "Square One," p. 72; Layish, "Mahkama," pp. 32–33.

75. Daqqaq, "Square One," p. 70.

76. For a detailed discussion of these developments, see Ma'oz, *Palestinian Leadership*, Chapter Five onward. See also E. Sahliyeh, *In Search of Leadership: West Bank Politics Since 1967* (Washington, D.C.: Brookings Institute, 1988), p. 24.

77. Interview with Hasan Tahbub, 3 May 1989.

78. Article 49. See also Article 6 (A, B), Charter of the Nuremberg Military Tribunal.

79. *Al-awqaf al-islamiyya, bayan, 1967–76* (Jerusalem: *al-awqaf al-islamiyya*, n.d.), p. 6. (Refered to as *bayan* I.)

80. Daqqaq, "Square One," p. 72.

81. Interview with Hasan Tahbub, 3 May 1989; Daqqaq, "Square One," p. 72. See also Farhi, "Muslim Council," pp. 7f who implies that this step was also taken to assuage the "rebelliousness" of regional religious leaders.

82. Daqqaq, "Square One," p. 72.

83. Interview with Shaykh Abd al-Hamid al-Sa'ih, 1989; Daqqaq, "Square One," p. 72. As regards the status of the shari'a court of appeal and the Awqaf Administration under Jordanian law, the relevant law (Shari'a Court of Appeal No. 20/1977, Art.2) was finally amended to provide for a shari'a court of appeal in Jerusalem, although the *qadi al-quda'* retained his title as acting *qadi al-quda'* until 1988.

84. Fees were collected in Jordanian dinars, which were sent to the *qadi al-quda'*s office in Amman. Farhi states that a separate account for court fees was set up in the summer of 1969 to give the courts some independence from Amman. Farhi, "Muslim Council," pp. 16ff.

85. Interview with Hasan Tahbub, 14 November 1985.

86. *Ibid.*

87. Daqqaq, "Square One," p. 73.

88. *Bayan* I, p. 3.

89. *'Idarat al-awqaf al-islamiyya al-'ama, bayan al-awqaf al-islamiyya fi al-dafa al-gharbiyya* (Jerusalem: *da'ira al-awqaf al-islamiyya*, n.d.), pp. 8–9. (Refered to as *bayan* II).

90. Despite the annexation of East Jerusalem by the Israeli government the headquarters of the Awqaf Administration remained in the old Supreme Muslim Council premises in the Madrassa Manjakiyya beside the Haram al-Sharif. The offices were renovated and partitioned into smaller units to accommodate the increase in staff over the years. Some offices such as the Department of Islamic Archaeology and the archival section of the Department for the Revival of Tradition and the Islamic Sciences are located outside the Haram area in waqf properties in other parts of the city. In general most of the departments of the Awqaf Administration are located in renovated monuments and historical buildings in or around the Haram compound.

91. *Bayan* II, p. 162.

92. Interview with Yunis Abu Hamdiyya, assistant to the director of the Department of Waqf Property, 4 October 1988.

93. Interview with Hasan Tahbub, 11 January 1986.

94. With regard to Christian holy sites, the Israeli government was more responsive to pressures from Western governments. See W. Zander, *Israel and the Holy Places of Christendom* (London: Weidenfield and Nicholson, 1971) for Israeli attempts to reassure Christian denominations.

95. The Holy Places Law states that:

> 1) The Holy Places shall be protected from desecration and any other violation and from anything likely to violate the freedom of access of the members of the different religions to the places sacred to them or their feelings with regard to those places. 2.a) Whosoever desecrates or otherwise violates a Holy Place shall be liable to imprisonment for a term of seven years. b) Any person who does anything likely to impair freedom of access to a Holy Place or to hurt the feelings of anyone to whom a place is sacred, shall be liable to imprisonment for a term of five years.

Under Israeli civil law all religious communities enjoy autonomous and equal status, see E. R. Cohen, *Human Rights in the Israeli-occupied territories* (Manchester: Manchester University Press, 1985), p. 209. For Military Order see Order Concerning the Protection of Holy Places (No. 66-1967), cited in Cohen, *Human Rights*, p. 269, n133.

96. No. 327 Concerning Protection of Holy Places in 1969 and No. 807 Concerning Religious Services in 1979. Military Orders Nos. 246 Concerning Antiquities Law, 1967, and 246 Concerning Inspectors of Antiquities, 1968.

97. Lesch, *First Two Years*, p. 39.

98. *Jerusalem Post*, 28 November 1967, and 1 October 1968, cited in Lesch, *First Two Years*, p. 39. See also Cohen, *Human Rights*, p. 215.

99. *Jerusalem Post*, 13 October 1968, cited in Lesch, *First Two Years*, p. 44. See also Cohen, *Human Rights*, p. 215.

100. Cohen, *Human Rights*, p. 215.

101. A. Lesch, *Political Perceptions of the Palestinians on the West Bank and the Gaza Strip* (Washington D.C.: The Middle East Institute, 1980) Special Study No. 3, p. 80. See also Cohen, *Human Rights*, pp. 215–16.

102. Lesch, *Political Perceptions*, p. 16.

103. *Bayan* II, p. 131.

104. *Bayan* I, p. 14.

105. *Ibid.*

106. Interview with Hasan Tahbub, 14 November 1985.

107. *Bayan* I, p. 13; *bayan* II, p. 131. No figures are given in either of the *bayan* as to what proportion of the income from West Bank sources is made up from rents, but it can be assumed that it forms the greater part. Nonetheless, despite the large quantities of land and property in the major towns of the West Bank that were endowed, the income from them is much less than their potential level. This is partly because many rents are frozen at their 1967 levels, as an expression of not recognizing the occupation, and partly because the Awqaf does not wish to

impose further hardships on the population under occupation. It could also be a means of securing the support of a substantial segment of the population. See Interview with Hasan Tahbub, 14 November 1985. As a consequence, by the 1980s, inflation had reduced many waqf rents to a nominal level providing little or no real income to the Awqaf Administration. In the early part of the occupation there was also a trend in the nonpayment of rents, since the Israeli controlled *nizami* (civil) courts did not enforce the decisions of the Jordanian-controlled shari'a courts. See Farhi, "Muslim Council," pp. 14–15. Furthermore, since there were no means to enforce payment of rents, some tenants began to deliberately default. However, when legal action was taken against defaulters visiting the East Bank, this trend was by and large reversed; Benvenisti, *Torn City*, p. 298.

108. *Hikr* usually refers to land rented out to tenants for long leases on the payment of an initial lump sum. Again, there are no figures given for this source of income but one can assume that since the leases tend to be for over twenty years and mainly for agricultural land, the income is extremely small. The main areas where the Awqaf Administration has *hikr* are in the Jerusalem, Nablus, Hebron, Bethlehem, and Bayt Jala regions; see *bayan* I, p. 13. This source is not mentioned in *bayan* II but may still be included under waqf rents (see p. 131).

109. When the Awqaf Administration has full management responsibilities it is entitled to 10 percent of the waqf's income; when it shares the management with the family it is entitled to 5 percent of the waqf's income. *Bayan* I, p. 13; also mentioned briefly in *bayan* II, p. 131. These arrangements are prevalent in Jerusalem, Nablus, Jenin, and Hebron. No exact figures are available but since profits for *dhurri* waqfs are largely from rented urban property, which are low, the proportion of the total income made up from these management fees is quite likely to be extremely low, too.

110. The only specific figures mentioned are in 1977 and 1982 when JD 149,712 and JD 102,440 were collected, respectively (*bayan* II, p. 141). In 1977 this constituted 39 percent of the Awqaf Administration's income and in 1982 it came to 28 percent and is therefore an extremely important source of income. (It is, however, subject to wide fluctuations, as the 1982 figure indicates, presumably a result of the drop in tourist trade following Israel's invasion of Lebanon.)

111. *Bayan* I, p. 14; *bayan* II, p. 141. No figures given in either *bayan* and it is difficult to estimate amounts involved.

112. The Jordanian government continued the practice of paying the annual grant even though it was not able to collect the agricultural tax because of the occupation. The first *bayan* states (p. 14) that the amounts were almost insignificant barely amounting to 5 percent of the Awqaf Administration's income.

113. *Bayan* I. A misprint on p. 14 refers to 22.2 percent. In 1967 the average wage of a mosque official was between JD 5 and JD 7 month; in 1976 it had risen to JD 35 a month. Thus, total salaries in 1967 amounted to JD 80,000; in 1975, they were JD 440,000. The second *bayan* gives no figures for total salaries, but since the number of employees almost doubled between 1977 and 1982, one can expect that the high proportion of the total expenditure spent on wages (i.e., 60 percent) was maintained. If 60 percent was the proportion, then one can deduce that in 1982 JD 1,384,491 were spent on wages.

114. *Ibid.*, p. 14.

115. The only figure available for construction work in this category is the 1974 figure of JD 45,747, or 9.5 percent of the total for that year. No indication is given whether this was a

typical amount. According to the former director-general, Hasan Tahbub, the amount was usually slightly more. (See Interview with Hasan Tahbub, 17 April 1989.) Such an assessment is borne out by the development projects undertaken by the Awqaf Administration in the late 1970s and 1980s.

116. By looking at the work of the Department of Construction and Repair (*al-'ansha'at w-al-siyana*, or popularly *al-handisa*) from 1967 onwards in the Nablus *mudiriyya* it is possible to obtain an idea of the nature of the Awqaf's work in this field. During the period covered by the first *bayan* (1967–76) the work of this department was relatively low key. It was responsible for the construction of fourteen warehouses (*makhazan*) in Qalqiliya and Tulkarm and ten shops and offices in Nablus itself providing a revenue of over JD 8,000 per year. In addition the *mudiriyya* exchanged a property belonging to the Nimr waqf under its management for a piece of building land on which it built some warehouses, for which it received JD 20,378 per year. Other work during this period included general repairs and the introduction of amplification into a number of mosques. The period covered by the second *bayan* (1977–82) indicates a stepping-up of activity, greater organization in the form of systematic construction projects and the participation of the Awqaf Administration in joint projects with other Islamic associations. For example, of the thirty-seven mosques built, thirty-two were in conjunction with other bodies. Similarly, two office complexes, and two out of the seven warehouses or shop projects that were completed were built in conjunction with other bodies. Other projects included the restoration of four mosques and two office or general utility buildings and the repair of five mosques, three warehouses and shops, and three offices and general utility buildings. *Bayan* II, pp. 58, 66, 72, 79, 84–85, 93.

117. Since these projects took place in the mid-1980s they do not appear in either of the *bayan* but information can be gleaned from other sources.

118. Shehadeh, Husan Mahmud, "al-zaria'at fi al-awqaf, limadha?" *Hoda al-Islam* (*rabia' al-awwal*/1984): 47–58.

119. Table, *Planting on Waqf Land*, produced by the Department of Waqf Land, Awqaf Administration, Jerusalem, 1987.

120. Repeated requests for comprehensive data were made to the central Awqaf Administration offices in Jerusalem but without success. It does appear that no centralized collection of information on the Awqaf Administration's *khayri* and *mulhaq* waqfs is publicly available. A pamphlet issued by the Department for the Revival of Tradition and Islamic Sciences on the Muslim waqf in Palestine, an official publication on this matter, carries no figures. See Department for the Revival of Tradition and Islamic Sciences, *al-awqaf al-Islamiyya fi filastin* (Jerusalem: Awqaf Administration and Islamic Affairs, 1984) Pamphlet No. 2. The same department manages an archive that contains many records and documents and from which an assessment could be made, but as yet no research has been carried out or been published. Some approximate figures were obtained from the Jerusalem *mudiriyya*, but not for other *mudiriyya*. Getting these figures would require extensive research into the files of each waqf province waqf office, which are not open to the public at this stage. Even less information is available on *dhurri* waqfs. Again, approximate figures have been obtained for the Old City of Jerusalem by interviewing a number of *mutawalli*s, but a West Bank survey would be beyond the scope of this book.

121. The total area of the West Bank is approximately 5,878 square kilometers or six million *dunums*; cited in Cohen, *Human Rights*, pp. 36, 152–53.

122. R. Shehadeh, *Occupier's Law: Israel and the West Bank* (Washington D.C.: Institute

for Palestine Studies, 1985), p. 37. For more detailed figures see M. Benvenisti, *The West Bank Data Project: A Survey of Israel's Policies* (Washington D.C.: American Enterprise Institute, 1984), pp. 23, 31.

123. Benvenisti, *Survey of Israel's Policies*, p. 30; see also Shehadeh, *Occupier's Law*, pp. 34–36; and Cohen, *Human Rights*, p. 154.

124. The practice of declaring unregistered land as state land was adopted by the Israeli military government after Palestinian landowners successfully contested the construction of an Israeli settlement, Elon Moreh, on privately-owned land near Nablus. See I. Lustick, "Israel and the West Bank after Elon Moreh: The Mechanics of *de facto* Annexation," *Middle East Journal* 35, No. 4 (Autumn 1981): 557–77. In court the Israeli government used its usually decisive argument that the settlement was necessary on security grounds. This argument previously had convinced the court to allow the Israeli military government to acquire areas for establishing army camps and training grounds and to set up a network of civilian settlements deemed necessary on security grounds; 30,000 dunums in the Jordan Valley had been confiscated on these grounds. See Cohen, *Human Rights*, p. 152; also J. Kuttab, "The Acquisition of Property in the West Bank," *Le Monde Diplomatique*, August 1983. These confiscations included waqf land around Jiftlik. (Interviews with Hasan Tahbub, 4 October 1988; Isam Anani, legal advisor to the Awqaf Administration, 30 July 1985; and Ala' al-Din al-Bakri, lawyer practicing in shari'a courts, 10 September 1988.) In the Elon Moreh case, however, this latter argument had been challenged by defense witnesses, including former senior reserve officers in the Israeli army. The Israeli government therefore sought other ways to acquire land and chose to interpret the Ottoman Land codes it inherited from the Jordanian government in a manner that would allow it to clear land that was legitimately its property.

125. See Shehadeh, *Occupier's Law*, pp. 22–33.

126. Shehadeh, *Occupier's Law*, pp. 25–27; see also Cohen, *Human Rights*, pp. 152–53.

127. See Goadby and Doukhan, *Land Law*, pp. 75–79, for an exposition of the different types of *miri mawquf*.

128. Interview with Hasan Tahbub, 2 October 1988.

129. Interview with Isam Anani, 30 July 1985.

130. Interview with Anwar Khatib, former Jordanian governor of the district of Jerusalem and *mutawalli* of the Tamimi waqf, 1 October 1988. See also Judgment of Special Tribunal held in Jerusalem, 2 February 1927 which ruled in favor of the Tamimi's family claim that its waqf was waqf *sahih* (available from archives of *qism 'haya' al-torath al-islamiyya* of the Awqaf Administration in Abu Dis, Jerusalem).

131. Interview with Anwar Khatib, 1 October 1980.

132. Shehadeh, *Occupier's Law*, p. 31.

133. Benvenisti, *Survey of Israel's Policies*, p. 25.

134. To strengthen the validity of these unattributed interviews, only data that could be verified by two or more sources has been included. They are referred to simply as Interviews.

135. See Lesch, "Dead End," p. 6; Roy, "Gaza Strip," p. 69. See also P. Cossali and C Robson, *Stateless in Gaza* (London: Zed Press, 1986), pp. 18–23.

136. Y. Meron, "The Religious Courts in the Administered Territories," in *Military Government in the Territories Administered by Israel, 1967–1986*, ed. by Shamgar (Jerusalem:

n.p., 1982), pp. 361–62.

137. Meron, "Religious Courts," pp. 355, 362.

138. Interview with Farraj Sarraf, 27 September 1988.

139. One scholar has estimated that in 1989 there were over 600 mosques in the Gaza Strip. Ziad Abu 'Amr, *al-Fajr* English Weekly, 30 January 1989, p. 11. This estimate appears to be excessive, approximating, as it does, one mosque per 1,000 dunums, not taking into account land confiscated for military purposes and settlement. Unless the figure can be confirmed by a survey, it would be safer to accept the waqf administration figure. Z. Shiff and E. Ya'ari, *Intifada: The Palestinian Uprising—Israel's Third Front* (New York: Simon and Schuster, 1989), p. 225, provides an undocumented figure of 160 mosques for 1987.

140. Shiff and Ya'ari, *Intifada*, p. 224. From the text one can assume that their source is Rif'at Abu Sha'ban, the former *ma'mur al-awqaf* of the Gaza Strip.

141. Interview with Farraj Sarraf, 27 September 1989. Residential rents are frozen at 1940 levels and commercial rents at 1941 levels.

142. One possibility under discussion is the development of the sites of some of the cemeteries in its care as commercial premises. Many of them are located in urban centers and would therefore bring in a substantial income. In Islamic law a site can be developed after thirty to forty years provided proper procedures are followed. Interview with Farraj Sarraf, 28 September 1988.

143. An illustration of this latter policy is the leasing to UNRWA of sixty-three dunums of land for eleven schools, one clinic, and two feeding centers for $3,500 per year when it could get much more if it set a commercial rate.

144. The Gaza Strip waqf administration is hesitant to enforce a ruling delivered in the Mandate period that would allow it to evict the tenants and draw up new leases. Such a move would entail the cooperation of Israeli police and would be politically unacceptable. One can also speculate on the extent to which such reluctance is due to the fact that the leading Gaza families who are at the same time part of the religious elite and also tenants on the disputed land may benefit from the irresolution of the dispute.

145. Roy, "Gaza Strip," p. 75, Table 1. This figure is derived by adding up all the cultivated land as well as another 7,000 dunums to take into account other categories in the table that have small amounts of cultivated land.

146. Roy, "Gaza Strip," p. 75.

147. Shiff and Ya'ari, *Intifada*, give a figure of 2,000 dunums of agricultural land (p. 224). From the text one can assume that their source is once again Rif'at Abu Sha'ban, the former *ma'mur al-awqaf* for the Gaza Strip.

148. Jordan Palestinian Joint Committee, *Achievements Report, 1979–1988* (Amman: Secretariat General of Joint Committee, October 1988), p. 60, table 7.

149. See Kafrawi, "abu khadr," p. 30.

150. Y. Litani, "Militant Islam in the West Bank and Gaza," *New Outlook* 32, nos. 11–12 (November–December 1989): 40–42. See also Shiff and Ya'ari, *Intifada*.

151. This policy change by the military government became more obvious during the intifada. See Shiff and Ya'ari, *Intifada*, pp. 227ff.

Notes to Chapter 5

1. The Israeli government termed the process "integration." In a speech to the UN General Assembly, former Israeli ambassador to the UN Abba Eban denied that it was annexation:

> [the term] annexation... is out of place. The measures adopted related to the integration of Jerusalem in the administrative and municipal spheres and furnish a legal basis for the protection of the Holy Places. These steps are aimed at improving the lives of the inhabitants, rebuilding the ruins, at civic cooperation, and at safeguarding the Holy Places and ensuring free access to them.

Cited in Benvenisti, *Torn City*, p. 122.

2. There were a number of guerrilla cells operating from the Old City in the early 1970s but most of their members were arrested and they are now defunct. See for example, "Two held for arson at Old City Jewish religious bookshop," *Jerusalem Post*, 18 February 1974.

3. See M. Brecher, "Jerusalem: Israel's Political Decisions, 1947–77," *Middle East Journal* 32, No. 1 (1978): 33, for policy implications as a result of the government's perceptions that its actions in East Jerusalem cause "marginal negative consequences for Israel's foreign policy and security interests."

4. K. Maquire, "The Israelisation of Jerusalem," *Arab Papers* (London: Arab Research Centre, 1981), Paper no. 7.

5. Farhi, "Muslim Council," p. 15. Farhi argues that senior officials in the Awqaf Administration were strongly opposed to this policy of deliberate neglect and tried in many cases to ignore it.

6. H. Lazarus-Yafeh, "The Sanctity of Jerusalem in Islam," in *Some Religious Aspects of Islam* (Leiden: Brill, 1981), pp. 58ff.; and H.S. Karmi, "How Holy is Palestine to the Muslims?" *Islamic Quarterly* 12, No. 2 (April–June 1970): 5–6. For a discussion of the reasons for the enhanced status of Jerusalem as a pilgrimage center see S.D. Goitein, "The Sanctity of Jerusalem and Palestine in Early Islam," *Studies in Islamic History and Institutions* (Leiden: Brill, 1968). Goitein disagrees with many of the points made by Lazarus-Yafeh. See also Peters, *Jerusalem*, on the growth of the sanctity of Jerusalem and its pilgrimage traditions, pp. 374–75. For a somewhat more ambiguous view of these traditions see also his later book: Peters, *Jerusalem and Mecca: The Typology of the Holy City in the Near East* (New York: New York University Press, 1986), pp. 44–45. The growing religious significance of Jerusalem also coincided with the spread of Sufism. Sufi shaykhs and their followers set up convents and hostels, or *zawiyas*, in the Old City. The tomb of Nabi Da'ud became a well-known convent. See Kupferschmidt, *Supreme Muslim Council*, p. 105; Massignon, "Documents," pp. 82–84; Trimingham, *Sufi Orders*, pp. 16–17. Furthermore, although Jerusalem never became renowned for its jurisprudence or religious learning as did Cairo, many schools and seminaries were established there. For the Mamluk period, for example, see Burgoyne, *Mamluk Jerusalem*, pp. 62–63, 70–74; and Peters, *Jerusalem*, p. 364. One of the main motivations was apparently the attempt by the Sunni establishment to train teachers, preachers, and intellectuals as a means to counter the spread of Shi'ism. See Peters, *Jerusalem*, p. 335; for the role of Sufis in Jerusalem during the Mamluk period, see Burgoyne, *Mamluk Jerusalem*, p. 63. Barron, *Mohammedan Wakfs*, pp. 7–8, writes that many Sufi institutions in Jerusalem were supported by the Khaski Sultan waqf. The Sinan Pasha waqf had properties throughout the eastern Mediterranean and a reader of the Quran in the Mosque of Omar was paid for out of funds from this waqf's property in Egypt; *ibid.*, p. 62, n17.

7. According to the Muslim historian and geographer of the Middle Ages, Muqaddasi, one of the earliest waqfs in Jerusalem was the pool of Siloam and the gardens it watered, just south of the Haram area. This was dedicated by Caliph 'Uthman ibn Affan as an endowment for the poor of the city between 644–656 CE. See Muqaddasi, *Description of Syria including Palestine*, translated from the Arabic by G. Le Strange, (New York: AMS Press, 1971) Pilgrims Text Society 3, pp. 48ff., cited in Peters, *Jerusalem*, p. 240.

8. One of the most important waqfs in Jerusalem was the Abu Madyan waqf that included most of the *harat al-magharib* (Moroccan quarter), founded in 1320 CE by well-known Moroccan scholar and ascetic, Shu'aib ibn Muhammed ibn Shu'aib, also known as Abu Madyan. Abu Madyan wished to provide for the needs of new Moroccan residents and poor Moroccans and ordered that two loaves be given daily during the three holy months of the Muslim calendar and that a meal be served at each of the three main Muslim feasts. Destitute Moroccans were also to be given a shroud and a funeral out of the waqf funds. Funds to meet these stipulations were obtained from the endowment of his agricultural land and property in the village of Ayn Karim and a property on Tariq Bab al-Silsila, the latter to be converted to a *zawiya* for male Moroccans. See *waqfiyya* cited in Tibawi, *The Islamic Pious Foundation in Jerusalem: Origin, History and Usurpation by Israel* (London: Islamic Cultural Centre, 1978), pp. 10ff. A smaller waqf but one that illustrates the attitude of the Mamluk exiled amirs mentioned above was the waqf created to support the al-Tashtimuriyya, a well-known school on the Tariq Bab al-Silsila in the Old City. The original *waqfiyya* no longer exists but the services it provided to the local community can be deduced by the architecture. See Burgoyne, *Mamluk Jerusalem*, p. 465. In addition to a tomb for the founder there was a *sabil*, a *kuttab* and a *madrasa*. Later endowments (1611 CE) reveal that fruit plantations around Jerusalem were converted into waqf in order to provide funds for water and lighting to assist passers-by. The *madrasa* was still functioning in late sixteenth century but it was subsequently converted into residences and is now administered by the al-Imam family as a *dhurri* waqf. See S. Graham-Brown, "Jerusalem," *Middle East* (December 1985): 51.

9. See for example the waqf of Khaski Sultan, which had villages in Lebanon and property in Tripoli endowed for the soup kitchen in Jerusalem; S.H. Stephan, "An endowment deed of Khasski el-Sultan, dated 24th May, 1922," *Quarterly of the Department of Antiquities in Palestine* 10 (1944): 183–86; and Peri, pp. 48–49. See *Architecture of Islamic Jerusalem* (1977), p. 14 for location; details of *waqfiyya* in K. al-'Asali, *mu'ahida al-'ilm fi bayt al-maqdis* (Amman: n.p., 1981), pp. 330ff. The waqf funded a new building complex in Jerusalem with a mosque headed by an imam from the Hanafi school; fifty-five rooms for pilgrims and residences; a *khan* for travellers; a soup kitchen providing food and bread for as many as 400 poor and needy Jerusalemites and pilgrims each day. In addition, more than twenty people were employed, from cooks to millers and dishwashers. See Stephan, "Khasski el-Sultan," pp. 187–93. Twenty-five villages in Palestine were endowed, sixteen in the *sanjaq* of Gaza (including Ramla and Lydda), eight in the *sanjaq* of Jerusalem (including Bethlehem, Bayt Jala, Issawiyya, and al-Jib), and one in the *sanjaq* of Nablus, as well as villages in Lebanon and properties in Tripoli. See Peri, "Waqf as an Instrument," pp. 48–49; Stephan, "Khasski el-Sultan," pp. 183–85. Income for the waqf came from taxes, tithes, and other dues.

10. Excluding minarets, *sabil*s and one-room *turba*s, thirty-nine of the forty-one monumental buildings mentioned in Burgoyne have waqf endowments. See Burgoyne, *Mamluk Jerusalem*.

11. For Ottoman neglect see Peters, *Jerusalem*, p. 480; and O. Grabar, "Al-Quds, B: The

Monuments," *Encyclopaedia of Islam* (Leiden: Brill, 1980) p. 343.

12. Heyd, *Ottoman Documents*, pp. 146–49. In 1552 Roxelana, the wife of Sulayman the Magnificent, made the first endowment for the Khaski Sultan waqf. Stephan, "Khasski el-Sultan."

13. Peri, "Waqf as an Instrument," pp. 48–49.

14. Peters, *Jerusalem*, p. 566; see also G. Baer, "The Dismemberment of Awqaf in early 19th Century Jerusalem," *Africa and Asia Studies* 13, No. 3 (1979). The Khalidi family is thought to have gained control over the *hamam al-'ayn* in the Old City in this way; see Burgoyne, *Mamluk Jerusalem*, p. 277.

15. Y. Reiter, *Waqf in Jerusalem 1948–1990* (Jerusalem: Jerusalem Institute for Israel Studies, 1991), p. 35.

16. G. Baer, "The Waqf as a Prop for the Social System (16th–20th Centuries)," paper presented to the International Seminar on Social and Economic Aspects of the Muslim Waqf, Jerusalem, June 1979, p. 5.

17. Baer, "Waqf as a Prop," p. 16. See also M. Kafrawi, "taqrir 'an waqfiyya al-marhuma: Amina Badr al-Khalidi," [A Report on the *waqfiyya* of the Deceased Amina Badr al-Khalidi], *Hoda al-Islam*, Nos. 8–9 (1985): 61–71.

18. Y. Reiter, *Waqf in Jerusalem, 1948–1990*, p. 38.

19. Kupferschmidt, *Supreme Muslim Council*, p. 110. Barron refers to list of waqf properties in Palestine as having been lost, see *Mohammedan Wakfs*, p. 56, n12.

20. When he included properties now confiscated by the Israeli government in the area redeveloped as the Jewish Quarter but excluding the Haram al-Sharif area (which is regarded as entirely waqf), Anwar Khatib, the former governor of Jerusalem estimated *khayri* at 30 percent and *dhurri* at 40 percent of the Old City. Interview with Anwar Khatib, Jordanian governor of Jerusalem, 13 January 1986. Hasan Tahbub, the former director-general of the Awqaf Administration estimated *khayri* at 30 percent but *dhurri* at no more than 15 percent. Interview with Hasan Tahbub, director-general of Awqaf Administration (1960–1983), 11 January 1988. From interviews conducted during 1986 with six *mutawallis* of major *dhurri* waqfs in the Old City, Khatib's figure for *dhurri* would appear to be too high. A figure between 15 and 20 percent would be much more accurate.

21. The Greek Orthodox Patriarchate owned 12.4 percent. Gosenfeld, "temurot bi-qehilat ha-'asaqim shel yerushalayim ha-mizrahit" [The ownership of commercial land in East Jerusalem] *Ha-Mizrah He-Hadash* 24 (1974): 274. This figure excludes residential and property for communal purposes. However, the high figure is partially confirmed by interviews with the former mayor of Jerusalem and Hasan Tahbub, who noted that much of the land to the north and east of the Old City is managed by the Awqaf Administration.

22. Y. Reiter, *Waqf in Jerusalem, 1948–1990*, p. 20.

23. To our knowledge no new endowments have been made in West Jerusalem since 1948. Prior to 1948 waqf property could be found in the Talbiyya Quarter, which was waqf *mundarisa*, or noted places like the former Supreme Muslim Council-run Palace Hotel on the Gershon Agron, which is now the location of the Israeli Ministry of Trade and Industry, or the nearby Mamilla pool and cemetery area, which has been converted into a public park. See Kupferschmidt, *Supreme Muslim Council*, p. 119. The former Palestinian village of Ayn

Karim, on the outskirts of Jerusalem but just inside the Israeli municipal boundaries of Jerusalem, was an endowment for the Abu Madyan waqf in the Moroccan quarter in the Old City. See note 10.

24. Notably the Law and Administrative Ordinance (Amendment) Law, and the Municipal Corporations Ordinance (Amendment) Law, see *Laws of the State of Israel*, vol. 21 (1966–67), pp. 75–76 respectively.

25. Benvenisti, *Torn City*, p. 92; see also p. 91 for Eshkol's speech.

26. See Farhi, "Muslim Council," p. 6.

27. Benvenisti, *Torn City*, p. 91.

28. Interview with Hasan Tahbub, 2 May 1989; see also Farhi, "Muslim Council," p. 6. Benvenisti refers to the closing phase of this episode tersely: "The visits to waqf offices were terminated," *Torn City*, p. 284, see also p. 287.

29. Interview with Hasan Tahbub, 2 May 1989. "I did not wish to go down in history as the one who allowed the Israelis to take over the waqf of Jerusalem."

30. Benvenisti, *Torn City*, p. 284.

31. *Ibid*., pp. 286–87.

32. See Y. Zvi Blum, "The Juridical Status of East Jerusalem," in *Jerusalem—Aspects of Law*, ed. by O. Ahimeir (Jerusalem: The Jerusalem Institute for Israel Studies, 1983) Discussion Paper No. 3, 2d rev. ed., pp. xxiv–xxviii for a defense of the Israeli government perspective.

33. See Chapter Two. There are some indications that the implementation of these steps were planned. Immediately after the occupation, posters appeared on certain buildings, such as the Khalidi Library, in parts of the Old City claiming that they now fell under the jurisdiction of the Custodian. Interview with Haydar Khalidi, 15 May 1985.

34. Legal and Administrative Matters (Regulation) Law (Consolidated Version) of 1970, *Laws of the State of Israel*, vol. 24, (1969–1970), pp. 144–52.

35. S. Jiryis, "Israeli laws as Regards Jerusalem," (n.p., n.d.), p. 187. Also in Arabic in *Shu'un Filastiniyah*, no. 106 (September 1980): 13–24. See also Y. Bar-Sela, "Law Enforcement in the Eastern Sector of Jerusalem," in *Jerusalem—Aspects of Law*, ed. by O. Ahimeir, Discussion Paper No. 3 (Jerusalem: Institute for Israel Studies, 1983), p. xx.

36. See Benvenisti for the intricacies of this system, *Torn City*, pp. 296–98; see also Bar-Sela who erroneously interprets this situation in the following way: "In this manner, the shari'a court has formally become part of the Israeli administration; but the arrangement is not regulated by legislation and in fact runs counter to the spirit and intent of the Israeli law," in "Law Enforcement," p. xxi.

37. Y. Reiter, *Waqf in Jerusalem, 1948–1990*, p. 17.

38. Interview with 'Isam Anani, 30 July 1985; see also Farhi, "Muslim Council," p. 14.

39. Dumper, "Muslim Institutions," pp. 429–34, provides a review of some of these problems based upon a series of interviews with Awqaf Administration officials and *mutawalli*s of waqf *dhurri* in Jerusalem during fieldwork between 1985 and 1987.

40. See for example resolution No. 15C/3.343 of October–November 1968, calling on Israel to preserve cultural properties especially in the Old City of Jerusalem, or UNESCO Decision No. 88 Ex/4.3.1. of 1971, calling upon Israel to preserve cultural properties, especially

Christian and Islamic sites in the Old City of Jerusalem and UNESCO Decision No. 89 Ex/4.4.1 of June 1972, deploring the continuation of Israeli archaeological excavations in Jerusalem. *UN Resolutions on Palestine, 1947–72* (Beirut: Institute for Palestine Studies, 1974), pp. 141ff. See also memoranda and letters sent to Israeli Military Commander by the Higher Islamic Board in Shaykh Sa'd al-Din al-'Alami, ed., *al-hay'at al-islamiya al-'ulya—watha'iq* (Jerusalem: Dar al-Tabi'a al-'Arabiyya, n.d.).

41. This emphasis on education is exemplified by the Jerusalem *mudiriyya* where Awqaf Administration runs a number of elementary schools and secondary schools, supports religious instruction in other non-Awqaf Administration secondary schools, and has established a shari'a college and several *dur al-qur'an* and *dur al-hadith*. See *bayan* I, pp. 20–25, and *bayan* II, pp. 12, 14. Many of these institutions are located in or around the Haram al-Sharif. It has also established a Department for the Revival of Tradition and the Islamic Sciences, which is collecting and publishing copies of ancient manuscripts, archival material, and commentaries. In addition a journal, *Hoda al-Islam*, on contemporary Islamic issues is published once a month and provides a forum for discussion and debate on contemporary Islamic affairs. Although not necessarily of a standard to rival other major seats of Islamic learning in the Muslim world, the result of this emphasis on education has been to generate, at least in the Haram courtyard, a visible atmosphere of study and discussion. One very important spin-off from these activities has been the attraction of significant numbers of young men to the Old City and the Haram courtyard the very physical presence of which serves as a deterrent against attempts by militant Israeli nationalists to establish some kind of Israeli foothold in the Haram courtyard. See "Police investigate al-Aqsa college," *Jerusalem Post*, 22 May 1987 (Saturday insert).

42. See *bayan* I, pp. 26–30, 45–47; see also Farhi, "Muslim Council," p. 15.

43. Interview with Hisham Asha'ir, 13 November 1985, who was at the time director of the Dar al-Aytam in Jerusalem and the West Bank.

44. Y. Reiter, *Waqf in Jerusalem 1948–1990*, p. 31.

45. *Ibid.*, p. 43.

46. *Ibid.*, p. 45.

47. Number of construction and repair projects undertaken by the Awqaf Administration in the Jerusalem province, 1977–82.

*Project**	*Year*					
	1977	1978	1979	1980	1981	1982
Mosques	32	20	19	22	13	22
Residential	20	10	15	22	19	30
Dar al Aytam Schools	15	14	4	1	4	12
Other schools	4	7	7	16	6	14
Monuments	6	2	4	4	1	2
Shops	1	1	1	3	-	1
Miscellaneous	15	36	25	28	15	23
Total Works	96	93	71	96	58	104

(Source: *bayan* II, pp. 51–54, 60–63, 68–71, 74–78, 81–83, 87–91.)

* No indication of the sums involved is given, which means that some of the projects may have been very minor.

48. See R. Nijm, *'ard tarikhi masawur 'an 'aham al-muqaddisa fi filastin w-al-'ijra'at alati tamat li-siyanat al-turath*, Fifth conference on the Holy Places, Tradition and Culture in

Palestine, Cairo, 1988, pp. 29–30. The renovation program of the Awqaf Administration benefitted from a widespread concern that the Israeli occupation of East Jerusalem was permanently damaging the Islamic character and architectural value of the Old City. Two surveys, one by the British School of Archaeology in Jerusalem (BSAJ) and another under the auspices of the Arab League, drew attention to the poor condition of many of these waqf properties. British School of Archaeology in Jerusalem, *The Architecture of Islamic Jerusalem* (London: British School of Archaeology in Jerusalem, 1976); and Burgoyne, *Mamluk Jerusalem*; also R. Nijm, ed., *Kunuz al-Quds*, (Amman, 1983). The Awqaf Administration began to receive financial support from other Muslim countries. For example, the Islamic Conference Organization established a Jerusalem Committee, which assisted in the financing of the Awqaf Administration's Department of Islamic Archaeology restoration program and the work of the Committee for the Restoration of al-Aqsa Mosque. The Jordanian government also established in the Shmeisani area in Amman a Center for the Preservation of Jerusalem to coordinate and direct these funds and projects. The Center never realized its full potential, possibly as a result of interministerial disputes since most of the funds are now directly channelled through the Jordanian Ministry of Waqfs and Islamic Affairs. The Center consists mainly of a Library and some administrative staff.

49. Interview with Adnan Hussayni, 27 July 1985; see also, M. Burgoyne, "The Continued Survey of the Ribat Kurd/Madrasa Jawhariya Complex in Tariq Bab al-Hadid, Jerusalem," *Levant* 6 (1974): 51. The Israeli Chief Archaeologist in Jerusalem argues that such damage is caused by the drying-out of the soil brought about by the proper drainage and sewage disposal introduced by the Israeli Jerusalem Municipality. Interview with Dan Bahat, chief archaeologist of Jerusalem for the Israeli government, 19 March 1987.

50. Interview with Adnan Husayni, 31 March 1987; see also S. Graham-Brown, "Jerusalem," *Middle East*, No. 136 (February 1986): 49.

51. See R. Thomas, "Demography and Settler Politics in the Old City of Jerusalem," *Khamsin* 1 (1989): 82–92, for a more detailed exposition of this argument.

52. Law of Antiquities, *Government Gazette*, 31 August 1967, p. 2159.

53. Interview with Dan Bahat, 19 March 1987.

54. A. Sharon, *Planning Jerusalem—The Old City and its Environs* (Jerusalem: Wiedenfield and Nicholson, 1973), pp. 82, 114, 117, and 123. See also M. Safdie, *The Harvard Jerusalem Studio: Urban Designs for the Holy City* (London: Massachusetts Institute of Technology Press, 1986), pp. 125–36, for discussion of development possibilities from the angle of Israeli and nonindigenous planners.

55. Safdie, *Urban Designs*, pp. 87–88.

56. See also Sharon, *Planning Jerusalem*, pp. 82, 114, 117, and 123, for plans to create open spaces around inside of the walls of the Old City.

57. This was a proposal to develop the area above three parallel suqs in the heart of the Old City, Suq al-'Attarin, Suq al-Lahamin, and Suq al-Khawajat. Municipality architects and planners argue that this is a neglected space that could be used as a park and garden area to ease the congestion in the Old City, particularly in the expanded Jewish quarter. They proposed that it should be paved and flower-beds and shrubberies introduced between seating areas to create a "promenade." Interview with Yitzhak Ya'acovy, 3 February 1987; see also D. Kroyanker, *Jerusalem, Planning and Development: New Trends, 1982–85* (Jerusalem: Jerusalem Committee, 1985), pp. 22–25. As managers of waqf shops beneath the area the Awqaf Adminis-

tration objected to the proposals on a number of grounds. First, the western-style design of the promenade was incompatible with the surrounding styles and would undermine the Islamic and Arab character of the Old City. It is interesting to note that the designs harmonized much more with the refurbished and expanded Jewish quarter, which is adjacent to the area. The project could be seen, therefore, as a form of architectural "Israelization" of the remaining parts of the Old City. Second, the Awqaf Administration did not wish to cooperate in relieving the congestion in the expanded Jewish quarter while the Israeli state still retained properties expropriated from the Awqaf Administration. More importantly, the Awqaf Administration was not prepared to relinquish responsibility for the maintenance of the roofs of the suqs, anticipating that it might lead to further encroachments by the Israeli government. This was particularly the case in view of the establishment of an Israeli settlement in the former Kolel Galicia beside the market area the members of which used the roof-top as their main access to the Jewish quarter (Interview with Adnan Husayni, 23 January 1986). In 1986, the Department of Islamic Archaeology began to carry out a simple retiling of the roof-top area without the walkways and plant-beds, as a preemptive measure and as a means of asserting its jurisdiction and control over the area.

58. The Legal and Administrative Matters (Regulation) Law (Consolidated Version) passed in 1970 states that inhabitants of East Jerusalem could not be regarded as absentee "in respect of property situated in that area" (Article 3a). Other articles overriding the provision of the Absentee Property Law and its amendments are Article 3b, 21b, and 28a. *Laws of the State of Israel*, vol. 24 (1969–70), pp. 144–52.

59. By taking figures for the total West Bank income of the Awqaf Administration in the years 1977 and 1982 (JD 382,389 and JD 362,437, respectively) and subtracting the figure given for the proceeds from entrance fees to the Haram al-Sharif (JD 149,712 and JD 102,440) one arrives at the sums of JD 232,677 for 1977 and JD 259,997 for 1982 for other, nonticket sources of income. See *bayan* I, p. 131. Given that rents are the chief source of this other income, one can estimate that between JD 180,000 and JD 200,000 are derived from waqf property, and given that Jerusalem, Nablus, and Hebron are the main areas for waqf property, one can also estimate, very approximately, that income in the Jerusalem *mudiriyya* is in the neighborhood of JD 150,000 or 40 percent of the total income of the Awqaf Administration.

60. Translation from Institute for Palestine Studies, *Resistance*, p. 12.

61. Benvenisti attempts to explain the action in the following manner:

> The move was the settling of an historic account with those who had harassed the Jewish people over the centuries, restricting and humiliating it at its holiest place, as well as with those who had prevented access to the wall for 19 years. The displaced inhabitants of the Mugrabi Quarter were not personally to blame, but it was their fate to be additional victims of the Arab-Israeli conflict.

Torn City, p. 307.

62. Tibawi, *Pious Foundations*, p. 38.

63. Interview with 'Isam Anani, 30 July 1985.

64. *Al-Fajr* English weekly, 17 May 1987, p. 14.

65. "Law Report," (Sapolinsky v. Minister of Finance), *Jerusalem Post*, 5 January 1975.

66. Interview with Antony Bakrijian, historian, former UNRWA official, and resident of Old City, 3 October 1989. See also Graham-Brown, "Jerusalem," *Middle East*, No. 136 (February, 1986): 48; Benvenisti, *Torn City*, p. 44; Tibawi, *Pious Foundations*, p. 38.

67. *Official Gazette*, No. 1443, 18 April 1968, cited in Tibawi, *Pious Foundations*, p. 37.

68. Statement by R. Khatib, deported mayor of Jerusalem, published in Dib and Jabber, *Violations*, document no. 67, p. 176.

69. See Dib and Jabber, *Violations*, p. 176.

70. Field work conducted between September 1985 and May 1986 consisting of interviews with *mutawallis* of the major Jerusalem waqfs and lawyers concerned with waqf cases. Other figures for *dhurri* waqf are as follows: Dajani–3, Hariri–1, Daqqaq–1, Abdo–1, Hallaq–1, Khatib–2, Husayni (one branch)–1, and Quttayni–3.

71. Cited in Dib and Jabber, *Violations*, p. 178.

72. See for example, "A bulldozer battle for Jerusalem," *The Christian Science Monitor*, 5 March 1975; "Arabs fighting ouster in Jerusalem Old City," *International Herald Tribune*, 21 April 1975; "Planners drive Arabs out of Jerusalem," *Tages-Anzeiger*, 2 June 1975; "The case of the hole in the wall," *Jerusalem Post*, 16 January 1977, and the letter by Anglican clergy in Jerusalem that this article prompted in *Jerusalem Post*, 31 January 1977.

73. Absentee Property (Compensation) Law, *Laws of the State of Israel*, vol. 27 (1972–73).

74. *Ibid.*, Article 14.

75. For a more detailed discussion of the background to Jewish settlement in the Muslim quarters of the Old City see Dumper, "Muslim Institutions," pp. 475–79.

76. Zacharia, *Jewish Institutions*, pp. 8–9.

77. Ben Arieh, *Old City*, pp. 382–83.

78. A bookshop, the Ben Arza, was opened on the site of a former Hungarian synagogue on the Tariq al-Wad, close to the underground passageway leading to the Western Wall plaza. Palestinian families were still being evicted from the enlarged Jewish Quarter adjacent to this area at that time, and the political sensitivity of such a development was illustrated by an arson attack on the bookshop in 1974. *Jerusalem Post*, 18 February 1974.

79. R.J. Friedman, "Jewish Zealots Plan `Redemption' of Arab Jerusalem," article from *Washington Post* in *Guardian Weekly*, 24 January 1988. See also Thomas, "Settler Politics," p. 88; Dumper, "Settler Groups in the Old City of Jerusalem," *Middle East International*, No. 375 (April 1990), p. 6. The groups are known as Ataret Cohanim, Torat Cohanim, the Young Israel Movement, and the Yeshiva Birkat Avraham. Torat Cohanim and the Young Israel Movement coordinate their settlement activities through a property development association known as Atara Leyoshna.

80. For Hammer, see *Davar*, 4 February 1987; for general confirmation see "A Bomb ticks in the Muslim Quarter," *Ha'Aretz*, 2 January 1987; for Ne'eman see *Kol Ha'ir*, May 1987.

81. See *al-Hamishmar*, 11 May 1987.

82. See Shragai, "Jews in the Muslim Quarter of Jerusalem: Who will buy, who will buy me a house?" *Ha'Aretz*, 23 April 1986; concerning the establishment of the commission see articles by Shragai in *Ha'Aretz*, 11 May 1987, and by Hadar Horesh in *Kol Ha'ir*, 1 March 1985 and 6 December 1985.

83. See report by Avi Temkin, "Yeshiva gets $40,000 to buy Muslim flats," *Jerusalem Post*, 27 March 1986; and Shragai, "Jews in the Muslim Quarter," *Ha'Aretz*, 23 April 1986.

84. See report by Dalia Shchori in *al-Hamishmar*, 11 May 1987. Sharon has also close connections with the Shuvu Banim yeshiva off the Aqabat Khalidi through the New York financier Avraham Dweik who met the yeshiva's legal costs in a dispute with the municipality. Report by Michael Eilan in *Jerusalem Post*, 14 and 16 December 1983 and following articles.

85. See the interview with Ne'eman in *Kol Ha'ir*, May 1987.

86. Observations during field work, 1986. In addition, support from Christian and Jewish groups abroad has been canvassed. An "American Friends of Ataret Cohanim" has been set up in the United States and produced a glossy brochure on the work and plans of Ataret Cohanim. The brochure contained endorsements from virtually all senior right-wing Israeli politicians.

87. J. Abu Shakr, *Israeli Settler Violence in the Occupied Territories, 1980–1984* (Chicago: Palestine Human Rights Committee, 1985), pp. 23–28. See also the following articles in the *Jerusalem Post*: "Police: Yeshiva men plagued beaten-up woman's husband," 6 April 1983; "Yeshiva students queried about attack on Aab's flat," 2 June 1983; and "Yeshiva men beat up two Arabs in Old City," 2 December 1983.

88. Interviews with Hasan Tahbub, 14 November 1985; Adnan Husayni, 6 August 1986; and Yusuf Natshe, 3 December 1986.

89. *Al-Fajr* English weekly, 21 November 1986 and 28 November 1986.

90. Interview with Yusuf Natshe, 3 December 1986. The intifada, beginning in December 1987, had stiffened the resolve of the residents to stay in the Old City.

Notes to Chapter 6

1. These means would include a decentralized communal structure with elected trustees. See also J. Abu Lughod, "Preserving the Living Heritage of Islamic Cities," in *Toward an Architecture in the Spirit of Islam*, Aga Khan Award for Architecture, 1978, p. 68, for references to possible role for the waqf in urban renewal. When such ideas were raised with a senior Awqaf Administration official they were dismissed as "trying to change the waqf into a kibbutz."

GLOSSARY

ahli • literally "family"; *waqf ahli* or family waqf, mainly Egyptian usage.

awqaf • plural of *waqf*, religious endowment.

caravanserai • an inn designed to accommodate large groups of travellers with their animals.

dhurri • literally "pertaining to the descendants"; *waqf dhurri* or family waqf, mainly Palestinian usage.

dunum • unit of land measure; four *dunums* equal approximately one acre or 1,000 square meters.

fatwa • a binding legal opinion based on *shari'a* law, usually issued by a *mufti*.

ghayr sahih (waqf) • waqf that was not wholly the property of the dedicator.

hadith • sayings attributed to the Prophet Muhammad.

Haram al-Sharif • The "Noble Sanctuary" in Jerusalem; site of the al-Aqsa Mosque and the Dome of the Rock, the third holiest shrine in Islam.

hay'a • a body, council, or board.

hikr • a long lease for waqf land, usually found in southern Palestine.

ijaratayn • a type of long lease involving an initial down payment with regular payments thereafter.

imam • the leader of the prayers in a mosque, often the chief functionary as well.

imaret • Turkish for a waqf institution of social welfare, usually a soup kitchen.

istibdal • an exchange of waqf property, usually for another of equal value.

khan • an inn or hostel for travellers; also a collection of warehouses.

khatib • the mosque preacher responsible for the Friday sermon.

khayri • literally "charitable"; *waqf khayri* or public waqf, as opposed to private or family waqf (see *ahli*, *dhurri*).

khulu • a form of endowment by which the cost of repairs of a waqf were reimbursed on a regular basis, often leading to the dismemberment of the waqf.

khutba • a Friday feast-day sermon in a mosque.

kuttab • a religious school at an elementary level.

madaris • plural of *madrasa*, school.

madbut • refers to waqfs taken over by the Ottoman Ministry of Waqfs and later by the Supreme Muslim Council; sometimes known as *mazbuta*.

madrasa • traditionally a religious school, in contemporary usage it refers to any secondary school.

majlis • a council; plural is *majalis*.

ma'mur awqaf • the manager of public waqfs in a given district.

mawquf • waqf of *miri* land of which only the usufruct could be dedicated.

mawsim • literally "season"; refers to local popular Islamic festivals.

mevkufe • Turkish for *mawquf*.

miri • tenanted land of the state.

mudiriyya • an administrative province.

muezzin • a mosque functionary who delivers the call to prayer.

mufti • religious scholar authorized to deliver interpretation of the *quran* and *hadith*.

mulhaq • privately administered waqf which became increasingly accountable to the Ottoman Ministry of Waqfs or the Supreme Muslim Council.

mulk • fully privately owned land.

mundaris • lapsed waqfs taken over by the Ottoman Ministry of Waqfs.

mutawalli • the manager of waqf property, usually private or family waqfs.

nazir • the manager of public or private waqf, a term frequently used during the Ottoman period, particularly in Egypt.

nizami • Ottoman courts of civil (that is, non-*shari'a*) law, established by the Tanzimat reforms.

qadi • a Muslim judge of the *shari'a* court.

quran • the holy book of Islam, the recitations of the Prophet Muhammad.

ra'is al-'ulama' • leader of the religious scholars, the *ulema*; official title of the President of the Supreme Muslim Council.

sadaqa • a (holy) gift.

sahih (waqf) • literally "genuine" waqf; waqf endowed from land or property wholly owned by the dedicator.

sanjaq • an administrative district of the Ottoman Empire.

shari'a • Muslim law derived from the *quran*, the *hadith*, and subsequent interpretations by religious scholars over the centuries.

sijill • the register of the *shari'a* courts.

Sufi • a Muslim mystic.

suq • a market area or bazaar.

tahsisat • a type of waqf, the annual income of which was collected by the state.

takiya • *Sufi* hospices, some of which accepted travellers.

Tanzimat • the Ottoman land, legal, and administrative reforms of the mid-nineteenth century.

tariqa • an order of brotherhood of *Sufi*s.

ulema • Muslim scholars, some of whom were also given important administra tive and legal positions.

vilayet • Turkish term for a province of the Ottoman Empire.

waqfiyya • waqf document authenticated by a *qadi* containing details and conditions of endowment.

waqif • the person setting aside a piece of land or property as waqf.

yeshiva • Hebrew term for religious seminary.

yishuv • the Jewish community in Palestine, often referring to its organizational structures.

zawiya • a *Sufi* convent or hostel, sometimes refers to a prayer-hall.

ziyara • a pilgrimage to a holy shrine.

BIBLIOGRAPHY

Works in English, French, and German

Abdullahi, A.A. "A New Definition of Waqf: A Basis on which the legal personality of Waqf is established." *Journal of Comparative Islamic Law* 7 (1978): 57–72.

Abel, F-M. "Jaffa au Moyen-Age." *Journal of the Palestine Oriental Society* 20: 6–28.

Abrahamovitch. "The Palestine Waqfs and the Supreme Muslim Council." In *Palestine and the Near East* (n.p., 1937), pp. 289–92.

Abu Lughod, J. "The Demographic Transformation of Palestine." In *The Transformation of Palestine*, edited by Y. Abu Lughod. (Evanston, IL: Northwestern University Press, 1971).

_____. "Preserving the Living Heritage of Islamic Cities." In *Toward an Architecture in the Spirit of Islam*, The Aga Khan Award for Architecture, April 1978, pp. 61–81.

Abu Lughod, Y., ed. *The Transformation of Palestine*. (Evanston, IL: Northwestern University Press, 1971).

Abu Shakr, J. *Israeli Settler Violence in the Occupied Territories, 1980–1984*. (Chicago: Palestine Human Rights Committee, 1985).

Ahimer, O., ed. *Jerusalem—Aspects of Law*. Discussion Paper No. 3. 2d rev. ed. (Jerusalem: Jerusalem Institute for Israel Studies, 1983).

Aly, M. Pacha. "Le Waqf, est-il une institution religieuse?" *L'Egypte Contemporain* 18 (1927): 385–402.

_____. "Le Probleme de Waqf." *L'Egypte Contemporain* 18 (1927): 501–24.

Anderson, J.N.D. "The Religious Element in Waqf Endowments." *Royal Central Asian Society Journal* 38, part 4 (October 1951): 292–99.

_____. "Recent Developments in Shari'a Law, IX: The Waqf System." *The Muslim World* 42, part 4 (1952): 257–76.

Arberry, A.J. *The Koran Interpreted*. (Oxford: Oxford University Press, 1964).

Architecture of Islamic Jerusalem. (Jerusalem: British School of Archaeology, 1977).

Aronson, G. *Creating Facts: Israel, Palestinians and the West Bank*. (Washington, DC: Institute for Palestine Studies, 1987).

Aruri, N., ed. *Occupation: Israel over Palestine*. (London: Zed Press, 1984).

al-'Asali, K., ed. *Jerusalem in History*. (London: Scorpion Publishing Ltd., 1989).

Asher, A. *The Elections in Israel—1973*. (Jerusalem: Jerusalem Academic Press, 1975).

Baer, G. "The Dismemberment of Awqaf in Early 19th Century Jerusalem." *Asian and African Studies* 13, No. 3 (1979): 220–41.

_____. *A History of Land Ownership in Modern Egypt, 1800–1950*. (London: Oxford University Press, 1962).

_____. "Jerusalem's Families of Notables and the Wakf in the Early 19th Century." In *Palestine in the Late Ottoman Period*, edited by D. Kushner (Jerusalem: Yad Izhak Ben-Zvi, 1986), pp. 109–22.

_____. *Population and Society in the Arab East*. (London: Routledge and Kegan Paul, 1964).

_____. "The Waqf as a Prop for the Social System (16th–20th Centuries)." Paper presented to the International Seminar on Social and Economic Aspects of the Muslim Waqf, Jerusalem, June 1979.

_____. "Waqf Reform in Egypt." *St. Antony's Papers* 4 (1958): 61–76.

Barclay, J.T. *The City of the Great King: or Jerusalem as it was, as it is, as it is to be*. (Philadelphia: n.p., 1858).

Barron, J.B. *Mohammedan Wakfs in Palestine*. (Jerusalem: Greek Convent Press, 1922).

Barry, B. "Review Article: Political Accommodation and Consociational Democracy." *British Journal of Political Science*, part 4 (October 1975).

Bar-Sela, Y. "Law Enforcement in the Eastern Sector of Jerusalem." In *Jerusalem—Aspects of Law*, edited by O. Ahimeir. Discussion Paper No. 3. 2d rev. ed. (Jerusalem: Jerusalem Institute for Israel Studies).

Bekhit, M. "De l'institution du waqf." Translated by J. Cassis. *L'Egypte Contemporain* 18 (1927): 403–31.

Ben Arieh, Y. *Jerusalem in the 19th Century: The Old City*. (New York: St. Martin's Press, 1984).

Ben Dor, G. *The Druze in Israel*. (Jerusalem: Magnes Press, 1979).

Bentwich. *Israel, Resurgent*. (London: Routledge and Kegan Paul, 1960).

Benvenisti, M. *The West Bank Data Project: A Survey of Israel's Policies*. (Washington, DC: American Enterprise Institute, 1984).

_____. *Jerusalem: The Torn City*. (Minneapolis: Israeltypset Ltd. and the University of Minneapolis, 1976).

Bliss, F.J. *The Religions of Modern Syria and Palestine*. (Edinburgh: T. and T. Clarke, 1912).

Brecher, M. "Jerusalem: Israel's Political Decisions, 1947–77." *Middle East Journal* 32, No. 1 (1978): 13–34.

Burgoyne, M. "The Continued Survey of the Ribat Kurd/Madrasa Jawhariya Complex in Tariq Bab al-Hadid, Jerusalem." *Levant* VI (1974): 51–64.

_____. *Mamluk Jerusalem: An Architectural Study*. (London: World of Islam Trust, 1987).

Bussons de Janssens, G. "Les Waqfs dans l'Islam contemporain." *Revue des Etudes Islamiques* (1951): 1–72.

Cahen, C. "Reflexions sur le Waqf Ancien." *Studia Islamica* 14 (1961): 37–56.

Cattan, H. *The Palestine Question*. (London: Croom Helm, 1988).

Cawson, A. *Corporatism and Political Theory*. (Oxford: Blackwell, 1986).

Cohen, A. *Political Parties in the West Bank under the Jordanian Regime, 1949–1967*. (London: Cornell University Press, 1982).

Cohen, E. *Integration and Separation in the Planning of a Mixed Jewish-Arab City in Israel.* (Jerusalem: Hebrew University Press, 1973).

Cohen, E.R. *Human Rights in the Israeli-Occupied Territories.* (Manchester: Manchester University Press, 1985).

Cossali, P., and C. Robson. *Stateless in Gaza.* (London: Zed Press, 1986).

Crouch, C. *State and Economy in Contemporary Capitalism.* (London: Croom Helm, 1979), pp. 14–53.

Daalder, H. "The Consociational Democracy Theme." *World Politics* 26 (1974): 616–17.

Daqqaq, I. "Back to Square One: A Study in the Re-emergence of the Palestinian identity in the West Bank, 1967–1980." In *Palestinians over the Green Line*, edited by A. Schölch. (London: Ithaca Press, 1983), pp. 64–101.

Dib, G., and F. Jabber. *Israel's Violation of Human Rights in The Occupied Territories: A Documented Report.* (Beirut: Institute for Palestine Studies, 1970).

Drory, J. "Jerusalem during the Mamluk Period (1250–1517)." *The Jerusalem Cathedra*, No. 1 (1981): 193–97.

Dumper, M. "Supressing a National Identity." *Middle East International* (January 1983).

_____. "Settler Groups in the Old City of Jerusalem." *Middle East International*, No. 375 (April 1990).

East Jerusalem Development Company. *Restoring the Old City of Jerusalem.* (Jerusalem: Alva Press, 1986).

Eicklemann, D.F. "Is There an Islamic City? The Making of a Quarter in a Moroccan Town." *International Journal of Middle Eastern Studies* 5 (1974): 174–94.

Eisenman, R.H. *Islamic Law in Palestine and Israel: A History of the Survival of the Tanzimat and the Shari'a in the British Mandate and the Jewish State.* (Leiden: E.J. Brill, 1978).

Erskine, B. *Palestine of the Arabs.* (London: Macmillan, 1937).

Esman, M., and I. Rabinovich, eds. *Ethnicity, Pluralism and the State in the Middle East.* (London: Cornell University Press, 1988).

Friedman, R.J. "Jewish Zealots Plan 'Redemption' of Arab Jerusalem." *Guardian Weekly* (24 January 1988), reprinted from the *Washington Post.*

Furlonge, G. *Palestine is My Country: The Story of Musa Alami.* (London: John Murray, 1969).

Gerber, H. *Ottoman Rule in Jerusalem, 1890–1914.* (Berlin: Klaus Schwarz Verlag, 1985).

Gerson, A. *Israel, the West Bank and International Law.* (London: Frank Cass, 1978).

Gibb, H.A.R., and H. Bowen. *Islamic Society and the West.* Vols. I and II. (London: Oxford University Press, 1957).

Gilbar, G. "Muslim Waqf and Economic Growth: Towards a Quantitative Analysis of Waqf, Investment and Productivity." Paper presented to the International Seminar on Social and Economic Aspects of the Muslim Waqf, Jerusalem, June 1979.

Gilbar, G., and J. Warburg, eds. *Studies in Islamic Society*. (Haifa: Haifa University Press, 1984).

Gilsenan, M. *Recognising Islam*. (London: Croom Helm, 1979).

Goadby, F.M. "Religious Communities and Courts in Palestine." *Tulane Law Review* 8, No. 2 (1934): 215–35.

Goadby, F.M., and M.J. Doukhan. *The Land Law of Palestine*. (Tel Aviv: Shoshany's Co., Ltd., 1935).

Goitein, S.D. "The Sancity of Jerusalem and Palestine in Early Islam." In *Studies in Islamic History and Institutions*. (London: Brill, 1968).

Goldman, Y. "Jerusalem Quartered." *Shma Yisrael* 1, No. 2 (Winter 1975).

Grabar, O. "Al-Quds, B: The Monuments." *Encyclopaedia of Islam*. (Leiden: Brill, 1980).

Graham-Brown, S. "The Economic Consequences of the Occupation." In *Occupation: Israel over Palestine*, edited by N. Aruri. (London: Zed Press, 1984), pp. 167–222.

_____. "Jerusalem." *Middle East*, No. 134 (December 1985).

_____. "Jerusalem." *Middle East*, No. 136 (February 1986).

Grannot (Granovsky), A. *Land Problems of Palestine*. (New York: Bloch, 1940).

_____. *The Land System of Palestine: History and Structure*. (London: Eyre and Spottiswoode, 1952).

_____. *Agrarian Reform and the Record of Israel*. (London: Eyre and Spottiswoode, 1956).

Hadawi, S. "Israel and the Arab Minority." International Organization for the Elimination of All Forms of Racial Discrimination, n.d.

Hadawi, S., and W. Lehn. "Zionism and the Lands of Palestine." International Organization for the Elimination of All Forms of Racial Discrimination, Paper No. 17, n.d.

Haidar, A. The Different Levels of Palestinian Ethnicity." In *Ethnicity, Pluralism and the State in the Middle East*, edited by M. Essman and I. Rabinovich. (London: Cornell University Press, 1988), pp. 95–120.

Halpern, S. "The Disorderly Universe of Consociational Democracy." *West European Politics* 9, No. 2 (1986): 181–97.

Hawari, N. "The Moslem Community." *New Outlook* 5, No. 3 (March-April 1962).

Heyd, U. *Ottoman Documents on Palestine, 1552–1615*. (London: Oxford University Press, 1960).

Himadeh, S.B. *Economic Organisation of Palestine*. (Beirut: American Press, 1938).

Hirst, D. "Rush to Annexation: Israel in Jerusalem." *Journal of Palestine Studies* 3, No. 4 (Summer 1974): 3–31.

Hodgson, M. *The Venture of Islam: The Expansion of Islam in the Middle Period*. Vol. II. (Chicago: Chicago University Press, 1974).

Hourani, A. "The Changing Face of the Fertile Crcsent in the XVIIIth Century." *Studia Islamica* 7 (1957): 89–122.

_____. "Ottoman Reforms and the Politics of Notables." In *Beginnings of Modernization in the Middle East*, edited by W.R. Polk and R.L. Chambers. (Chicago: Chicago University Press, 1968), pp. 41–68.

Hourani, A., and S.M. Stern. *The Islamic City*. (London: Oxford University Press, 1970).
Jerusalem Committee. *Out of Jerusalem* 4, No. 1 (n.d.).

Jiryis, S. *The Arabs in Israel*. (London: Monthly Review Press, 1976).

_____. "Israeli Laws as Regards Jerusalem." (n.p., n.d.). [In Arabic in *Shu'un Filastiniyah*, No. 106 (September 1980): 13–24.]

de Jong, F. "The Sufi Orders in Nineteenth and Twentieth Century Palestine." *StudiaIslamica* 58 (1983): 149–81.

Karmi, H. "How Holy is Palestine to the Muslims?" *Islamic Quarterly* 12, No. 2 (April-June 1970).

Karmon, Y. "Changes in the Urban Geography of Hebron during the Nineteenth Century." In *Studies on Palestine during the Ottoman Period*, edited by M. Ma'oz. (Jerusalem: Magnes Press, 1975), pp. 70–86.

Kedourie, E., and S.G. Haim. *Palestine and Israel in the 19th and 20th Centuries*. (London: Frank Cass, 1982).

Kesten, A. *Survey of Old Acre*. (Tel Aviv: Government Printers, 1962).

Khatib, R. "The Judaization of Jerusalem and its Demographic Transformation." In *Jerusalem: The Key to World Peace*. (London: Council of Europe, 1980).

Khoury, P.S. *Urban Notables and Arab Nationalism: The Politics of Damascus, 1860–1920*. (London: Cambridge University Press, 1983).

Kozlowski, G.C. *Muslim Endowments and Society in British India*. (London: Cambridge University Press, 1985).

Kroyanker, D. *Jerusalem: Planning and Development, 1982–1985: New Trends*. (Jerusalem: Jerusalem Committee, 1985).

Kupferschmidt, U. *Supreme Muslim Council: Islam under the British Mandate for Palestine*. (Leiden: Brill, 1987).

Kushner, D. *Palestine in the Late Ottoman Period*. (Jerusalem: Yad Izhak Ben Zvi Press, 1986).

Kutcher, A. *The New Jerusalem—Planning and Politics*. (London: Thames and Hudson, 1973).

Kuttab, J. "The Acquisition of Property in the West Bank." *Le Monde Diplomatique*, August 1983.

Landau, J. *The Arabs in Israel: A Political Study*. (London: Oxford University Press, 1969).

Lapidus, I.M. *Muslim Cities in the Later Middle Ages*. (Cambridge: Cambridge University Press, 1967).

Layish, A. "Mahkama." *Encyclopaedia Islamica*. (forthcoming).

_____. "Muslim Religious Jurisdiction in Israel." *Asian and African Studies* (Journal of the Israel Oriental Society) 1 (1965): 49–79.

_____. "The Muslim Waqf in Israel." *Asian and African Studies* (Journal of the Israel Oriental Society) 2 (1966): 41–76.

_____. "Qadis and the Shari'a Law in Israel." *Asian and African Studies* (Journal of the Israel Oriental Society) 7 (1977): 237–72.

_____. *Women and Islamic Law in a Non-Muslim State.* (Jerusalem: Israel Universities Press, 1975).

Lazarus-Yafeh, H. "The Sanctity of Jerusalem in Islam." In *Some Religious Aspects of Islam.* (Leiden: Brill, 1981).

Lehn, W., and U. Davis. *The Jewish National Fund.* (London: Kegan Paul International, 1988).

Lesch, A. *Arab Politics in Palestine, 1917–1939: The Frustration of a Nationalist Movement* (London: Cornell University Press, 1979).

_____. "The Gaza Strip: Heading toward a Dead End." *USFI Reports*, part 1, No. 10 (1984).

_____. *Israel's Occupation of the West Bank: The First Two Years.* (Santa Monica, CA: RAND Advanced Research Project Agency, 1970).

_____. *Political Perceptions of the Palestinians on the West Bank and the Gaza Strip.* (Washington, DC: Middle East Institute, 1980). Special Study No. 3.

Lijphart, A. "Consociationaliam: the model and its application in divided societies." In *Political Cooperation in Divided Societies*, edited by D. Rea. (Dublin: Gill and Macmillan, 1982), pp. 166–86.

_____. *Democracy in Plural Societies: A Comparative Exploration.* (New Haven and London: Yale University Press, 1977).

Litani, Y. "Militant Islam in the West Bank and Gaza." *New Outlook* 32, Nos. 11–12 (November-December 1989).

Little, D.P. "Jerusalem under the Ayyubids and Mamluks, 1197–1516 AD." In *Jerusalem in History*, edited by K. al-`Asali. (London: Scorpion Publishing Ltd., 1989).

Lundsten, M.E. "Wall Politics: Zionist and Palestinian Strategies in Jerusalem, 1928." *Journal of Palestine Studies* 8, No 1 (Autumn 1978): 3–27.

Luke, H., and E. Keith-Roach. *The Handbook of Palestine and Transjordan.* (London: Macmillan, 1934).

Lustick, I. *Arabs in the Jewish State: Israel's Control of a National Minority.* (London: University of Texas Press, 1980).

_____. "Israel and the West Bank after Elon Moreh." *Middle East Journal* 35, No. 4 (Autumn 1985): 557–77.

_____. "Stability in Deeply-Divided Societies: Consociationalism versus Control." *World Politics* 13, No. 3 (April 1979): 325–44.

Magil, A. *Israel in Crisis.* (New York: International Publishers, 1950).

Maguire, K. "The Israelisation of Jerusalem." *Arab Papers*, No. 7 (London: Arab Research Centre, 1981).

Makhoul, N. *Guide to Acre.* (Jerusalem: Government of Palestine, Department of Antiquities, 1941).

Manna', A. "The Sijill as Source for the Study of Palestine during the Ottoman Period, with Special Reference to the French Invasion." In *Palestine in the Late Ottoman Period*, edited by D. Kushner. (Jerusalem: Yad Izhak Ben Zvi Press, 1986), pp. 351–62.

Ma'oz, M. *Ottoman Reform in Syria and Palestine.* (London: Oxford University Press, 1968).

_____. *Palestinian Leadership on the West Bank.* (London: Frank Cass, 1984).

_____, ed. *Studies on Palestine during the Ottoman Period.* (Jerusalem: Magnes Press, 1975).

Mattar, P. *The Mufti of Jerusalem, al-Hajj Amin al-Husayni and the Palestinian National Movement.* (New York: Columbia University Press, 1988).

Massignon, L. "Documents sur certains waqfs des lieux saints d'Islam." *Revue des Etudes Islamiques* (1951): 73–120.

Mayer, L., and Pinkerfield. *Some Principal Muslim Religious Buildings in Israel.* (Jerusalem: Government Printer, 1950).

Meron, Y. "The Religious Courts in the Administered Territories." In *Military Government in the Territories Administered by Israel, 1967–1986*, edited by Shamgar. (Jerusalem: Alpha Press, 1982), pp. 353–67.

Middlemas, K. *Politics in Industrial Society.* (London: Andre Deutsch, 1979), pp. 371–82.

Migdal, J. *Palestinian Society and Politics.* (Princeton, NJ: Princeton University Press, 1980).

Mogannam, E. "Developments in the Legal System of Jordan." *Middle East Journal* 6 (1952): 194–206.

Muqaddasi. *Description of Syria including Palestine.* Translated from Arabic by G. Le Strange. Pilgrims Text Society 3. (New York: AMS Press, 1971).

Muslih, M.Y. *The Origins of Palestinian Nationalism.* (New York: Columbia University Press, 1988).

Nakleh, K. "Cultural Determinants of Palestinian Collective Identity: The Case of the Arabs in Israel." *New Outlook* (October-November 1975): 31–40.

Pearl, D. *A Textbook of Muslim Law.* (London: Crrom Helm, 1979).

Peres, Y., and N. Yuval-Davis. "Some Observations on the National Identity of the Israeli Arab." *Human Relations* 22, No. 3 (1969), pp. 219–33.

Peretz, D. *Israel and the Palestinian Arabs.* (Washington, DC: Middle East Institute, 1958).

_____. *The West Bank: History, Politics, Society and Economy.* (Boulder, CO: Westview Press, 1986).

Peri, O. "The waqf as an instrument to increase and consolidate political power: The case of Khasseki Sultan waqf in late eighteenth-century Ottoman Jerusalem." In *Studies in Islamic Society*, edited by G. Gilbar and J. Warburg. (Haifa: Haifa University Press, 1984), pp. 47–62.

Peters, F.E. *Jerusalem.* (Princeton, NJ: Princeton University Press, 1985).

_____. *Jerusalem and Mecca: The Typology of the Holy City in the Near East.* (New York: New York University Press, 1986).

Porath, Y. *The Emergence of the Palestinian Arab National Movement, 1918–1929.* (London: Frank Cass, 1977).

_____. *The Palestinian Arab National Movement, 1929–1939: From Riots to Rebellion.* (London: Frank Cass, 1977).

Reiter, Y. *Waqf in Jerusalem* (Jerusalem: Jerusalem Institute for Israel Studies, 1991).

Resistance of the Western Bank of Jordan to Israeli Occupation. (Beirut: Institute for Palestine Studies, 1967).

Reudy, J. "The Dynamics of Land Alienation." In *The Transformation of Palestine*, edited by I. Abu Lughod. (Evanston, IL: Northwestern University Press).

Richardson, J.P. *The West Bank: A Protrait.* (Washington, DC: Middle East Institute, 1984).

Ritter, C. *The Comparative Geography of Palestine and the Sinaitic Peninsula.* (Edinburgh, n.p., 1866).

Roy, S. "The Gaza Strip: Critical Effects of the Occupation." *Arab Studies Quarterly* 10, No. 1 (Winter 1988): 59–103.

Safdie, M. *The Harvard Jerusalem Studio: Urban Designs for the Holy City.* (London: Massachusetts Institute of Technology Press, 1986).

Sahliyeh, E. *In Search of Leadership: West Bank Politics since 1967.* (Washington, DC: Brookings Institute, 1988).

van Schendelen, M.P.C. "The views of Arend Lijphart and collected criticisms." *Acta Politica* 19, No. 1 (1984): 19–55.

Schmitter, P.C. "Still the Century of Corporatism?" *Review of Politics*, No. 36 (1974): 85–131.

Shamgar, ed. *Military Government in the Territories Administered by Israel, 1967–1986.* (Jerusalem: Alpha Press, 1982).

Sharon, A. *Planning Jerusalem—The Old City and its Environs.* (Jerusalem: Wiedenfield and Nicholson, 1973).

Shehadeh, R. *Occupier's Law: Israel and the West Bank.* (Washington, DC: Institute for Palestine Studies, 1985).

_____. *The West Bank and the Rule of Law.* (New York: International Commission of Jurists and Law in the Service of Man, 1980).

Shiff, Z., and E. Ya'ari. *Intifada: The Palestinian Uprising— Israel's Thrid Front.* (New York: Simon and Schuster, 1989).

Shlaim, A., "The All-Palestine Government." *Journal of Palestine Studies* 20, No. 1 (Autumn 1990): 37–53.

Schölch, A., ed. *Palestinains over the Green Line.* (London: Ithaca Press, 1983).

Shokeid, M. "Strategy and Change in the Arab Vote: Observations in a Mixed Town." In *The Elections in Israel—1979*, edited by A. Asher. (Jerusalem: Jerusalem Academic Press, 1975): pp. 145–66.

Sofer, N. "The Political Status of Jerusalem in the Hashemite Kingdom of Jordan, 1948–1967." In *Palestine and Israel in the 19th and 20th Centuries*, edited by E. Kedourie and S.G. Haim. (London: Frank Cass, 1982).

Stendel, O. *The Minorities in Israel.* (Jerusalem: Israel Economist, 1973).

Stephan, S.H. "An endowment deed of Khasski el-Sultan, dated 24th May, 1922." *Quarterly of the Department of Antiquities in Palestine* 10 (1944): 170–94.

Thomas, R. "Demography and Settler Politics in the Old City of Jerusalem." *Khamsin* 1 (1989): 82–92.

Tibawi, A.L. *The Islamic Pious Foundation in Jerusalem: Origin, History and Usurpation by Israel.* (London: Islamic Cultural Centre, 1985).

Tobler, T. *Denkblatter Aus Jerusalem.* (Constance: n.p., 1853).

United Nations Resolutions on Palestine, 1947–72. (Beirut: Institute for Palestine Studies, 1974).

The West Bank and Gaza: Israel's Options for Peace. (Tel Aviv: Jaffee Center for Strategic Studies, 1989).

Williamson, P. *Corporatism in Perspective: An Introductory Guide to Corporist Theory.* (London: Sage Publications, 1989).

Vesey-Fitzgerald, S. *Muhammedan Law, an Abridgement.* (London: Oxford University Press, 1931).

Van Arkadie, B. *Benefits and Burdens: A Report on the West Bank and Gaza Strip Economies since 1967.* (New York: Carnegie Endowment for International Peace, 1977).

Volney, Comte de, C. *Voyage en Syrie et en Egypte pendant les annees 1783, 1784, et 1785.* (Paris: Jean Gaulmier, 1958).

Young, P.W. *Scientific Social Surveys and Research.* 4th ed. (New Jersey: Prentice-Hall, 1966).

Zander, W. *Israel and the Holy Places of Christendom.* (London: Weidenfield and Nicholson, 1971).

Zureik. *The Palestinians in Israel: A Study in Internal Colonialism.* (London: Routledge and Keagn Paul, 1979).

Zvi Blum, Y. "The Juridical Status of East Jerusalem." In *Jerusalem—Aspects of Law*, edited by O. Ahimeir. Discussion Paper No. 2. 2d rev. ed. (Jerusalem: Jerusalem Institute for Israel Studies), pp. xxiv–xxviii.

Works in Arabic

al-'Alami, Shaykh Sa'd al-Din, ed. *al-hay'at al-islamiya al-'ulya-watha'iq* [Documents of the Higher Islamic Board). (Jerusalem: Dar al-Tabi'a al-'Arabiyya, n.d.).

al-'Arif, 'Arif. *mufassal tarikh al-quds* [Introduction to the History of Jerusalem]. (Jerusalem: Ma'aari Printers, 1986).

al-'Asali, K. *mu'ahida al-'ilm fi bayt al-maqdis* [Institutions of Learning in the Holy City]. (Amman: n.p., 1981).

Furani, F. *difa' al-judhur* [Defending the Roots]. (Nazareth: matba'at al-sha'biyyat, 1984).

Husayni, M. *al-munhal al-safi fi-al-waqf w-ahkama.* (Jerusalem: matba'a al-watani, n.d.).

Kafrawi, M. "al-waqfiyya dar 'a'sha and and makram abu khadr" [The Waqfiyya of the Aisha and Makram Abu Khadr Family]. *Hoda al-Islam* (September 1985).

_____. "taqrir 'an waqfiyya al-marhuma: 'Amina Badr al-Khalidi" [Report on a well-known waqfiyya: Amina Badr Khalidi]. *Hoda al-Islam*, Nos. 8–9 (1985): 61–71.

Natshe, Y. *al-turba al-kilaniyya* [The Kilaniyya Mausoleum]. (Jerusalem: Islamic Waqf Department, 1979).

Nijm, R. *'ard tarikhi masawur 'an 'aham al-muqaddisat fi filastin w-al-'ijra' at alati tamat li-siyanat al-turath* [An illustrated presentation of the Holy Places of Palestine and the measures taken to preserve the heritage]. Paper presented at the Fifth Conference on the Holy places, Tradition and Culture in Palestine, Cairo, 1988.

_____, ed. *qunuz al-quds* [The Treasures of Jerusalem]. (Amman: n.p., 1983).

al-Sa'ih, Shaykh Abd al-Hamid. "al-hay'at al-islamiyya l-'ulya fi al-quds" [The Higher Islamic Board]. *al-Quds al-Sharif*, No. 1 (April 1985).

Shehadeh, Husan Mahmud. "al-zira'at fi al-awqaf, limadha?" [Why Waqf Agriculture?] *Hoda al-Islam, rabia' al-awla* (1984): 47–58.

Saysalim, M., et al., eds. *majmu' at al-qawanin al-filastiniyya* [Collected Laws of Palestine]. (Gaza: n.p., n.d.).

Works in Hebrew

Farhi, D. "ha-mo'atza ha-muslemit be-mizrah yerushalayim u-vi-yehuda ve-shomron me'az milhemet sheshet ha-yamin" [The Muslim Council in East Jerusalem and in Judea and Samaria since the Six Day War]. *Ha-mizrah He-hadash* [The New East] 28 (1979): 3–21.

Gosenfeld. "temurot bi-qehilat ha-'asaqim shel yerushalayim ha-mizrahit" [The Ownership of Commercial Land in East Jerusalem]. *Ha-mizrah He-hadash* [The New East] 24 (1974): 261–79.

Hirschberg, H.Z. "be'ayot ha-shari'a bi-medinat yisra'el" [Islamic Legal Problems in the State of Israel]. *Ha-mizrah He-hadash* [The New East] 1, No. 2 (1950): 97–108.

Reiter, Y. "An Assessment of the Reform in the Muslim Waqf Institution in Israel: Acre as Case Study." Draft of English summary of article in *Ha-mizrah He-hadash* [The New East] 32 (1988).

Shimoni, Y. *'arvey eretz-yisra'el* [The Arabs of Palestine]. (Tel Aviv: n.p., 1947).

Vashitz, Y. *ha-'aravim be-eretz-yisra'el* [The Arabs in Palestine]. (Meravya: n.p., 1947).

Zacharia, S. *Jewish Houses and Institutions in the Muslim Quarter, the Old City, Jerusalem.* [In Hebrew, unofficial translation]. (Jerusalem: n.p., 1985).

Dissertations

Barnes, J.R. "Evkaf-i Humayun: Vakif Administration under the Ottoman Ministry for Imperial Religious Foundations, 1839–1875." Ph.D. diss., University of California, 1980.

Dumper, M.R.T. "The Palestinian Muslim Waqf: A Study in the Transformation of a Religious Symbol." M.Phil. diss., University of Lancaster, 1983.

Khayat, H. "Waqfs in Palestine and Israel—From the Ottoman Reforms to the Present." Ph.D. diss., The American University, Washington, DC, 1962.

Reiter, Y. "mosad ha-hikdesh ha-muslimi b-akko." [Muslim Endowments in Acre]. M.A. diss., The Hebrew University, Jerusalem, 1986.

Official Documents, Reports and Pamphlets

A. MANDATORY

Civil Appeal No. 108/41. Signed judgment in the possession of the author. Photocopy.

Committee for Muslim Religious Affairs (Government of Palestine, 1921).

Hope-Simpson, J. *Palestine: Report on Immigration, Land Settlement and Development*. Command Paper 3686. (London: Her Majesty's Stationery Office, 1930).

Judgment of Special Tribunal held in Jerusalem, 2 February 1927. Available from archives of qism 'haya' al-torath al-islamiyya of the Awqaf Administration in Abu Dis, Jerusalem.

Report by His Britannic Majesty's Government to the Council of the League of Nations on the administration of Palestine and Transjordan for the year 1926. Colonial Paper No. 26. (London: Her Majesty's Stationery Office, 1926).

Report by His Britannic Majesty's Government to the Council of the League of Nations on the administration of Palestine and Transjordan for the year 1928. Colonial Paper No. 40. (London: Her Majesty's Stationery Office, 1929).

Supreme Muslim Council. *muwazanat al-awqaf l-sanat, 1947*. (Jerusalem, 1947).

B. ISRAELI

Civil Administration, Judea and Samaria. *Annual Report*.

Information Bulletin of the Communist Party of Israel, December 1980.

Islamic Initiative Committee. *Islamic Waqfs in Israeli Mixed Cities*. 31 August 1988.

Judgments of the Supreme Court.

Koenig, Israel. "The Koenig Report." Translated in *Journal of Palestine Studies* 6, No. 1 (Autumn 1976): 190–200.

Laws of the State of Israel.

Statistical Abstract of Israel.

Statistical Yearbook of Jerusalem. (Jerusalem: Jerusalem Institute for Israel Studies, 1986).

C. JORDANIAN, WAQF ADMINISTRATION, AND PLO

Department for the Revival of Tradition and Islamic Sciences. *al-awqaf al-Islamiyya fi filastin*. Pamphlet No. 2. (Jerusalem: Awqaf Administration and Islamic Affairs, 1984).

Department of Occupied Territories Affairs (PLO). *al-awqaf al-islamiyya taht al-ihtilal: 1948–1985*. (Amman: dar ibn rashid, 1987).

Department of Waqf Land. *khutat al-amal l'il-aradi al-waqfiyya al-zira'iyya* [Workplan for the Cultivation of Waqf Land]. (Jerusalem: Awqaf Administration, 1987).

'idarat al-awqaf al-islamiyya al-'ama, bayan: al-awqaf al-islamiyya fi al-dafa al-gharbiyya, 1967–76. (Jerusalem: da'ira al-awqaf al-islamiyya, n.d.).

'idarat al-awqaf al-islamiyya al-'ama, bayan: al-awqaf al-islamiyya fi al-dafa al-gharbiyya, 1977–82. (Jerusalem: da'ira al-awqaf al-islamiyya, n.d.).

'idarat al-awqaf al-islamiyya al-'ama, "suq al-qattanin—dirasat muqadima l-lsayid mudir al-awqaf al-'am". (Jerusalem: n.p., 1972).

Official Gazette of the Hashemite Kingdom of Jordan.

Newspapers

A. ENGLISH

al-Fajr (weekly)

Jerusalem Post

B. ARABIC

al-Ittihad

al-Fajr (daily)

C. HEBREW

Kol Ha'ir

Ma'ariv

Ha'Aretz

Yediot Aharanot

Interviews

Subjects' positions and titles are those at the time of the interview.

Abu Hamdiyya, Yunis. Assistant to the director of the Department of Waqf Property. Interviewed on 4 October 1988.

Asha'ir, Hisham. Director of the Dar al-Aytam in Jerusalem and the West Bank. Interviewed on 13 November 1985.

al-'Asali, Walid. Lawyer and *mutawalli* of the al-'Asali waqf. Interviewed on 9 September 1985.

Bahat, Dan. Chief archaeologist of Jerusalem for the Israeli government. Interviewed on 19 March 1987.

al-Bakri, Ala' al-Din. Lawyer practicing in shari'a courts. Interviewed 10 September 1988.

Bakrijian, Antony. Historian, former UNRWA official and Old City resident. Interviewed on 3 October 1989.

al-Dajani, Awni. Beneficiary of the Shaykh Ahmad al-Dajani waqf, international lawyer and former legal advisor to King Idris of Libya. Interviewed on 22 November 1989.

Dana, Nissam. Director of the Muslim and Druze Division of the Ministry of Religious Affairs. Interviewed on 3 May 1989.

Daqqaq, Ibrahim. Member of the Higher Islamic Board and director of the Arab Thought Forum; former engineer for the Al-Aqsa Resoration Committee. Interviewed on 9 September 1988.

Fityani, Ali. Shopkeeper and *mutawalli* of the Shaykh Khalili waqf. Interviewed on 31 August 1985.

al-Husayni, Adnan. Director of the Department of Engineering and Maintenance. Interviewed on 27 July 1985.

al-Husayni, Sayed. *Mutawalli* of one of the Husayni family waqfs. Interviewed on 16 November 1985.

Khalidi, Hayder. *Mutawalli* of Khatib waqf *dhurri* (1967–1987). Interviewed on 23 May 1985.

Khatib, Amin. *Mutawalli* of Khatib waqf *dhurri*. Interviewed on 31 August 1985 and 15 January 1986.

Khatib, Anwar. Former Jordanian governor of the district of Jerusalem and *mutawalli* of the Tamimi waqf. Interviewed on 1 October 1988.

al-Khatib, Ruhi. Mayor of Jerusalem until 1967. Interviewed on 12 April 1989.

Natshe, Yusuf. Director of the Department of Islamic Archaeology. Interviewed on 27 July and 8 August 1985.

Nummari, Jihad. Architect and Islamic designer in the Department of Islamic Archaeology. Interviewed on 28 July 1985.

Qupti, Mazen. Lawyer with cases in the Old City of Jerusalem. Interviewed on 12 January and 21 January 1986, 2 February, 11 February, 13 February, 25 May, and 3 June 1987.

Quttayni, As'ad. Beneficiary of the Quttayni waqf *dhurri*. Interviewed on 9 November 1985.

al-Sa'ih, Shaykh Abd al-Hamid. Former Chairman of the *hay'at al-islamiyya al-ulya* and acting *qadi al-quda'*. Interviewed on 13 September 1989.

Sarraf, Farraj. Lawyer to the Gaza Strip office of the *ma'mur al-awqaf*. Interviewed on 27 September 1988.

Tahbub, Hasan. Former director-general of the Awqaf Administration (1960–1983). Interviewed on 4 October 1988.

Ya'acovy, Yitzhak. Director of the East Jerusalem Development Company. Interviewed on 3 February 1987.

Zu'mot, Nabil. Property Department, Jerusalem Diocese, Episcopal Church in Jerusalem and the Middle East. Interviewed on 1 October 1988.

INDEX